Derek Maling

The Rose and Crown Library

No. 2

Men and Memories

1900–1922

volume 2

MEN AND MEMORIES

RECOLLECTIONS

OF

WILLIAM ROTHENSTEIN

1900–1922

✳ ✳

'But it makes no matter, it shall serve the
turne; *men are not wise at all times.*'
THOMAS WENTWORTH,
EARL OF STRAFFORD

LONDON
FABER & FABER LIMITED
24 RUSSELL SQUARE

FIRST PUBLISHED IN APRIL MCMXXXII
BY FABER & FABER LIMITED
24 RUSSELL SQUARE LONDON W.C. I
NEW EDITION
IN THE ROSE AND CROWN LIBRARY
APRIL MCMXXXIV
PRINTED IN GREAT BRITAIN
AT THE UNIVERSITY PRESS CAMBRIDGE
ALL RIGHTS RESERVED

TO
HERBERT ALBERT LAURENS FISHER

CONTENTS

Contents

CHAPTER I

AUGUSTUS AND IDA JOHN

ONE day, during 1900, John and Ida came to see us; they had been married that very morning, they said. How pleased we were, and what mysterious things Ida and my wife had to talk over! We gave a small party to celebrate their wedding, to which Ida and her mother, Ida looking exquisitely virginal in a simple white dress, Conder, Gwen John, Steer and Tonks, McEvoy and my brother Albert came; but of John there was no sign. Someone said he had met John early in the afternoon on his way to take a bath; and then John arrived, in a check suit, with earrings in his ears. During the evening charades were played; one scene represented the Slade, with Steer teaching. He who played Steer looked long in silence at a canvas on an easel, then turned to him who played the student and remarked 'How's your sister?' This, John swore, was a perfect version of Steer's teaching!

Orpen didn't come to the party. He wrote:

My dear Rothenstein,

Thank you very much for the drawing received this afternoon. I am just going out to get it framed. I fear I can do nothing in return, but if perchance you would care for a drawing, painting or anything I have, it is yours with my heart.

I was very sorry not to have been at your party. I hear it was a great success. Miss Grace was not at all well all the afternoon after you left, and went to sleep, from which I did not like to wake her. I did not get back from Highgate till nearly 10, so it was too late to go. I pray the marriage may be a splendid thing for both parties, as I am sure it will. With many thanks for the drawing,

Yours affectionately,

WILLIAM ORPEN

'Miss Grace' was my wife's youngest sister; ever since the summer at Vattetot she and Orpen had been meeting, and we were not surprised when, some time after John's marriage, Grace Knewstub and Orpen became engaged. 'I want to see you very much to tell you how happy I am. Yr. affectionate Orpen', he wrote, with a charming drawing on the back of his note.

I had already painted Grace Knewstub in a picture *The Browning Readers*; she had then worn a dress belonging to my wife. I disliked the high collars, and the *gigot* sleeves which women wore, and my wife dressed in a way that pleased us both, somewhat after the style of the Pre-Raphaelite ladies. My wife sat to me for most of my pictures, and my sister-in-law copied her clothes, and sat likewise to Orpen. Thus, for a time, Orpen's pictures were confused with mine; indeed I think Orpen would have agreed that at this period he was somewhat influenced by my 'interiors'. But Orpen was much more skilful than I was; his merits won immediate recognition. The paintings he had done at Cany, which he showed at the New English Art Club, all found purchasers, and the brilliant little picture of the *Girl with a mirror*, now in the Tate Gallery, which he showed the same year, was purchased by Croal Thomson at the Private View. Then came several commissions for portraits, and I had no doubt that a brilliant career awaited Orpen. Robbie Ross used to say that people came into Carfax and prostrated themselves before a John, but always went off with an Orpen. With McEvoy things went slowly. He was, in those early days, a leisurely and fastidious painter. He made a remarkable copy of a Titian in the National Gallery; and he studied closely the methods of the Dutch painters, and of the English Pre-Raphaelites.

2

A charming person was McEvoy, affectionate, intelligent and extremely sensitive to beauty.

But John, whose first exhibited paintings were very 'messy', was beginning to show astonishing promise as a painter too. Such power, combined with a marvellous subtlety, such drawing, astonished me more than ever; no one living had his range of sensuous, lofty and grotesque imagination. There seemed to be no limit to his improvisation. Quite suddenly he achieved a wonderful portrait of an Italian girl, a Miss Cerutti, who lived in the house where he lodged. The splendour of the drawing and modelling took my breath away. This portrait was followed by another of Rosa Waugh, and one of his wife, holding a basket of flowers, the hands of which were beautiful, though finally he spoilt the freshness with bad glazing. That was the worst of John; he was impetuous, undisciplined, and had scant respect for his materials. But I thought this portrait of his wife masterly; and when it was shown at the New English Art Club, I persuaded my brother Charles to buy it for £100. Steer and Tonks were critical, deeming it wrong for one so young to ask so large a price, forgetting that they were bachelors, and both had comfortable posts at the Slade School.

Frederick Brown understood John's difficulties better, and bought several of John's pastels. But John was producing such beautiful work at this time that I could not understand the attacks of the critics and the reluctance of the more enlightened artists to recognise his genius. Even George Clausen wrote to me after seeing an exhibition of John's work at Carfax, that it was deplorable. Yet John's drawings at this time were very finished, and probably no such drawings had as yet been produced by an Englishman. But for all his genius, John found it difficult to support himself and Ida in London. His work antagonised people; it was deemed *deliberately* ugly. Were people altogether blind to beauty? I asked myself. And when one could draw and paint nudes like John, nudes so lyrical, endowed with such subtle and vivid grace, who would choose to carp at him? John poured out designs, with figures enough to people earth, Heaven and Hell.

I remember sitting one evening at the Café Royal with Steer and George Moore. Moore was ridiculing my praise of John's drawings. 'Why, the man can no more draw than I can! Ingres could draw, Degas can draw; when I see a drawing I know at once whether a man can draw', and so forth, when John himself strolled in, and seeing us, sat down at our table. Truth to tell, John had been dining well. He took no notice of Moore, though I dare swear he knew who was with us. Moore tried to engage his attention, but John remained silent, while he took out a sketch book, and made as if to draw, doing nothing, however, but scribble. Moore, flattered, imagining John to be sketching him, sat bolt upright, not moving a muscle. When John, tired of scribbling, shut up his book, Moore asked to see it, and turning over the pages, said unctuously, 'One can see the man can *draww*'. O tempora! O Moore! I said to myself, inwardly laughing. And Steer, too, shook gently.

Since he was now married, John needed more money than hitherto, and being invited to take charge of the drawing and painting at Liverpool University, he decided to go north, for a time at least. At first he wrote cheerfully enough:

4 *St James' Rd.*
Liverpool.

My dear Wilhelm,

Liverpool has its fine sides. The docks are wondrous. The college is quite young, so are its professors and they are very anxious to make it an independent seat of learning. The German professor called on us, and proved a very pleasant man. He also teaches Welsh and Irish which he learnt at Leipsig.

Mackay—Prof. of History—is delightful—the leading spirit of the College—he avoids coming to a practical point most tenaciously—when arranging about taking these rooms, he refused to consider terms but referred us to the Swedish

Consul—who was extremely surprised when Ida spoke to him on the subject.

We dined with two artistic people called MacNair, who between them have produced one baby and a multitude of spooks—their drawing room is very creepy and the dinner table was illuminated with two rows of nightlights in a lantern of the 'MacNair' pattern. The 'MacNair' door knocker is most popular with the children of the neighbourhood who by its means keep themselves in constant touch with the most advanced Art movement. However the MacNairs have a homely way of conversing which immediately sets people at their ease.

Ida is pleased to foregather with her new newly married friends. This town is full of Germans, Jews, Welsh and Irish & Dutch. Do write and tell the news—I have been painting a great deal lately.

Yrs. JOHN

The German Professor was Kuno Meyer, a great Celtic scholar, with whom John became intimate. But his chosen friend was John Sampson, the University Librarian. Sampson's knowledge of Romany astonished John, who had picked up a fair knowledge of Romany from Welsh gipsies, and he became his aptest pupil; when Sampson published a Romany translation of Omar Khayyam, John provided an admirable frontispiece. Sampson's outlook, and his ways of life, were unusual for a university don, and he and John would escape together to Wales, sleeping under hedges, dodging policemen, and feasting on hedgehogs with gipsies.

Ida John, too, settled down in Liverpool, though since she and John wrote from several addresses, settled down is perhaps a euphemism. My wife heard from her soon after they left London:

4 *St James Rd.*
Liverpool.

My dear Alice,

I long for Gwen; have you seen her lately? We have callers pretty often, university men & their wives. Our room is always in disorder when they come, as Gus is generally painting—but they survive it. Everyone is very kind. We have bought a funeral wreath. A most beautiful thing. The flowers are made of porcelain, & it cost 7/-. I was to wear it for a drawing, but it is too small.

I am doing a little painting—& have an old man model, who goes to lectures on Dante, & takes parts in play readings. He sits like a rock, occasionally wiping his old eyes when they get moist. There are a great many negroes & other foreigners here. One sees them sauntering about in groups.

How are you feeling? I am afraid I haven't started a baby yet. I want one. My sister Ethel is coming home this week. Perhaps I shall go up to town to see her in a week or two.

Give my love to Will. I shall doubtless see you if I come to London. I'm afraid Gussie won't come too. He works very hard. Remember me to Albert. With love.

I am

Yrs. IDA

John was by no means idle at Liverpool; on the contrary, he produced some excellent work, and, as usual, discovered remarkable models; from one especially he drew, painted and etched, planning too some large paintings. More than one exhibition of John's drawings and pastels was held at Carfax. John depended on this little firm, which served him well; and again he wrote: 'I would paint any man a nice big picture for £50 if he paid down £25 first'. But no one bit. Yet this Liverpool period was a fruitful one; one of John's best portraits, that of Mackay, was done for the University; other portraits followed. But to teach became more and more irksome.

CHAPTER II

BERLIN

AMONG my brother Albert's friends at the Slade School were Innes, and Spencer Gore. Innes I thought specially gifted; his figure drawings were poor, but his landscapes, then mostly in water-colour, were remarkable. Gore too, was better at landscapes than at figure drawing.

Sickert at this time was much interested in my brother and in Gore and Innes. Sickert and Albert used to be at home once a week in Sickert's studio, where they showed their paintings. Walter had many friends, who delighted in his wit; but he still got absurdly small prices for his pictures. I remember my anger with an American, who was anxious to buy some slight studies by Whistler, which Sickert then owned. He took no trouble to hide his small regard for Sickert's own work, though he offered a trifling sum for one of his pictures, as an inducement to obtain the Whistlers, a sum Sickert was ready to accept, though I insisted on his getting at least double the price offered, a small enough sum even then. Sickert's modest view of the value of his paintings always surprised me. We saw much of Sickert in those days. For a time he had a studio in Robert Street, and when we visited him he would take us to a little public house with a sanded floor, where we would dine off kippers; both public house and bill of fare suiting Sickert's taste perfectly. He delighted in the rough and racy talk of his studio neighbour, an obscure sculptor called Winter. Winter was a typical old-fashioned artist, who spelt art with a small a. He made little speculative busts of statesmen and Royalties, with whom, in his unpretentious way, he had established relations. Through some member of the Court, he obtained an interview with the Prince of Wales (afterwards King Edward). He was getting on splendidly with the Prince, he said, when someone came in and interrupted the talk—'Just'—said Winter—'*when I was chatting him into a bronze*'; a phrase which enchanted Walter.

During 1901 Steer painted some admirable pictures. His achievement was now evident, and it seemed to me that the time had come to show how highly we esteemed him as an artist; and Tonks who looked on Steer as his special charge offered worthy advice: 'if anything in the form of a dinner is given to him, it should be attended *only* by admirers of his *work* and should not be open to mere friends of himself as some of them are so foolish. Let there be as many speeches in praise of Steer as you like, but it would be simply unkind to ask Steer to reply as I know he hates it so'. 'And the rag-tag and bob-tail', Tonks added, 'ought not to be allowed: they only in their hearts, at least many do, hate what he does.'

Sargent also wrote:

> 31, *Tite Street*,
> *Chelsea*, *S.W.*
> *Dec.* 6th

My dear Rothenstein,

I will be delighted to join in doing honour to Steer, and I note the 21st—let me know where the dinner is to be and at what time.

My only misgiving is that if there are to be speeches (& I scent them in the air) one might be expected from me, and I am utterly incapable of saying a word. I dare say this is a recognised fact by this time and that I need not fear being asked.

> Yours sincerely
>
> JOHN SARGENT

I should like very much to show you my decorations but this is my month at the R.A. schools, morning & evening, and I rarely get to Fulham Rd. Later on I would be glad to give you your choice of time for coming.

The dinner was duly held, with Sargent in the chair; it was

more than a private affair; a large number of artists came to do Steer honour. Both Sargent and Steer were assured that no speeches from them were expected; but Sargent even found it difficult to say, 'I rise to propose the health of our guest', so tongue-tied was he. The emphatic nature of our tribute did something, I think, to establish Steer's reputation.

In 1901 our first child was born. We named him John. Augustus John was pleased to think we had him in mind:

My dear Will,   *Southbourne, Tenby*

Thank you for a letter which has imparted to me a good deal of its beautiful exuberance. I was feeling rather meta-grabolized this morning in contemplation of an oppressive breakfast when my hungry eye lit on your missive. And then Oh Heaven! with what appetite did I fall to & devour, gulp, guzzle, chew, toss off & roll under the tongue those most streaky fat morsels of paternity bacon & soul dripping you had so cunningly packed stamped addressed & despatched me in a five by four inch parcel of goods.

And you have called him John. My vainest of hearts refuses to deny itself the gratification the pride you have un-wittingly but fatally laid in its way, like a snare, tho' my mind is well aware of your intention in thus reviving & propitiating the memory of that distinguished figure John of Gaunt (or can it be Prester John?). I hope in confessing such weakness I exonerate myself from a portion of it.

You will like Corfe castle I think. I'm so glad to know you no longer drag Carfaxian fetters[1].

We go back to L'pool the 23rd September. They have raised my dole to a smug £200 and a day less in the week than last term. So we hope to find a place in the country and a studio in town.

You have not said explicitly how Alice & little John are, so I infer the best.

Saluez de ma part Alys, blonde et belle et chère (maintenant plus que jamais) avec mes souvenirs les plus tendres, en elle

[1] I had written to tell John I had left Carfax.

assurant de mon dévouement, fort comme jadis et toujours croissant. (I have taken to nitric acid like a duck to water & send you one of the first grubby fruits of my needle.)

The new English Art Club was now at its zenith. Steer was doing his best work, while John, Orpen, Innes and McEvoy were beginning a new chapter of the Club's history. John was then, and has remained, a staunch admirer of Steer.

My very dear Will,   66 *Canning St.*

A letter from you at last! I feel less an exile now. Nothing of late to remind me of home but grave epistles from Michel Salaman. Give you joy of your sturdy brat!

I take no interest in my own beyond grudging him the room he takes up (or she). My dear! a bang in the head has never & will never down me. Au contraire I feel double the *uebermensch* with a great patch on my nose! I have paraded it before my students with great effect. At the Sketch Club the other night it must have been grand to see me point a dislocated finger of scorn & turn up a broken nose at these purblind gropings in pictorial darkness. Tonks has kindly written me pricking my pride (not conscience) with his New English pricker. I daresay I shall send an etching or two. I refuse to hurry up my 'fair chandler' for English New or Old. I should like you to see her—you'ld rave! As Sampson sings:

> "Tu jinsa so si men koná
> O dush te dukerela men
> Te sasa shukar—Vela yek
> O wafriben ta Kashiben!"

I really must come up to town & see what my contemporaries are about.

. . . . . .

I too love Steer & Tonks in carpet slippers strolling unconcerned through the pêle-mêle of life.

Pour nous autres, ça n'est pas la même chose.

Yrs always

JOHN

John's babe was at first called Honoré, after Daumier, but finally David. Ida wrote one of her adorable letters:

138 *Chatham St.*
Liverpool

Dear Alice,

I do sympathise with you in having more to do than you can manage. So have I. Baby takes so much time—& the rooms we are in are not kept very clean, so I am always dusting & brushing—also we have a puppy, who adds to the difficulties.

I think I enjoy working hard really. I have not sat to Gus for ages. I wonder what Will is doing of you. Perhaps I am coming to London in about a month or 6 weeks. Really I cannot tell you the baby's name, as we can't decide. Gus has said Pharaoh for the last few days. But it changes every week. I don't mind what it is. I like Honoré very much. I wish you would tell me something of your baby. Does he often cry? Ours *howls*. He is howling now. I have done all I can for him, & I know he is not hungry. I suppose the poor soul is simply unhappy. He is very fat & strong & heavy—& gains 1 lb. nearly every week! So there cannot be much wrong with him.

Give my love to Will. I can't write again till he has written to me.

I should like you 3 to be photographed. We are going to be.

Yr. affectionate

IDA

Fortunately, too, at this time things were going well for John; I was able to tell him of the sale of some of his pastels to the Hugh Hammersleys:

138 *Chatham St.*

Beloved Will,

You know how nothing delights my soul more than your laudation! you have made me tickle & thrill, & gulp brought tears to eye & water to lip. And have my poor girls served me so well! Blessings on you Maggie & Ellen Jones![1] Daughters of Cardigan I thank ye! And you Quean of the Brook whose lewd leer captured me in my dreams, may your lusty honest blood be never denied the embrace it tingles for! To-morrow morn—Monday, I'll dispatch & send you what I have of good. To-day I cannot go to my studio having lost the street door key.

By the bye the things I send you were those rejected by the Liverpool Academicians. And am I to be trumpeted in print & by your clarion voice! I shall be drunk with delight to see *your* name at the end of the notice!

I leave the choice of reproductions to you. I hope they will be well done. I can't remember my birth but my father sent me many happy returns of the day last 4th January on my 24th birthday. I hail as you know from Tenby. I must have been 17 or so when I came to the Slade & stayed there I think 4 years.

I pant to do a superb decoration.......The 3 days I prostitute to foul faced commodity weigh on my soul terribly. My conscience is awakening and I see the evil of my ways.

The arrival of Honoré gives me to see I cannot thus dally with destiny, & temporise with Fate. I will repay you your confidence in kind, mon très cher. Ida shall have golden underclothing if she cares, & may be we shall have time to build a city such as one perceives to crown a rocky hill in the background of a picture by Mantegna & I shall be able at last to do homage to Alice in terms of gold, frankincense & myrrh. Honoré is becoming a surprising bantling with muscles like an amorillo.

My love to Alice & Johnny   always yrs—JOHN

Would you care to have a portrait of me in? There is the etching I did and there are one or two drawings at Carfax would do—with a black hat.

[1] Two Liverpool models.

A Norfolk holiday

The summer of 1901 we spent at Hingham in Norfolk. The country was flat, but beautiful; nearby was Wymondham, with its twin-towered church, and near Norwich we came upon a village, Shotesham, a hamlet which Gainsborough might have painted. Its picturesqueness pleased us so much that we nearly hired a house there; the property thereabouts belonged to an old Squire Fellowes, whom we met, a squire of the old school, who put me in mind of Fielding.

While we were in England, John was abroad: 'Adey told me of your removal to Hingham. Let me know, I prithee, how you are getting on my dear Triolet,' he wrote; 'I've been etching a good deal. I should like to hie down to see you. We didn't go for a walk but instead went to Bruges and stood amazed before the works of Van Eyck & Memling. The Belgians are as shoddy as they were formerly magnificent. Maeterlinck needs all his second sight.'

I heard again from John after his return to Liverpool:
'This school breaks up in a week I think. If you were in town then I would certainly hie thither for a day or two. Inform me, beloved scribe, of your movements. Do not haste unduly to the German capital. I would like to follow you there and see the pictures. I have started some startling pictures. Ah! if they would emerge triumphantly from the ordeal of completion!... Sampson is publishing a Romany translation of Omar Khayyam, to which I contribute a drawing.'

I had written to John that I was asked to have a one-man show in Berlin, at Schulte's, a well-known picture dealer. Lavery was invited at the same time. Schulte's was then the most visited of the Berlin galleries, and my friend von Hofmann advised me to accept.

While my show was on, I stayed with von Hofmann, who was now married. The exhibition received a good deal of notice, both in the Press and from artists, and though none of the paintings were sold, the Print Room of the Kaiser-Friedrich Museum acquired some prints, and Max Lieber-

13

mann bought some of the drawings. At the von Hofmanns, I met a Norwegian artist, Berndt Grönvold, an ardent admirer of Adolf von Menzel, whom Grönvold took to my exhibition. Then came a message from Menzel: 'He was glad to find a young man who still took pains over his work; he would be glad to see him at his studio'.

Grönvold told me, too, that Menzel would sit for a drawing; he had praised my portraits. I had admired Menzel's drawings ever since, when a boy, I had copied some of his illustrations to Kugler's *History of Frederick the Great*. To my mind, Menzel stood alone among German draughtsmen. His reputation in Germany was not unlike that of Degas in France, for Menzel was famous, too, for his grim repartees, though unlike Degas, he had been most of his life a court painter.

As I mounted the long flights of stairs that led to his door, I wondered at Menzel's endurance; for he was a very old man and there was no lift. In answer to my knock, Menzel himself appeared and led me into a large and untidy studio. I am small enough, but beside Menzel I felt tall, so short was he; and he had short arms and very small hands. His head was large and quite bald, while his mouth was still firm; his eyes, slightly clouded, most showed his age. I told him how highly he was esteemed in England; that Millais and the Pre-Raphaelites had studied his early drawings, which, in fact, had inspired their own. The old man flushed and said: 'Really, am I so well known in *Grosse England*?'

He knew and admired Millais' early drawings, and Charles Keene's, which he praised highly. He also thought well of Bernard Partridge's work. Of his own drawings he said, 'Well, I early cultivated the habit of drawing things as though I were never to see them again'. I thought this admirable. I was inwardly excited while drawing Menzel, and after a preparatory study of his head, said I would like to do a better one. This Menzel understood; 'One is often nervous during a first sitting; *nicht wahr?*' I might come again, once, twice; he had plenty of time to spare; better make a good job of what one was doing. But next time I must stay for lunch.

Well, next time, after sitting, old Menzel began to show his drawings, which he took from countless paper folios. We went through a number of these, forgetful of time. Suddenly Menzel looked at his watch. His face fell, and he seemed embarrassed; would I mind, he asked, lunching below in the Friedrichstrasse? But of course I didn't mind, and he took me to a famous restaurant where he was treated with marked attention. He drank his bottle of Rhenish wine with his lunch: not bad, I thought, for a man of his age. For he was 87. He was born the year of Waterloo, he said with pride, and had known many of Blücher's veterans; and he told me how, when he was painting historical pictures for Kaiser Wilhelm I—'My Kaiser', he called him—some of the great generals and courtiers were inclined to be difficult, but 'the Kaiser, he would always do exactly as I wanted, and sit or stand without any complaint, keeping his pose, until my study was done'. We talked of Degas—'Da ist ein tüchtiger mensch!' and he told me how he had attended an artists' banquet in Paris as an honoured guest, and had met all the famous French painters there, among them Puvis de Chavannes, whom he had shaken warmly by the hand, saying 'Grand payssachiste! Grand payssachiste!'

After a while the old man began to get sleepy, but he would not return to his flat before he had taken me past the Palace, where the guard, he being an Excellency, stood to attention as he passed. He was pleased, I think, that I should see him thus honoured. He took my arm as I walked back with him to his door; and now he had all those stairs to climb! I went on to the Pariser Platz, to the Liebermanns. A singular thing, I told them, that an old man like Menzel should go out to lunch at a restaurant, down all those stairs and up again. Liebermann was highly amused. 'Don't you know what happened?' he said. 'Menzel lives with a sister, as old, or still older than he; *eine alte hexe*, who rules him with a rod of iron. If he is a minute late the dining room door

is shut against him, and he must go out for his lunch!'
Incredible! a man of his age and fame to be treated thus!

I was eager to acquire one of Menzel's drawings; but he
wouldn't hear of such a thing. One must spend one's money
on models, on good paper, on mounts and frames, and if one
wants drawings, well, nowadays there are good reproductions, and photographs. But he would give me a drawing to
take back to England; and after sitting he got out some of his
folios. I was too shy to ask for any particular drawing, leaving
it to Menzel to choose one he could spare. But he lovingly
handled each drawing in turn and slipped it back; and after
some time, remembering what happened before, I prepared
to take my leave; alas, Menzel either forgot his promise, or
could not decide to part with anything. 'You should have
taken one', Liebermann said afterwards. 'He would have
been quite pleased; but he can't ever make up his mind to
part with any special study; besides, that old devil of a
sister tries to prevent him giving his drawings away; she is to
inherit everything; though Menzel might well outlive her.'
But in the end 'the old witch' outlived her brother.

Liebermann agreed with me about Menzel's supremacy as
a draughtsman, though the young painters Corinth, Lepsius,
Slevogt and others ran Menzel down. Foreign fashions, it
seemed to me, were the ruin of German painting. German
artists leapt at whatever was novel or bizarre, as fish leap at a
painted fly. Liebermann, though vain and easily flattered,
was too sound an artist to be deceived about Menzel though
he was somewhat jealous of Menzel's powers. I remember,
once at lunch, discussing modern painting with Liebermann's
nephew, Walter Rathenau, who spoke of Sargent as a mere
fashionable portrait painter. When I claimed greater qualities
for Sargent, others at the table supported Rathenau; but
Liebermann came to my aid. I was quite right, he said; one
had to count with Sargent. But Liebermann himself failed to
understand Whistler. 'Ein cocotten-geschmack', he said.

Liebermann was very generous; in addition to several of
his drawings—and he made admirable drawings—he gave

me a painting, one of a series he was doing then of men and horses by the sea. His house was a quiet retreat, full of paintings by Manet, Degas, Pissarro, Monet and Menzel, presided over by Frau Liebermann, a wise and charming woman. Young Rathenau, Liebermann's nephew, was constantly there, a thoughtful and fastidious person for a man of affairs; and there were always artists buzzing round Liebermann. Old Josef Israels came on a visit from Holland, a little, shrunken man, genial withal, but very bitter against England, on account of the Boer War. With Israels, I was Liebermann's guest at a dinner of the Berlin Secession. At this dinner I first met Harry, Count Kessler. I had often heard of Kessler as a generous friend to poets and painters, who knew everyone worth knowing, and who missed nothing that was either new, curious or vital in the literary, artistic and theatrical world. Rodin had spoken of him; and I remember that, with Freiherr von Bodenhausen, he was co-editor of *Pan*. Kessler, who was then in the early thirties and very good looking, had perfect manners, and perfect English.

While we were in Berlin, Rodin came over to London. He was much fêted, a dinner was given him by old and young artists, of which Adrian Stokes sent me an amusing account:

> *Dolphin Hotel,*
> *Beer,*
> *Nr. Axminster.*
> 21 *May* 1902.

I was glad to hear from you & hope your wife came safely to Berlin, also John.

It seems long since you left & things have been dull—and now it's raining raining raining—which perhaps makes me look more for the dull side of them than I need. In Scotland the fishing was bad & the luxury bad for me. Poverty seems worse after it, almost unbearable.

You are prospering I trust and appreciated—work and all —& commissions pouring in. Otherwise you would have come to the Rodin dinner. It was a great evening. You would have enjoyed some of the speeches. Wyndham, MacColl & the French Ambassador were admirable, the Frenchman exquisite—Rodin read his dear little schoolboy effusion from half sheets of note paper pinned together & constantly lost his place. Then boys from the Slade & South Kensington pulled him in a cab from the Café to the Club—Sargent on the box. Everyone, boys & all, were invited to supper, Wyndham again presiding & magnums of champagne were still flowing when I left.

They say that Tweed is going to Paris to work for Rodin & that a house has been built for him & his wife in the garden of the maître.

Harrison[1] came over for the affair & I took him to the Club where he introduced me to the great man who by some odd chance had been left all alone, in a corner of the big drawing room. I told him how happy & proud we all felt to have an opportunity of expressing our etc etc & he said 'Oui oui— Oui oui'. I could not for the life of me help thinking of an old nursery jingle that ends 'some little piggies said um um um & some little piggies oui oui'.

My exhibition was not a pecuniary success, while Lavery's was. But I was asked to paint a picture of Herr and Frau von Kekulé in their sitting room; after a few weeks I returned to Berlin; and later my wife joined me there with nurse Adkins and our small son. The first news my wife told me was that poor Stirling was dead. I was shocked, for I cared deeply for Stirling.

I should have spoken of Stirling ere this. Cunninghame Graham had written to me in 1897:

'God is great (as you know) but very careless as I know. Therefore I write this to introduce my friend Mr Stirling. He is a Scotchman and an architect in whom there is no guile. He has written an extremely interesting book on 'Phallic Worship' (vous voyez ça d'ici) and I have written the preface. Mr Quaritch was to have published it (including my preface), but at the last moment a difficulty cropped up as to

[1] Alexander Harrison.

the terms. Mr Stirling had heard of Hacon & Ricketts and had, I think, approached them. I write then to ask you to take your cane in your hand and take Mr Stirling and introduce him to Hacon, who is I suppose Hacon Llewellyn— this I know you will do, not only for me as a friend, but to help a friend of mine, and also because the book is a most curious one and should be published by a good man like Hacon'. . . .

I found in Stirling an exquisite and lovable nature. He was self-sufficing and knew scarcely anyone. An architect without work, he devoted himself to scholarship. He had curious views and theories—how far they were supported by evidence I did not know—about the gospels, and the building of early churches; in his view the ground plans of early churches were always symbolic. He was full of the subject, making researches and spinning theories which he embodied in a book, *The Canon*. I was too ignorant to have an opinion on the subject; but I could appreciate the fineness of Stirling's nature; he was one of those men who made others, however gifted and famous, appear coarse by contrast. I have met only two or three men of equal sensibility—all, like Stirling, unknown to fame.

In pursuit of his subject, Stirling was an ardent collector of books; I suspected, indeed, that he starved himself in order to buy them, so frail he looked, and I began to see symptoms which made me uneasy. For Stirling talked as though he were being spied on, and this mood grew upon him. He had lodgings in York Buildings, where someone, he said, had lately taken rooms and was watching his movements. I became anxious, and one day sought out his fellow lodger; I found him to be a young actor, lately come to London—one Granville Barker—and it was evident that Stirling's suspicions were groundless. Just before I left London for Germany Stirling came to see me, bringing me a copy of his book. As he bid me adieu, he lightly touched my cheek with his fingers, and it crossed my mind that he thought he would never see me again. I remembered this when my wife told me the tragic news. Stirling had left me his papers, about which I consulted Yeats; he had been greatly interested in Stirling, and felt as I did about him, but having 'no great trust' in his speculations:

Coole Park
Gort
Co. Galway
Oct. 17.

My dear Rothenstein

Your letter has only just been sent on by my housekeeper. I would like very much to see Stirling's manuscripts when I get back to London in November—my eyes are too bad to read MS. but I will get one of my little mystical community to read it out to me.

Stirling's death was a terrible thing—sooner or later he was certain to do good work—he showed me a quantity of designs for some sort of a heathen temple which seemed very imaginative—I couldn't follow his numerical speculations & indeed had no great trust in them, but he lit on all sorts of interesting things by the way—

Yours sincerely

W. B. YEATS.

Nor could Yeats make anything of Stirling's papers; they were too scrappy and inchoate.

CHAPTER III

A VISIT TO HAUPTMANN

PEOPLE in Berlin were friendly and hospitable. We were much entertained by, among others, the Lippmanns. Friedrich Lippmann was Head of the Print Room of the Kaiser-Friedrich Museum. He was proud of his early German paintings, which were hung on a gold background, and he asked me to paint him and his wife (a lady whose substantial proportions were as striking as his) sitting beside his pictures. I made what excuses I could; I was not an illustrator of fairy tales, and the subject of such a picture could only have been that of strange monsters guarding fine treasures.

Lippmann, whose reputation as an expert stood high, was outspoken, at times crude. One night, at a dinner-party at his house, Lippmann, becoming impatient with tedious talk of orders and decorations, a common topic in official society, 'Herr Rothenstein', he bellowed in his loud, guttural voice, 'Give me your Rembrandt drawings for the Museum, and you can have any Orders you like!' Later in the evening, there was music; Lippmann preferred to talk, and retired, with some of the men, to another room. Presently a lady knocked at the door: 'Herr Geheimrath, do you mind speaking a little lower? We can hear every word you are saying in the next room'. 'Tell that fellow to play a little lower then', Herr Geheimrath replied, 'We can hear *every note* in here!' Being unmusical, I sympathised with Lippmann; I cannot believe that people really want to hear music after dinner, unless as a relief from tiresome talk, a reason which is kind neither to composer nor player.

I happen, too, to dislike opera as a form of entertainment, but meeting Mrs Charles Hunter and her sister Miss Ethel Smyth, in Berlin, by them I was taken to the first night of Miss Smyth's opera, *Der Wald*. It was the only opera, they told me, written by a woman that had been produced at the Berlin Opera House—a feather in Miss Smyth's cap. But the German composers, she complained, were jealous that this exception should be made in favour of an English-woman; hence a conspiracy of silence. The Emperor was present and the British Ambassador, and the boxes were full of gorgeous officers and glittering ladies. I, in my innocence, thought the opera quite well received, but not so Miss Smyth, who wanted the praise of musical, rather than official, Berlin.

Ida John had a sister studying music in Berlin and wrote to tell me so—

138 *Chatham St.*
Saturday.

My dear Will—

I have never sent you one single message, even of thanks for all the lovely things you have said to me. They were so lovely. I am writing late at night. Gus has gone to sleep in the studio because he has lost the key of the outer door & cannot get in on Sundays without it. Also he wants to keep up the stove, as that model, Lizzie, with the yellow hair— such a beauty—is sitting for him tomorrow. M. Honoré is asleep, thank the Lord. He has been very cross all day. He is a fat old thing—& when asleep he looks magnificent. But awake he is a little paltry-looking. You are a dear good friend to Gus.

Dear Will—It is Sunday morning, & I am just going to bath the baby. We have a puppy, &, between the two, life just now is rather perplexing. I suppose you wouldn't have time to see Ethel while you are in Berlin. Her address is Lützow Str. 82^{iii}, I think she would love to see you. I do not think we feel about our babe like you do about yours. I have not had any ecstasies over him. He is a comic little fellow, but he grumbles such a fearful lot. I think he would very

22

much rather not have been created. You know your wedding present is one of the few things we take with us everywhere. At any rate to me she is most important & wonderful & wise. I seem to have known her always. Dear Will I must stop now, as there are so many things to do. I send my love to Alice.

Your affectionate

IDA JOHN

I saw a good deal of one of Lippmann's assistants in the Print Room, Herr von Loga, who was writing a book on Goya; very thorough he was, and he had found out many things which threw fresh light on Goya's life.

I had just finished my portrait of Herr and Frau von Kekulé, when I met Gerhart Hauptmann. What a beautiful appearance! a strong, well-shaped nose, and a sensitive, finely chiselled mouth, and hair brushed back from a radiant forehead. An immediate sympathy sprang up between us; Hauptmann was then a mere name to me; I had read none of his plays, but felt at once that here was a man. He pressed us to come to the Riesengebirge, in Silesia, where he lived; I would find the landscape inspiring, he promised. The von Hofmanns were coming, but with wife, nurse and child, he would find room for us all, either at his house, or else at a forester's cottage close by. We liked the idea of the forester's cottage, so then the von Hofmanns would stay at the house.

We took train to Hirschberg, and from there drove up to Agnetendorf. It was early spring, and the orchards were in full flower, the grass bright emerald; behind were the Riesengebirge, ringed by dark pine woods. The sun was shining; it was our first sight of snow-covered mountains, and the higher we got the higher our spirits rose also. Hauptmann's house was newly built, standing four square to the winds of heaven, overlooking valley and mountains. Inside the house were ample rooms, very German in character, with high ceilings and bright, painted beams. The forester's cottage was on the edge of a deep pine wood; the boles of the great trees, bare and erect, put one in mind of a vast cathedral. Our rooms were spotless, their floors scrubbed white, like the decks of a ship.

Agnetendorf, with its beautiful little farmhouses, low, thatched, with small gay-coloured shuttered windows, each with its orchard, was ideal for a painter. What a happy change it was from Berlin! And what splendid hosts the Hauptmanns were! Hauptmann's views on life were large and generous. Artists, he held, should live proudly, as Dürer and the great German craftsmen had lived, putting on fur-lined gowns and gold chains as it were at the end of each day's labour. We had neither fur-lined gowns nor gold chains; but every day we sat down to a table glistening with silver and glass. We drank choice Rhenish and Mosel wines out of great Venetian glasses; huge salmon were handed round, boar's head or saddle of veal, dish following dish; I was put in mind of the feasts in Harrison Ainsworth's *Windsor Castle*, of which I had read as a boy. Never before had we fared so richly.

One evening, when the wine had gone round more often even than usual, Hauptmann asked who was for the Schneekoppe? The Schneekoppe! four or five hours' walk, and it was already night! 'But there is a moon', cried Hauptmann. I was willing, so was Marguerite Hauptmann, and we started out. I shall never forget that walk up the mountain through the woods, the drooping arms of the pine trees, heavy with snow, turned to silver here and there, as the moonbeams caught them. How still it was! a stillness broken only by the crunching of our feet in the thick crust of snow, and by the singing of the mountain streams running down into the valley.

It was four in the morning when we reached the little *gasthaus* near the top, and roused the inn-keeper with loud knocks upon his door. When he came down and recognised Hauptmann, he at once made us welcome. Cold meat, rye bread, cheese and hot coffee quickly appeared—then we were glad to find our bedrooms. Late next morning we walked down the valley to the *Goldener Stern* at Schmiedeberg. Hauptmann was everywhere recognised, and respectfully greeted; sometimes a group of young men would even cheer. I couldn't imagine this happening in England to a young writer, to Kipling for instance; for Hauptmann was then no more than forty. But his play, *Die Weber*, had roused enthusiasm for the cause of the labouring classes in Germany, and thereby brought him the hostility of the Kaiser and the court circles. *Die Weber* was followed by *Der Biberpelz*, a brilliant satire on the Junker class, which increased his unpopularity in the official world. Their idol was Kipling. Indeed, their enthusiasm for Kipling's poems may well have encouraged Germany's ambition to possess a great navy. Strange paradox, if this be true, that the national poet of one country should rouse the patriotism of a rival people. Hauptmann himself thought Kipling the most powerful poet of the time; I could not convince him that England had other writers of merit. In Germany, as in France, the Boer War had undermined English prestige. Nevertheless, when the day before our departure from Agnetendorf, I asked Hauptmann, as we sat pledging one another in German champagne, or maybe in *Mai-bowle*, what I could do in return for his noble hospitality, he replied: 'Lieber freund, a man must be as generous in what he takes as in what he gives'. But when I insisted, he said at last, with a flourish of his glass, 'I should like to be a Doctor of the ancient University of Oxford'. A romantic whim, prompted by the moment, or else the *Mai-bowle*.

Soon after our return to England, while staying with Walter Raleigh at Oxford, I asked him would he do me a favour, and get a degree for a distinguished German? That was for Gerrans to decide, Raleigh said—Gerrans knew all about Germans. Gerrans was consulted and at once approved; a letter was duly despatched from the Vice-Chancellor, but when it reached Hauptmann, why, it was one of my jokes! a good joke! It was not until Hauptmann chanced to show the letter to a friend, that he was assured of its genuineness; and when the time came, Hauptmann found himself in truth a Doctor of Oxford.

CHAPTER IV

RECONCILIATION WITH CONDER

FOR some time now I was occupied with 'interiors'; my wife figures in many of these; artists' wives have a hard time, sitting; mine certainly had; and, like most artists with their first child, I made countless studies of babes, and of mother and babe. I continued to draw my friends, Thomas Hardy, Bowyer Nichols, Henry Tonks, John, Gordon Craig, and Max Beerbohm. One day a stranger came, a young Australian, who wished to be drawn. Frederic Manning was his name; he admired the poets and writers I knew, Max especially, and since I had drawn so many poets, he had sought me out. He was an attractive youth, a little precious and frail, looking wise for his years. I found him to be very intelligent; he came almost daily, then he disappeared. Manning had no money it transpired; he believed his father would pay for the drawing I did of him, and for other extravagances; not so his father. And now he was afraid lest I might take proceedings against him. I reassured him, his father would pay some day; if not, what matter? For some years Manning lived with Arthur Galton, a rare scholar under whom Manning became well nigh as familiar with classical as with modern authors. When his *Scenes and Portraits* appeared, Max Beerbohm said that he knew no better short stories in English. A few people agreed with this verdict; so, later, did T. E. Lawrence, but until it became known who had written *Her Privates We*, Manning's name was rarely mentioned.

About this time, a young Slade student, Wyndham Lewis, came often to see us. Stirling had shown me some poems he

had written, which I thought strange and interesting, and
Wyndham Lewis would bring me his poems to read. Lewis
was striking looking (an early etching by John shows him as
he then was) and even then showed signs of a formidable
personality. He hesitated between writing and painting,
meanwhile he made sensitive studies of the nude; I recall no
compositions by Lewis—the imaginative and romantic side
of his nature he put into his poems and into his daily life.
He liked to shroud himself in mystery. After hiding for
weeks he would suddenly reappear, having been, he would
declare, in Sweden, or in some remote country; and he would
hint at a conquest. His 'conquests' seemed for the most
part to be Swedes, Germans, Poles or Russians, shadowy
figures whom one heard of, but never met. I was never sure
whether, indeed, he ever had left England—perhaps John
knew. He certainly went later to join John in Paris. Lewis's
relations with John recalled mine with Conder, an intimacy
frequently disturbed by violent quarrels and again renewed.
This year D. S. MacColl produced his book on 19th
century art, the best English work, I thought, on the
subject that had yet appeared. I had long admired MacColl's
articles in the *Spectator* and then in the *Saturday*, but in
these, beautifully written as they were, he was advocate or
prosecutor. In his *Nineteenth Century Art*, he allowed himself to be absorbed by each artist upon whom he wrote and
got into their skins, as it were, so that he was here less critic
than artist. I wrote a review for the *Saturday* wherein I
expressed my admiration. 'Your review', wrote MacColl,
'I got on the way down here. It is a most generous word, &
you let me off far too easily for the glaring & lesser defects of
a too hastily executed sketch. If I have the good fortune to
rouse in well disposed minds any of the feeling that was
ready to vibrate in yours for those artists, I shall not regret
the work & worry of the thing.'

My only regret was that the book was so large and so
expensive that but few would read it. My fears proved true,
for to-day this admirable work is rarely mentioned.

In 1902 we began to think of leaving our delectable cottage; another baby was expected, and the cottage would be too small. I suffered from bilious headaches, both in Chelsea and Kensington, and was advised to live in Hampstead. In my Slade days I thought, if ever I were rich, I should live in Church Row, a perfect Queen Anne street. I was far from being rich, but a house there that had once been Gilbert Scott's, who had put it into perfect order, was now to let. The rent was £120—but what should have concerned me more, a block of flats, which shut out direct light from the house I coveted, had lately been built. We took the house notwithstanding. A month later our second child was born.

Soon after came a note from Conder:

Dear Will

I must be writing on my familiar note-paper—judging from the pictures in the next room. And my next difficulty is to explain why I am writing at all—but perhaps you may be able to read between the lines & understand that there has been a long silence between us. I went to bed to-night but came down again to write this letter which is to say that you are the friend that I miss most.

C. CONDER.

P.S. I think you may reply & come & stay a week & meet my wife if Mrs R can come too, in any case let us be as we should have been, good friends.

I had seen little of Conder since the episode I related earlier. For a time I had felt bitter, so bitter that I wanted to get rid of the paintings I had of his—to efface all signs of our friendship. But his letter touched me, and I answered it at once, & there followed an affectionate letter:

Hotel Baudy
Giverny
Eure
21 *April* 1902.

My dear Will

I was delighted to get your letter with its friendly assurances & kind messages to us both & am more glad than I can tell you that a quarrel with one of my oldest friends has come to an end. I often felt very much to blame about the whole thing & had often meant to write before—for some time past I have tried in every way both in London & abroad to be a strong partisan of yours & I am so glad to tell you how very good I think your work is & what great pleasure it always gives me to see it.

I was so glad to hear about the baby & nearly wrote from Paris at the time—I am very happy although I haven't a baby & my wife is such a good sort & I am sure you will like her. We only intend to stay a week or ten days in London (from the 3rd May till the 10th) as it costs such a lot & we have had to move from Paris—which costs a fortune.

We expect to be installed in a house in Wellington Square by about the end of the year so I may not see you after all if you only arrive in town by the middle of May—most likely I am going to Les Petites Dalles in May. I am feeling *really* upset about my work & intend for some time to work out of doors.

Even if I don't produce any good work I am sure it will be a good thing in every way—and you will understand how difficult it is for me to know exactly what to do when I tell you that I feel somewhat played out. Although it may only be my imagination. Espérons.

Goodbye

Yours affectionately,

CHARLES CONDER.

I found Conder greatly improved by marriage—happier, gentler and more sober; and so he continued until serious illness came; and glad I was then that there was no longer coldness between us. But Conder still had three years to live with his wife before his health broke up entirely. His wife had means, and Conder was able to take a beautiful house in Cheyne Walk, where he gathered round him many old and new friends. Two fancy dress balls they gave were famous, so daring were the dresses in which people came; but Conder would steal up to his workroom, for work was becoming a mania; as though he had forebodings of the little time left to him.

CHAPTER V

FRANCIS DARWIN AND OTHERS

CONDER, who was frequently in Paris, gave me some bad news. 'It is very sad about poor Lautrec—shutting the man up when he is no more mad than you or I. We all hope to get him out. They do *not* all things better in France, and I for one think it somewhat of a barbarous country.' I had not realised how excessive Lautrec had become; his habits with women I knew too well, but though he would drink much more than was good for him, I was unaware to what a state he had brought himself. His work was done, but few foresaw the importance that was to be given to his prints and paintings.

Anquetin, I heard, had almost given up painting. Through his scholarship, his study of Rubens especially, he had come to despair of achieving anything worthy to rank with the work of past masters; yet Conder and I both thought that Anquetin would bring a more masculine force into modern painting. He was soon to retire to the Gobelins factory, where a traditional baroque still survived which, though enfeebled, appealed to Anquetin.

Much as I admired Anquetin in my early Paris days, when I came across some posters he had made in the manner of Daumier, I saw that he had failed to understand the main principles of Daumier's form; yet formerly, not having grasped these myself, I had believed Anquetin's Daumieresque work to be admirable. We are easily deceived by the seeming likeness of imitative work to that which inspired it; but imitation is *not* the sincerest flattery, and disciples may

30

miss the essential and maintain the superficial. Who among Cézanne's followers has taken the time and the pains to match the delicate values, the scrupulous quality of the paint, that preoccupied Cézanne himself? Indeed, the same may be said of Whistler's disciples, of whom I was one. But the influence in England of Cézanne was not yet. The most vital of the younger painters still knocked for admittance at the door of the New English Art Club. Sickert was still to found his Camden Town group. The Slade school, where all the most promising young men and women worked, was turning out competent draughtsmen by the score, leaving South Kensington, and the Royal Academy School, far behind. MacColl was delivering rude shocks against Burlington House with his verbal battering ram. The 'decadent' school was dead, and a more vigorous opposition to the Academy was growing. But the social prestige of the R.A. was still great, as I was to find at Bradford. Social prestige, however, seemed far from the thoughts of John, Orpen and McEvoy. I remember McEvoy describing a dinner which he found so intolerably pompous, that he got up from the table and danced a jig. This was the Victorian end of the scale; there was also the fashionable Edwardian-bohemian.

X and his wife, whose means scarcely permitted their entertaining, were anxious to have a salon, and gave supper parties, but would ask too many people. A friend, on leaving, commented on the meagreness of the fare; he could get neither enough to eat nor to drink. Most of us, I remarked, have skeletons in our cupboards, but X brings his out every Sunday and invites his guests to pick the bones. But on one occasion at least we must have supped well with X, for on Max and myself walking home, we talked of our childhood, when we rang front door bells and ran away. A sudden impulse seized us—we rang and knocked violently at a couple of solemn Georgian doors, and then ran as hard as we could —straight into the arms of a policeman! He would not see the joke, and threatened to take us to the nearest police station.

Now on one occasion John did find himself in a cell for the

night; for one morning a telegram came: 'Bail me out, Vine St., John'. I had never yet acted as 'Bail', I must look solid and respectable, so I bought myself a new pair of gloves on the way; but when I got to Vine Street, John had been set free—Michel Salaman had arrived there before me.

Hampstead delighted me; why hadn't we come there before? There was the Heath, and immediately beyond it was open country. Golders Green was not yet, and the view from the White Stone Pond was not unlike that which Constable saw. And such charming old lanes and houses and cottages! At first I was happy about the house, with its panelled rooms, carved staircase and noble Queen Anne fireplaces. But I came to feel its very beauty to be a defect; it was all *too* perfect, too stylish; for I was aiming at something more elemental than a Queen Anne interior. I was painting wife and child, and wished to suggest every-wife and every-child; and Queen Anne got in the way, while for portraits the light was too diffused. I painted Francis Darwin at Church Row, and W. H. Hudson, Steer, Sargent and Tonks, when Sargent advised me to get a studio; the lack of direct light was a serious drawback.

I had met Francis Darwin two or three years earlier at the Protheros, and staying with him at Cambridge I became greatly attached to him and to his wife. His wife, a Miss Crofts of Leeds, sister to Ernest Crofts the painter, had been brought up at Bolton Abbey, where her father was Rector. Their daughter, Frances, was a sort of pupil of mine; as a young girl, a child almost, she had won my heart: the nut-brown maid, I used to call her, for nut-brown she was, dark-eyed, dark-haired and russet-browed. She both drew and wrote poems with a simple sincerity, and was wise beyond her years. So often I stayed with the Darwins I got to know Cambridge as well, almost, as I already knew Oxford. Through them, too, I met William Bateson and his wife. Bateson I held to have one of the finest minds in England. He was too outspoken to be popular, but I have ever found unpopular people to be among the most attractive. Certainly those who knew Bateson well revered his character. I stayed often, too, with Henry Jackson, in the gorgeous guest rooms at Trinity College.

While painting Francis Darwin I noticed how strong a resemblance there was between him and his father, Charles Darwin. He had, too, much of his father's directness and simplicity. There was never any doubt about what he disliked nor whom he liked and disliked. He used expressions which pleased me: he spoke of certain ladies as being 'rather the worse for dress'.

I referred earlier to an aristocracy of virtue; well, the Darwins had that—a sort of yeoman integrity and downrightness, and a fastidious sense of conduct, which one thinks men like John Hampden possessed.

Darwin, one of the sweetest and gentlest of men, was moved to anger by cruelty, cruelty to animals especially. Nor could he be indifferent to attacks on his father, which he thought unfair. He was at first prejudiced against W. H. Hudson, because as a young man Hudson had criticised Charles Darwin in one of his books. But when he and Hudson met, each recognised the other's charm, and the small hatchet was quickly buried. Francis Darwin's objection to Samuel Butler was more emphatic. Butler, he thought, had behaved very ill to his father. Festing Jones gave me an account of the quarrel between Butler and Darwin, which was new to Francis; and the misunderstanding was finally explained in a pamphlet written before his life of Butler appeared, a pamphlet wherein Francis Darwin as well retracted some of the hard opinions of Butler he had formerly published; for Darwin was happier liking people than nursing a grievance; though when once convinced of the unworthiness of anyone, he could not meet him.

Francis Darwin thought I should make a drawing of Alfred Russel Wallace, his father's old friend, who was living at Parkstone near Bournemouth, and Hudson, who knew him too, wrote to Wallace, who readily consented, and asked me to stay for a week-end. I knew of course that Wallace had discovered the theory of evolution at the same time as Charles Darwin, and I had read his later writings, of a political and social sort. He had written too about spiritualism, so much he had changed. On this account I expected to find someone more warm hearted than I found him to be. Perhaps age had dulled him, and the years had damped down a once brightly burning fire. His appearance, too, was less that of a man of science than that of a Nonconformist preacher, and he had little charm. His house was rather like a schoolmaster's, containing nothing of beauty, and I was amused to see a poor faded photograph of Charles Darwin, in a cheap frame, the only sign of their association. He spoke chiefly of his hopes for the future, and of spiritualistic experiences which had impressed him; and he told me also why, early in life, he had gone to South America. Being threatened with consumption, he was sent to a warmer climate, and on the way had met a young doctor, a Doctor Salisbury, who said he could cure him. The cure was simple: to eat nothing but lean beef, chopped fine, and to drink hot water; and Wallace assured me that he had cured himself thus, and followed this diet ever since. He was then well over eighty.

After I had drawn Wallace, Francis Darwin sent me to draw Sir Joseph Hooker, another distinguished friend of his father. Sir Joseph Hooker was still older than Wallace, and much less robust. How handsome he must have been as a young man I saw from one of Mrs Cameron's photographs in the Darwin's house; but he now showed his age. In the Hooker's house hung an entertaining picture of a very Victorian young Hooker, with side whiskers and sun helmet, receiving, in a tropical landscape, the fruits of the earth from kneeling savages.

Another eminent Victorian I drew was John Morley, Lord Morley as he now was. He too was rather dry and somewhat cold; but I was cheered on going to lunch with him to find on his dining-room walls nothing but engravings of Millet's pictures. I expressed my pleasure at finding that he too admired this great artist—the most significant artist, I held, of his time, 'Tut tut', said Lord Morley, 'You must not exaggerate!' I silently asked myself why, then, he had hung these particular pictures round his room.

From Lord Morley came a phrase I have since often heard quoted (other men must have said a similar thing) 'that a man can do a deal of good in the world if he doesn't mind who gets the credit for it'.

Besides these several portraits, I now discovered a new subject matter. Having business in the city with a solicitor, a brother of Solomon J. Solomon, and on his asking whether I chanced to know the Spitalfields synagogue, in Brick Lane (a curious sight, he assured me, well worth seeing), I accompanied him there. My surprise was great to find the place crowded with Jews draped in praying shawls; while in a dark-panelled room sat old, bearded men with strange side-locks, bending over great books and rocking their bodies as they read; others stood, muttering Hebrew prayers, their faces to the wall, enveloped from head to foot in black bordered shawls. Here were subjects Rembrandt would have painted— had indeed, painted—the like of which I never thought to have seen in London. I was very much excited; why had no one told me of this wonderful place? somehow I must arrange to work here. But to draw in a synagogue, I was told, was out of the question, was against the Law. The Jews here, I saw, were suspicious of strangers; they had lately come from the ghettos of Russia and Galicia, and were fanatically strict; so strict that they rejected the authority of the Chief Rabbi who, in their eyes, was unorthodox. I was suspected, since I was ignorant alike of Hebrew and of ceremonial, of being a missionary from a society for the conversion of the Jews. They believed that if I painted them, I would sell the pictures to churches. Now and then a few good-for-nothing rogues were converted for a handsome price, I was told. The simple but narrow-minded Russian and Galician Jews could not be tempted to leave what was almost a ghetto, for the ghetto is almost as much a Jewish as a Gentile arrangement. Determined not to waste a subject so precious, I took a room close by in Spital Square, where at last I persuaded 3 or 4 men to sit. Here I worked for two years, painting eight pictures in all.

Whitechapel has a vigorous life of its own. I haunted the Jewish quarter, where one observes astonishing types of men and women. The orthodox Jews from Russia and Galicia never shave, and some of the younger men put me in mind of portraits of Titian; for beards give breadth and radiance to a face. The old gray-bearded men, noble in mien if ignoble in dress, wear the pathetic look of Rembrandt's Rabbis. It was the time of the Russian *Pogroms* and my heart went out to these men of a despised race, from which I too had sprung, though regarded as a stranger among them. The men who sat to me, emigrants from the Russian ghettos, were rigidly orthodox, extremely poor and feckless; but their children would, belike, get on in the world, for they in no wise follow the ways of their fathers. Though the men were small, some of their daughters were magnificent creatures. No wonder Sargent admired the women of the race; though when Sargent went to Palestine he was little impressed by the people, a decadent generation, he thought. But this was before the Zionist Colonies. Sargent wanted to join me at Whitechapel, but he never found time.

Speaking of Whitechapel, I had a characteristic encounter with Joseph Pennell. Aitken, who was then director of the Whitechapel Art Gallery, had arranged an exhibition of modern paintings, including a number of pictures by younger men, which group in the catalogue was called the group of the New English Art Club. In consequence Pennell wrote a violent letter to Canon Barnett, which the latter sent on to me. Pennell complained that 'the artists who add distinction to this room are mostly *not* members of the New English, *never* have been, have in *some cases* no *sympathy with* it, and in other cases *belong to other societies*', and, considering that he noticed on the Committee (for this exhibition) the names of three members of the New English Art Club, he can only conclude that 'they have also taken no active part in the Show or else have lent their names to the publication of false statements.... If I am no longer a member of the Committee I would point out these matters for your information as I am afraid, if they are not corrected you will be rather severely dealt with by the small section of the British press which has any knowledge of British Art'. A reply of some kind was sent to Pennell, who grumbled again that it was no question of Painters exhibiting at the N.E.A.C. or the International—it was a mere question of fact and telling the people, whom Canon Barnett and Aitken profess to educate, the truth, and not making incorrect remarks. '...As a matter of fact the N.E.A.C. in almost every case owes what reputation or notoriety it possesses to cribbing the ideas of two or three of the artists whom you have grouped with them. True almost all have shown with the N.E.A.C. but are now opposed to their methods.' However he was glad that to a certain extent Aitken had altered matters, 'as otherwise I fear the consequences might have been serious!'

This kind of dog-in-the-manger attitude was characteristic of Pennell; he growled and snapped so often; but his manners were so well known that no one minded them.

CHAPTER VI

CONRAD AND HUDSON

CHARLES FURSE had lately married Katherine Symonds, John Addington Symonds's daughter, and the two had settled down at Camberley, in a house built for them by Reginald Blomfield. There they entertained largely; Charles Furse would meet his guests, driving a tandem; and when they left, would convey them thus to the station. It was a matter of pride with Furse to get there as the train came in. But once at least he just missed the train, as he did when driving Miss Terry Lewis, who had to get back for an early rehearsal; but dear Charles didn't mind, bless him, for the horses had gone so beautifully. The high dry air of Camberley suited Furse, and if, now and then, there were ominous symptoms, and he had to rest for a while, his energy and zest for work would drive him back to his studio. But the dread disease had not lost its hold, and he had to spend long weeks at Davos.

A visit to the Furses at Camberley brought us new friends, the Frederick Olivers and the George Calderons. The Calderons lived in an old-fashioned cottage, with a large garden, in the midst of the Vale of Health. The son of Philip Calderon the painter, George was partly Spanish, and his Spanish blood gave an element of passion to an otherwise Rugbeian character. Calderon, on leaving Oxford, thinking that but few people knew Russian, went to Russia, supported himself there, and returned with so apt a knowledge of the language that he was appointed Slavonic librarian of the British Museum. Scholar, writer, athlete, politician, reformer, anti-suffragist, dramatist, above all else Calderon loved discussion, deeming the spoken word greater than the written one. With his friends, and, since I was so near a neighbour, with me perhaps most of all, he daily practised dialectic. Calderon sometimes annoyed people who did not understand his character, by waving, so to say, a red flag in their eyes; he annoyed Conrad; and he failed to rouse any response in A. E. Housman. I remember how Calderon, after meeting Housman at our house, remarked, as I accompanied him downstairs: 'Well, William, so far from believing that man wrote *The Shropshire Lad*, I shouldn't even have thought him capable of reading it!'

It is true Housman neither looked nor talked like a poet. He prided himself on this, I think; he was grim and dry and seemed to disdain the artist in himself, to be contemptuous of temperament. But Housman and W. H. Hudson had an attractive quality in common; they were the only two men I knew whose opinions on any subject could never be gauged beforehand. Housman had few friends; but to those he admitted to intimacy he was very faithful. These he entertained usually at the Café Royal; the food and wine were carefully chosen; for Housman had a superfine palate. After dinner came a box at the play. Housman had formerly lived at Highgate, from whence he travelled daily by train to Gower Street. But the story goes that one day someone jumped into the carriage in which he was, and tried to get into conversation with him; upon which he moved to Pinner.

Housman sat to me more than once, never failing to tell me how repellent he appeared to himself in my drawings. One day, finding ourselves in the neighbourhood of Pinner, my wife and I called on him, to his housekeeper's alarm; such a thing had never happened before, but Housman made us welcome nevertheless. Housman, Hudson and Conrad, whose acquaintance I made then, I think of especially in connection with our house in Church Row. Hudson I had met many years before, at Mrs Bontine's; but it was not until 1903 that we became intimate with him; his writings were now familiar—I associated them, why I don't quite know, with Conrad's; perhaps because both were friends of Robert Cunninghame Graham, who spoke of them constantly.

Hudson would walk in with his strange, rather crab-like walk; very tall he was, a little awkward as he sat himself down and disposed of his long limbs, folding his large, beautifully formed hands across his knees. He had haunting eyes, brown with yellow lights, eyes that scarcely moved in their orbits, but remained level, fixed on no particular point, held rather by memories of things past, than by what was before them. His cheek-bones were wide and prominent (once he said he had Indian blood in his veins), and his jaw seemed narrow by comparison, a narrowness emphasised by the shape of his beard. His fine, slightly narrowing brow was deeply fur-rowed, and his nose was that of a predatory bird. Yes, he put me in mind of those sad, caged eagles at the Zoo, whose motionless eyes look out beyond the bars of their cages, as they sit, desolate prisoners, their wings unused and drooping, through the long dull days.

One could listen to Hudson for hours; he could describe, and make absorbingly interesting, things, people, animals; incidents he had observed, whether lately or long ago, made no difference to the vividness of his account. The things he noticed were perhaps common things such as others pass by, though he would talk, too, of less usual adventures, especially when he spoke of his early days in the Pampas. Once he told us, I remember, that he had known an old woman who as a girl had been carried off by Indians, with whom she had lived for many years as a squaw, at which John, who was with us, exclaimed: 'Lucky woman!'

I never tired of drawing Hudson. He was a willing sitter, though he disliked my drawings, thinking I made him look too old and worn. He could not bear the idea of growing old and concealed his age. He was very fond of Morley Roberts, Edward Thomas, Edward Garnett and George Gissing. One day I got a letter from Hudson:

'No doubt you have by now seen poor G. Gissing's death

in your paper. At Xmas his brother wrote to me that he had better news of his health. Wells went to France to see him, and on Sunday wired to Morley Roberts to go at once. He went that night, but whether he was in time to see his friend alive or not, I have not yet heard. I was one of Gissing's half a dozen closest friends, and feel very badly about it.'

Later Wells told me about Gissing's sad end; he died just as he had found happiness with the woman who understood and loved him. This was like Wells, to go straightway to the South of France directly he heard Gissing was seriously ill. Sargent too, when Robert Brough, a young painter he admired, was terribly injured in a railway accident, went up to Scotland to comfort him. I had thought once that most men would act thus, but now I know this is not so.

I had drawn Gissing some six years before, and his brother Algernon now came to see me, to say how much he valued my portrait. Sometimes too, when others have died, their relatives have said how they wished I had drawn them, while there was still time. Yet how few have ever asked me to make drawings—not fifty, I should say, during 40 years. It has nearly always been I who have asked people to sit.

Ford Madox Hueffer, coming in one day while I was drawing Hudson, suggested I should draw Conrad, and seeing Conrad shortly afterwards, for Conrad was living at The Pent, the farmhouse where Crane had stayed, which now belonged to Hueffer, he spoke to him about sitting. Whereupon Conrad asked me down for a week-end. The Pent was a small farmhouse, with farm buildings round it. It provided modest quarters for Conrad, his wife and little boy, and a room where he could put up a friend. The walls were hung with drawings and cartoons by Madox Brown.

One sees more of a man by staying with him for a week-end than by meeting him a dozen times at London parties. Conrad had known few painters and was curious about the painter's outlook on life. With his piercing eyes and keen, deeply-lined bearded face, in some ways he looked like the sea captain, but his nervous manner, his rapid, excited speech,

his restlessness, his high shoulders, did not suggest the sailor.
I accepted him at once as an artist; never, I thought, had I
met anyone with a quicker apprehension, with such warmth
of intellectual sympathy, sympathy which came half-way to
meet everything one said. This warmth, not uncommon
between young artists, was rare in a man so much my senior
as Conrad was; but as a practising artist I, Conrad pointed
out, was *his* senior; for I began to paint before he ever
thought of writing.

On the Sunday, Wells, who was then living at Sandgate,
was expected to lunch. We waited and waited, looking out
across country; each time Conrad caught sight of a distant
figure he would say, le voilà! But Wells never came. Well, I
must meet him later, Conrad said, and must get to know his
friend, Jack Galsworthy, too. 'Of course you couldn't have
heard of Jack. Our first meeting was when I ordered him out
of the way; he was a passenger on my ship, you know; he is
such a good friend; but insists on writing, poor fellow.
Writing is a treadmill; he doesn't know it yet. I shall be
coming up next week to see Pinker—Pinker is my agent; he
believes in me—wants to pull me out of my difficulties—an
idealist, you understand. You must meet Pinker too. And
may I bring Jessie? she would like to meet your dear wife.'
And before the visit was over we had become fast friends.
We met again very soon. Conrad wrote generously about
the portrait I did of him during this visit.

*Pent Farm
Stanford, Near Hythe
Kent.
13th Oct 1903.*

My dear Rothenstein—

You are exceedingly kind. My wife is delighted with her
Hudson both as to work and the inscription. You have got
the man there in a striking way. We are impressed for as it
happens we have both seen him in just that way; or, may be,

the force of the rendering imposes your conception of the personality. Anyway it is triumphant.

Of myself in black and white (I mean without colour) I do not speak. Hueffer prophesied to me how effective it would be—and it is.

I am so profoundly satisfied that I cannot help fearing you've flattered me—not in feature vous concevez—but in the suggestion. At any rate I accept your vision of that head, eagerly. The contemplation of it m'a remonté le moral: for you must know I have been tormented by gout for three weeks and brought morally, intellectually, temperamentally to the lowest ebb.

P.S. Have you found that Pinker can be of any use to you? Or is he no good?

Through my painting, through my desire to wring all I could out of my subject, to aim at what was beyond me, rather than to achieve an easier and more attractive result, I could sympathise with Conrad's difficulties. For Conrad wore himself out in his struggle for *le mot juste*, for words that should glow with a white heat; Conrad would often despair, and one needed all one's energy to pump faith and hope into him. He was then writing *Nostromo*, and working himself into a fever. In addition he suffered terribly from gout, and his wife, Jessie, had trouble with her knee. 'I can't get anything out of myself quickly,' he said, 'it takes me a year of agony to make something like a book—generally longer. And, my dear fellow, when it is done there are not more than twenty people who understand *pourquoi on se tue pour écrire quelques phrases pas trop mauvaises.*' There was always an element of strain in Conrad—an excitability, which may have been individual, or may have been Polish—I cannot say. Perhaps something of each. But I sympathised with him acutely in his desire to impress the passion of life on to his pages. This sympathy was, I think, the basis of our friendship; for Conrad seemed to understand what I too was aiming at in my painting. It was a fascinating friendship;

Conrad's charm, his mental energy, were inexhaustible. And Conrad understood everything; in him I had at last met a man of a passionate nature, who yet understood that a sane view of life is not a matter of compromise; but, as the *mot juste*, the phrase which shows neither weakness nor exaggeration, is the quest of the writer, so the sane opinion, the just action, are the signs of the enlightened man.

I leaned more towards radicalism than Conrad, and he often brought me up sharply with a contemptuous remark. Conrad was, by birth and by choice, an aristocrat; he believed that the object of life was the perfection of individual conduct—the education of man's own spirit. For panaceas of human perfection he had neither patience nor respect. Social idealists, pacifists and their like roused his anger. Hence he couldn't abide Bernard Shaw. Conrad knew that Cunninghame Graham was more cynic than idealist, that he was by nature an aristocrat, whose socialism was a symbol of his contempt for a feeble aristocracy, and a blatant plutocracy.

While Conrad was extremely courteous and understanding by nature, his nerves sometimes made him aggressive, almost violent; and like most sensitive men, he was strongly affected, either favourably or disagreeably, by others. Poor Conrad was always in difficulties over money. His books brought him insufficient for his needs; needs which were perhaps not quite so simple as he believed them to be. There was an extravagant side to Conrad, characteristic, I thought, of his former profession; he was like a sailor between two voyages, ready to spend on land what he couldn't aboardship; and he had a wife in one port only, for whom nothing was too good. His gallantry to his Jessie was a true sailor's chivalry. What others had, she should have too.

CHAPTER VII

RODIN IN ENGLAND

DURING 1903 Rodin came to England again. I took him down to Lewes House, to meet Warren, and to see the Greek bronzes, gems and marbles. These delighted him so, it was with difficulty he was persuaded to leave them. At table the talk naturally led to the subject of beauty. Warren, like so many archaeologists of that day, believed beauty to be a monopoly of the Greeks. Rodin, who would go into rhapsodies over Greek marbles and bronzes, but was a creative artist first and foremost, getting somewhat impatient with the table talk, 'Let me go out into the street', he said, 'and stop the first person I meet; I will make a work of art from him'. 'But suppose he were ugly,' Warren replied; to which Rodin: 'If he were ugly, he would fall down.' This was beyond Warren, and the talk took another turn.

I remember another episode in connection with Rodin's visit. Frederick Oliver and his wife were eager to meet Rodin; so they gave a party in his honour. All went well until roast beef was handed round. It was the middle of summer, and it became obvious to everyone that the beef was tainted—to everyone that is save Rodin, who, with squared shoulders and his massive head bent down, continued to attack his plate with energy. Mrs Oliver tried to explain: 'Non, non, il est excellent, excellent; le vrai rosbif anglais'. It was with difficulty he was persuaded to put down his knife and fork.

Rodin had now become an European figure; going from capital to capital, receiving homage, sitting at banquets and,

45

what was still more agreeable, selling his work to the great museums. It is perhaps as well that a good artist should have his measure of success early, for coming later, success may take too important a place in his life. It did in Rodin's; his head was a little turned, he played up to worshippers and became something of a social lion and, worst of all, he spent overmuch time as his own showman. He employed, moreover, Italian workmen who turned out too many works in marble unworthy of Rodin's genius. Whenever I stayed with him, I wondered at his patience with fools, and with adoring, exotic ladies. But I naturally knew little of such temptations. With artists, at least, Rodin was sincere enough; still, I felt that in future I would wish my friends success, but not too much success.

I was now less in touch with Paris, though I still corresponded with French friends. Rodin wrote charmingly, after another short visit to London:

182 *Rue de l'Université*,
4 *février* 1904.

Mon cher ami,

Je n'ai pu vous voir en Angleterre et n'ai pu aussi aller avec vous voir la collection Warren. Ce qui a été de toutes façons un crève-cœur pour moi, mais vous savez que je suis si bête sans savoir parler que je suis entre les mains de ceux qui sont avec moi.

Il y a donc eu des moments de perte, que j'ai tant regrettés, quand j'aurai pu être si heureux près de vous, et de MacColl que je n'ai vu non plus.

Mais vous savez bien combien mon esprit est avec le vôtre, et mon cœur aussi.

Votre maison et votre caractère me semble un portique de temple, et je sais chez vous que les dieux vous sont amis, vos réflexions toutes de sagesse, ravissant mon intelligence, et ne pas vous voir c'est perdre pour moi.

Votre dévoué
AUG. RODIN.

Arthur Symons much wanted to meet Rodin.

134, *Lauderdale Mansions,*
Maida Vale,

My dear Rothenstein,

Will you do me a favour? I have offered *The Fortnightly Review* an article—which they have accepted—on Rodin for the June number, and we are going over to Paris for a fortnight on Sunday, mainly in order that I may refresh my memory of his work. I have been to see him, at intervals, for some ten years, and I had an article, in French, on his drawings, in the book issued by *La Plume*; but I am only a vague sort of acquaintance. Will you, who know him so well, write & tell him that I am coming over in order to do this article as well as I can, and ask him if he will let me come to and fro to his studio, and just look and think, without disturbing him? You will do me a great kindness. If he answers, you might let me know. I suppose he is still at 182 rue de l'Université? and has he also the other studio, 117 boul. de Vaugirard?

Yours, ARTHUR SYMONS.

Are not all Moreau's things to be seen, is it at rue de la Rochefoucauld?

Of course I gave Symons the letter he asked for; he was a veritable amateur of artists, and collected them with the passion others have for china and pictures, poring over his impression of their characters like a connoisseur over his treasures.

Kessler, one of Rodin's warmest admirers, was often in London. On one occasion he brought Meier-Graefe with him. I had met Meier-Graefe in Paris, but did not take to him. He was now writing a book on modern painting, and wished to see English collections, that of Dorchester House especially; so I took some trouble, since he was Kessler's friend, to oblige him. When the book appeared, I found he spoke slightingly of English art, for which indeed he had little understanding.

Now there appeared a new figure on the scene, one Hugh Lane, a conjuror, who swore he had nothing up his sleeve, yet produced a quantity of pictures from his hat, and from other people's pockets, the artists' among them. These pictures were for Dublin, he said; for though Ireland had a National Gallery, she had no modern paintings; nor was there an Irish school of painting. But there had been numbers of Irish painters in England like Maclise, and to-day there were Hone, Jack Yeats, Orpen, Shannon, Lavery, Dermod O'Brien, and a host of others who were, if not wholly, part Irish at least. Surely John must have some Irish blood, and could not Steer, Tonks and I trace Irish ancestors? For Lane was bent on founding a great gallery of modern art in Dublin, and he begged and bought wherever he went. And he grew and prospered, finding a Titian at Christies, buying Manets and Monets, commissioning portraits and getting himself, at last, painted by Sargent, for the glory of God, Ireland and Hugh Lane. He found an 18th-century house in Harcourt Street, Dublin, which he filled with pictures, and gave to the city. He took too a great house in Chelsea, where he hung up masterpieces, and piled up treasures of Queen Anne and of Kien Lung, adding to the collection in Harcourt Street the while. He was made Director of the National Gallery of Ireland, became an arbiter of taste, was knighted, and had the world at his feet; then he went down with the Titanic and was no more. A great loss was Hugh Lane, though 'twas whispered his lungs were weak, and that in no case would he have had a long life before him. Perhaps he knew this, and hurried; for in truth his was a hectic nature, to which indeed he owed a part of his surprising success. Like others, he was no prophet in his own country; Dublin showed him small gratitude; and for a time he despaired of Ireland, and spoke of leaving his pictures to England instead. He did in fact make a will in this sense, but I believe this was a gesture only, to make Ireland, his true love, jealous, that he might have his way with her. So I have always felt that despite the letter of the law, the Lane pictures should be returned to Dublin.

Before the summer I went with my brother Albert for a change to France. We bicycled through Sens to Vézelay, of which happy memories remained; I had long wanted to revisit the old hill town. At the inn there we met a young Slade student, Noel Rooke, with his father, T. M. Rooke. The latter was Burne-Jones's faithful friend and assistant, and an admirable painter in water-colours. Ruskin had left a sum of money, the interest on which was to purchase each year a painting of an architectural subject by Rooke, who was a master of this kind of work. Rooke was now painting the Cathedral at Vézelay and the church of S. Pierre down in the valley. I marvelled at his patient integrity, and at his knowledge of the intricacies of building; no wonder Ruskin had chosen him out. Rooke's modesty was almost embarrassing; and while he was faithful to Pre-Raphaelite principles, he shared William Michael Rossetti's respect for the younger generation. He was pleased, therefore, when I offered to take his son, Noel, into my studio.

The elder Rooke was interested in a simple system I used for measuring while drawing or painting. I was surprised it should be new to him; he wrote to me later that he was 'taking sights with T square & inch rule after your manner which I am trying to adopt, as it seems such a good one. I see it wants the accustomed eye & mind, & that first it is a case of finding out all possible developments & then of simplifying them'.

My eye for proportion was untrustworthy, hence my frequent recourse to measuring. I found this useful for portraiture; for to establish the place of the eye in the head, and the relation between height and width gives a sense of confidence, and without a plumb-line it is difficult to make a figure stand well on its feet. Sargent depended entirely on his eye; but his great friend, Mancini, did more than measure; he used two nets, one hung in front of his model, the other applied to his canvas. The older painters used similar systems. Dürer used a glass frame, squared up; and there are two illustrations in Abraham Bosse's book on the engravers' art, of an artist drawing with a squared sheet of glass in front of his model, and his paper squared out before him, while between him and the sitter hangs a plumb-line.

Letter from Rooke

I had a charming letter from the elder Rooke on my
return:

Vézelay
15th Sept. 1903.

My dear Rothenstein

It is extremely good of you to write me such an encouraging sympathetic letter and to spare me some of your stored
up paper and be at the wearisome trouble of sending it me.
I hope to put it to good use for my last Vézelay sketches.

Indeed we should like to see you in Hampstead & in
Bedford Park too, and your brother, and it is one of the
things we look forward to in starting home, to help to reconcile us to departure; always a hard tug at the heart strings.
A sensation that makes me think my nature rises not high
over a pussycat's. We two are still at it, as weather will
permit; and perhaps not hindered as much as we imagine, for
fine weather when continuous gets wasted & undervalued
& when rare is made the most of.

. . . . . .

We had a splendid fortnight that wound up with the
hottest day of all the summer on Saturday week & since then
have had to pay for it.

From trying how little we could manage to go about in &
from creeping into every crack of shadow; we have, within
a week, got to trying how much we can put on & what
gleams of sun there may be to warm ourselves in. The
poor folk of the *pays* have given up their grapes for lost;
after having had them half destroyed a month ago in the
finest hailstorm I have ever seen. The street when we look
out of window on going to bed is of incredible & mediaeval
blackness, no lamps in it & only a very rare thin crack of
light through window shutters. Once on getting home in the
dark it did seem to me that the municipality had decided to
thoroughly blind us by having a blazing light half way up
the street but it proved to be the light of a vehicle & moved
off so restoring my sight, to my joy.

. . . . . .

We saw *a house* on Sunday, looking over Pierre Perthuis & in full sight of Vézelay. If any one wants to set up for a Count, or write a novel of a deserted manor, or do a thousand pleasant things there is the chance of doing it, cheap possibly, but at the trouble of much doing up. Young trees were growing out of the deserted steps, mounds marked the garden beds, shutters hung loose, fruit trees were neglected in a garden built up out of the hill side overlooking the river; and we had to be content with imagining ourselves the restoring possessors, or repairing I must say, as an anti-scraper, & go off.

Many thanks about the publishing suggestion.... I suffer equally with you about choice of work, am now very much doubting about selection of it here. It is the plague of the free born un-priestridden British artist; such as counts himself pleased at the newly gained pleasure of being,

Yours sincerely

T. M. ROOKE.

Rooke wrote admirable letters. He knew, too, much about older methods of painting; and I begged him to put down all he knew about these, before they should be forgotten.

I heard from time to time of Whistler, of how ill he was, and miserable. My heart went out to him. He had never recovered from the shock of his wife's death. I remembered how happy he had been with her. Now he had taken C. R. Ashbee's house—a house with a beaten copper door, arty-and-crafty, too, inside. I wondered at his choice. Soon he was complaining of incessant noise—building was going on outside the house, and his heart was troubling him. Next I heard talk of swelling of the legs. Then came the news that he was no more. I was greatly affected by Whistler's death; he, and his art, had counted for much in my life; and he drew from me from the first, loyalty and devotion. Now I deeply regretted the difference which had prevented my giving him such to the end.

I went to the funeral service at Old Chelsea Church. Later,

the International Society held a memorial banquet, when
Walter Raleigh read an oration. The oration was well
enough; but somehow the many speeches rang false. For
praise comes from equals, flattery from inferiors. I remembered a story of some Spaniard who, instead of presiding
at a meeting, sent his stick to be laid in his place. I felt that
Whistler's stick was, spiritually, present.

CHAPTER VIII

A BRADFORD EXHIBITION

Towards the end of the year 1903, I was asked to make a pastel-portrait of Leslie Stephen, who was hopelessly ill, for Trinity Hall, Cambridge, his old College. So near was he to death, I felt awed in his presence. He looked painfully worn and sad, but resigned; while every word he spoke was significant, for me, from the knowledge that he was soon to leave the world. While drawing Leslie Stephen I was engaged on an almost sacred task. With age we grow accustomed to death; but how alarming its nearness is in youth! In earlier times death was a familiar figure, striking alike at young and old; hence death is a subject constantly met with in medieval poetry and painting. I felt that I venerated Stephen the more from knowing that he was a stoic and an agnostic. Stoical too were his children. Vanessa Stephen was then studying at the Slade School. Pre-Raphaelitism was by now forgotten, and she impressed me, when I met her in houses where the older ideas still lingered, with the quiet courage of her opinions. She looked as though she might have walked among the fair women of Burne-Jones's *Golden Stairs*; but she spoke with the voice of Gauguin.

This year, too, Craig got a chance he had long been waiting for. He had already shown new possibilities of beauty and dignity in his staging of Housman's *Bethlehem*, of Purcell's *Dido & Aeneas* and Handel's *Acis and Galatea*; but these productions, lovely as they were, were seen by few people. In 1903 Ellen Terry took a lease of the Imperial Theatre,

Westminster, and appointed her son her producer. He chose, for her opening night, Ibsen's *Vikings*, and so beautifully was the play staged, so nobly were the figures grouped in scene after scene, that I felt something important had happened to the English stage. But no one, not even Max[1], made mention of this; and I was impelled to write to *The Saturday Review* to say that what Craig had done would surely affect the European theatre. Craig wrote from the Imperial Theatre:

Your letter to the Saturday Review was as pleasant as it was unexpected. Max didn't quite manage it. Tell him when next you see him that if possible I shall put my next production round a realistic play. *Much Ado* will please the others a bit...I don't think any will be able to giggle about it—

I am especially glad you saw & liked the Vikings...for you see & dislike so much. Do you care to use these 2 stalls for *Saturday* next? 1st night of *Much Ado*.

Come round after the play, will you? The Vikings will run for 200 nights 10 years hence...the thing I shall try for is to get the decent theatre built—& soon. It ought to be easy enough.

                                        Yours GORDON CRAIG.

Send me full title & address of your friend & Count. I can't lunch with him to-morrow.

But notwithstanding the unique beauty of the production, *The Vikings* ran for little more than a fortnight; *Much Ado About Nothing* followed. This again was a glorious production. Ellen Terry herself played with her wonted grace and charm; but her season proved a failure, and no other London manager beckoned to Craig. But keen-eyed Kessler saw what Craig was after; I must bring Craig to see him; he must get him to Weimar. However, the Weimar plan didn't

---

[1] Max wrote to me after reading my letter in *The Saturday Review*....'when I read my own article I thought I had not been nearly enthusiastic enough—I must buy some sort of patent pen that will run away with me. Meanwhile—floreant "qui" post "nos nostra" non dicta "dixerunt"!'

materialise; instead of Weimar, Craig went to Berlin. He wrote to me while I was in Yorkshire:

I've had a long charming letter from Count Kessler—& I don't seem to be able at all to show him that I feel certain that my visit to Weimar would merely end in my returning after a very pleasant waste of time.

I can do nothing talking to Dukes and Grand Duchesses & Poets with a court actress or two thrown in—

I have had so much experience of these *discussions* about a production.

If only he or the duke would make me a definite offer I would then make a definite answer.

As I have told him I can do nothing without first reading the play—secondly I can do nothing unless he can assure me that absolute power will be given me over *play*, *actors* & *actresses*, scenery costume & every detail in the production.

You see, my dear Will, it is the only way to do the work & probably the Grand Dook will see me to 'ell before he'll give me full powers. His poets, & actors AND *actresses* and even horses would all be up in arms against the idea—there would be mutterings of resignation & Weimar's actors would all leave in a body for Berlin—

But if I am to do the work some definite proposal can *easily* be made same as in any business affair—& I can then take it or leave it.

Do you see that they have refused Duse a license for the 'Citta Morta'? That's another thing—I have to be here in October to see Duse about a play or something.

Meanwhile I'm sticking to this 'Passion' work. Its tremendous & worth the doing for no other gain but the pleasure.

But I feel suffocated today. It's hot & this is a chill I think.

Yours GORDON CRAIG.

We went to Yorkshire for the summer, to Hawksworth, a village but a few miles from Bradford. We were thus able to see my parents, and old friends. I found the country as dramatic and austere as it had always remained in my memory. There was a deserted stone quarry at Hawksworth, which I painted; and the yellow, stone farmhouses and barns, stone-roofed, and the stark mill buildings, also of stone, with grim moorland around, reminded me of my childhood. We stayed at a farm; the farmer, 'Farmer Bell', was a rugged old Yorkshireman, whom I had known as a boy.

Hawksworth Hall was an Elizabethan stone house belonging to the Fawkes of Farnley; Turner had stayed there more than once, it was said, as the guest of Squire Fawkes. Some friends who lived at the Hall told us, as though it were a significant thing, that on the night of Queen Victoria's death one of the plaster rosettes (a Tudor rose) fell from the drawing-room ceiling!

While we were at Hawksworth, Craig sent me one of his enchanting letters:

> 13 *Trafalgar Studios*
> *Manresa Road*
> *Chelsea.*

Ow be ye, varmer Bill? I asked your little brother to-day where you were & he tells me you'r *there*—on the moors—where that huge fire of Heathcliffe & Cathy burned itself out. I feel I would give anything to be off there & get near the place.

I can't. I *have* to be here doing masque again & preparing to go to Berlin.

Would you be annoyed if I took it into my head to move towards Hawksworth in a week or so—if I *can*? They have made me a splendid offer from the Lessing Theater, Berlin—for September. I think I shall go there for a week first *soon*. I was excited to hear you were where you are. Never read that extraordinary thing about Wuthering Heights till a week ago—& now you are there—& why that should be exciting I don't know, but it is—& there's an end of it. God—what a sensible fellow you are to get out of this town—along with that dear extraordinary wife of yours & to go there—*That* is sheer genius.

The paintings—you know about, I don't.

It's quite decent here—warm, & a nice black night & black trees & quiet in a way but I would give hundreds to be *now* c/o Farmer Bell—'Where is your brother' I asked & I get the reply here in this funny town—'Oh—near Wuthering Heights—c/o Farmer Bell—' Lord it's enough to send one crazy.

I wrote you a day or two ago to Hampstead—asked where Max lived now. Can you give me his address? It's easier to find you on a moor than him amongst these houses.

Yours G. C.

During this summer Bradford opened its new Art Gallery, and wished to mark the occasion with an important exhibition of pictures. They asked Masefield, who had organised the Wolverhampton Exhibition so well, to act as secretary. 'The Bradford folk', he wrote, 'wish to arrange for a London committee of artists to meet and settle the scope and tendency of the Bradford Art Exhibition. They wish the committee to be composed of Mr Strang, Mr Steer, Mr Shannon, Prof. Brown, Mr Swan, and, if you will be so good as to serve, yourself.' We got together what was probably the best exhibition of contemporary art that had ever been held in Yorkshire, not without opposition from Bradford however. They thought we were being too revolutionary. Some members of the Academy must have frightened them, for all of us then, except Swan, were outside the fold. As for Swan, he backed out before the exhibition opened. The exhibition, however, drew crowds of people, and was a great financial success. Steer, Tonks, MacColl and Count Kessler came up to Bradford to see it, and Steer stayed with my parents; my parents liked Steer's restful ways. He seemed so safe from the slings and arrows of his fellows. Never enthusiastic about anything or anyone, he suffered fools more gladly than most of us did; he praised no one unduly, nor did he blame, so he made no enemies. For I have noticed that to single out a few men for praise is to gain the hostility of many. Steer had the wisdom of the slow and steady pulse, disturbed neither by undue ardour nor anger; nor did curiosity for the ways of men, for books, for science, or for the theatre tempt him from his safe ways: a pretty model, a quiet morning's painting, a rest after lunch, a little more painting, a ramble round the bric-a-brac shops, and early to bed.

Every summer he would go away to paint landscape, with Frederick Brown and Coles, never with anyone else; though Tonks on rare occasions would join them for a while. It was essential to find a place with subjects suited to his taste, and rooms nearby, so that he should have no distance to carry his easel and canvases.

If Steer was satisfied, Brown and Coles were content.

I tried to persuade the Bradford Committee to use some of the money they made out of their exhibition to purchase a Steer and a John, but without success. There was Alfred Stevens's portrait of Colman, too, to be had for no more than £200. 'I had a letter this morning from Wood', wrote Masefield, 'saying that the question of buying the Stevens should be discussed as soon as the new Art Committee has been appointed by the Council. It is possible that they will buy it. It would be a good and wise purchase.' Among other pictures they might have bought was a Whistler; but finally the Bradford committee purchased nothing, and afterwards Ricketts and Shannon bought the Colman portrait.

Masefield, who was then unknown to fame, was not too well treated at Bradford. 'I would like to thank you', he wrote after the exhibition, 'very much indeed for all your kindness to me during what was quite the most abominable week I have ever experienced. I think that but for you I should have gone home long before the Saturday. I would like to thank you also for your very generous help in the gallery, & over the correcting of the catalogue proofs, & for the very real pleasure your art gave me, in the brief moments I had for the enjoyment of the things about me. I shall always have a pleasant memory of our work together.'

Masefield in Manchester

Soon afterwards Masefield was asked by C. P. Scott to help him on the *Manchester Guardian*. 'I have been talking with Scott, the editor of this paper, on the subject of illustration. We both thought that a paper of this kind ought to print only the very best portraits obtainable. He wished me to ask you whether you could allow him, in case of need, to reproduce some of your lithograph portraits, and whether you know of any process by which the delicacy of a lithograph might be given to the reproduction? If Rodin, or Yeats, or Shannon, or Max Beerbohm, or Conrad, or any of the people who have sat to you were to come to Manchester, it would be so much nicer to print the portrait of a distinguished artist than the photograph of a journalist's camera. Perhaps you would be pleased to see your work helping to banish the base art of newspaper portraiture. Will you please let me know?...I am afraid I haven't put it very nicely, but I am so tired I can hardly write. It is past one in the morning. This late work is still a little trying.'

At this time newspaper illustration was in its infancy; and four days later Masefield writes again: 'We are told by the workmen here that they cannot make a good reproduction of your lithograph. They have been trying to reproduce your Rodin, but have failed wretchedly so far. Scott asks me to ask you if you know of any suitable process, or if you have pen drawings of the portraits, which might be reproduced instead of the lithographs. Will you be so very kind as to let me know? It would be a great pity if the project had to be abandoned'. But it was not many years before process reproduction became a common feature of newspapers.

Scott rated Masefield's services to the *Guardian* very highly, but Masefield did not remain long at this work. His poems and stories were beginning to catch the public ear. I sent one of his books to Count Kessler, who wrote an enthusiastic letter about it.

'I know of few books so *picturesque* in the Flaubert sense of the term, every phrase teeming with colour and movement and suggestion. That seems to be the essence of Masefield's singularity: picturesqueness of feeling and language. His talent is quite different from Conrad's, who has caught the force and bare sublimity of the sea. I linger over each phrase of Masefield's, while with Conrad I hurry on breathlessly to seize the whole. They seem to me both equally wonderful in having curbed such a monstrous thing as the sea to produce art. I know of only one other man in our time to compare to them: Corbière, whose *Amours Jaunes* Verlaine must have talked to you about. They possess the supreme quality of art, to exhilarate instead of deadening by what is terrible and enormous and tragical. Such a thing of cruel magnificence and terror as the sea becomes through them the friend of life. I am profoundly grateful to you for having pointed out to me Conrad, whom else I might not have read.'

I passed this letter on to Masefield who modestly disclaimed the high qualities which Kessler discerned in his writing:

My dear Rothenstein,

Thank you very much for your letter, and for sending me that of Count Kessler, and for telling me about the halls at Bradford. It was a very deep pleasure to me to receive such praise from a critic so distinguished; but Count Kessler judges my work too kindly. I have my own little boat, stuck full of gimcracks and little gay flags, but I am not fit to be mentioned in the one breath with Conrad. I am not in the same sea with him. He has a disciplined imagination, & I have a disordered fantasy. However, I am going through a mill of prose drama, the strictest discipline a writer can have, so that my work in future may keep more closely to life, and away from dreams and nightmares, and the adornments and dress of life. It is a mark of decadence in our writers, that they try to get, in their particular arts, either prose or verse, the quality of other arts, such as painting or music. It is a great temptation, to any sensuous person, to do so; but if they do it, they should do it very sparingly, for wherever it has been done by great men in the past, as by Shakespeare, or Fletcher, it is a weariness, it is like an Archbishop playing knucklebones. Perhaps in a few months' time I shall have more stories ready, & these new ones please me more than the old.

Masefield was not alone in his admiration for Conrad. While I was at Hawksworth I heard from Conrad. His letters sometimes made painful reading, so harassed he was by expenses—worse still, by old debts. When I returned to town, I spoke to various friends and Hugh Hammersley, Henry Newbolt, W. P. Ker, Gilbert Murray and others helped to relieve Conrad of some of his pressing difficulties. Later Henry Newbolt and Edmund Gosse approached Mr Balfour—was there no fund for such a man as Conrad? Balfour went off to Scotland, taking with him half a dozen of Conrad's books which so impressed him, that he arranged for a substantial sum to be put at Conrad's disposal. Mr Balfour appointed Newbolt as a kind of trustee for the money, an arrangement which Conrad found somewhat irksome. Conrad, as often happens in like cases, had underestimated the sum needed to pay off his debts, and was not therefore relieved from worry, as I had hoped. Indeed, Conrad was for long obsessed by thoughts of money, and feared lest he should die, and leave his wife and two children penniless. He was then finishing *Nostromo*, and wrote from the Pent Farm:

3rd. Sept. 1904

My dear Rothenstein—

The book is finished; it has been finished for a couple of days now, but I have been too tired, too flat to write to you at once. The last month I worked practically night and day; going to bed at three and sitting down again at nine. All the time at it, with the tenacity of despair.

What the book is like I don't know. I don't suppose it'll damage me; but I know that it is open to much intelligent criticism. For the other sort I don't care. Personally I am not satisfied. It is something—but not *the* thing I tried for. There is no exultation, none of that temporary sense of achievement which is so soothing. Even the mere feeling of relief, at having done with it, is wanting. The strain has been too great; has lasted too long.

But I am ready for more. I don't feel empty, exhausted. I am simply joyless—like most men of little faith. To see you would do me good. I count the days. I must take Jessie to London to see Watson Hood. I am sorry to say that her heart seems to be troubling her again of late. She is very cheery however. Your dear wife's letter has brightened her up.

Plans of work with ideas of getting away for the winter jostle in my head. I won't say anything more now. Only our dear love to you four people with the hope of meeting soon for a day or so.

Ever yours J. CONRAD.

Hudson, too, was very poor, but he spent much time wandering about the countryside, and needed little. It was some time before we discovered that Hudson was married. One day he spoke of his wife. 'Married!' said my wife, 'and you never told us. How long have you been married?' 'As long as I can remember', was Hudson's answer, the gloomiest verdict on married life I have ever heard. Hudson had met, early in life, a singer, a friend of Adelina Patti, with a great career before her; Hudson, in love with her and her voice, induced her to marry him. Then something happened; she lost her voice, and was never to sing again, a tragedy for both of them.

Mrs Hudson owned a large, dreary house at Westbourne Grove, of which she and Hudson occupied two floors; the rest of the house they let to lodgers. Poor Hudson, so fastidious as a writer, lived with the most forbidding furniture, the commonest pictures and china, the ugliest lace curtains and antimacassars. No wonder he chose such poor illustrations for his books. It irked me to see a man of a nature so elemental, living in this lodging-house atmosphere. His peculiar, mysterious charm was indescribable; something about him tore at one's heart, so lovable he was. Yet he never invited affection; he was a lonely man, with something of the animal about him, walking away, and returning with the nonchalance of an animal, and then disappearing again.

I had from the first admired Hudson's writings. His *A Naturalist in La Plata* and *Idle Days in Patagonia* I thought wonderful; then came *El Ombú*, and a little later, *Green Mansions*. I talked of these books, of the last especially, wherever I went. Many of my friends laughed at *Green Mansions*, though a few cared for it as I did. But Hudson affected to disdain his own writing. He was really absorbed in literature, and cared for good books, and liked to discuss them; but he would affect a contempt for the writer's trade. Once when I asked him to write on a mutual friend, he answered:

'It grieves me not to be able to do what you want; but I can't tell lies & what you want is an appreciation, with books & *not the man* as the thing to be appreciated. And I dislike all books—excepting purely informative ones like Kelly's Directory & the Almanac. Most of all my own. I do like them for as long as they remain unwritten, but the liking declines when I am writing them, & no sooner are they finished, printed & published than my only feeling about them is a desire to kick them out of the house & forget all about them. Of course you will refuse to believe that; but I don't mind since no one who speaks the truth can expect to be believed. Nevertheless, it is the literal truth that I love my friends in spite of the books they write. Imagine then what my feelings are at this time when I have been compelled (in fulfilment of an old contract) to revise the proofs of a book—my first book on birds of S. America, first published *thirty years ago*!'

I painted Hudson at Church Row, and drew him often. Wells also came to sit; and when, not being satisfied with what I did, I wanted to draw him again, he wrote:

Spade House,
Sandgate.
9. XI. 04.

My dear Rothenstein

There's no need for you to be hardened this time. We both like the portrait enormously. You have penetrated the mere superficialities of my personal appearance & shown me how I should like to look. And my wife, who displays that very human resentment of wives when the camera with its facty emphasis brings home to them, with all the indisputableness & wrongness of statistics, what it is they have really centred their poor dear lives upon—my wife I saw approves of it too.

Here at any rate it's a success, & it will go far to efface the painful memories of Max Beerbohm's little joke.

Yours ever

H. G. WELLS

John sat again at Church Row, where he made some remarkable drawings of me.

Through Professor Jack I met another of the scientific Titans, Lord Kelvin, of whom I made several portraits. Of the greatness of his mind I was assured; but a duller man, from my ignorant point of view, I had never met.

I was, perhaps, exigent in the matter of mental gymnastics: Sickert, Max, Craig and Conrad set a high standard. I came on a letter from Frederick Oliver: 'I have a strange party on Tuesday 15th—to drop tears over my newspaper's inability to come into the world:—the Chancellor of the Exchequer & the Edr. of Morning Post, Telegraph & St James. Also Chas. Whibley. To leaven this mass of letters I am asking you and Ian Hamilton. Do come if you can. 'Tis a rich dinner'. I always looked forward to dinner-parties where I might hear the opinions of statesmen and men at the centre of things, though I was as often as not disappointed. The polite rule of conversational setting to partners is usually fatal to good talk. Moreover the enlightenment one finds among poets and artists is rare. The minority, it is said, is always right; and often I have found myself, when among the great and famous, pretending to agree with ideas of which, in my own heart, I am ashamed.

John and Conrad seemed to me so far above most of the men whose praise one heard so often. John had a show at Carfax, with his sister, Gwen. He greatly admired his sister's paintings, as, indeed, did others among us. He wrote in reply to a letter of mine:

> *c/o Mrs McEvoy*
> *Westcott*
> *Wantage, Berks.*

My dear Will—

Very glad I was to have your letter. I was wondering how you were for I heard you had been far from well. I trust you are yourself again. Oh yes, Gwen has the honours or *should* have—for alas our smug critics don't appear to have noticed the presence in the Gallery of two rare blossoms from the most delicate of trees. The little pictures to me are almost painfully charged with feeling; even as their neighbours are painfully empty of it. And to think that Gwen so rarely brings herself to paint! We others are always in danger of becoming professional and to detect oneself red-handed in the very act of professional industry is an humiliating experience.

I have fled the town and my studio; dreary shed void of sunlight and the song of birds and the aspirant life of plants. Nor shall I soon consent to exchange the horizons that one can never reach for four mournful walls and a suffocating roof—where one's thoughts grow pale and poisonous as fungi in dark cellars, and the breath of the Almighty is banished, and shut off the vision of a myriad worlds in flight. Little Egypt for me—the land without bounds or Parliaments or Priests, the primitive world of a people without a history, the country of the Pre-Adamites! All the same I hope to see you in Hampstead before long.

Une bonne poignée de main!

Yrs JOHN.

Lines from Conrad

How generously Conrad could praise may be seen in the letter following, written to my wife after a visit to a one-man show of paintings:

> *Pent Farm*
> *Stanford, near Hythe,*
> *Kent.*
> 18 *Ap.* 1904.

... Just a word of thanks from myself and of love from Jessie who, you may be sure, is as grateful as I am myself for all your kindness to us.

Notwithstanding my half dead condition I went to see the pictures, and was recalled to life in all its fullness and force. What in art, could do more! I felt myself in the presence of something profoundly significant and masterfully comprehended. I wonder what people write about him? What ineptitudes they find to say? I would be sorry to parade my own; I only know that standing before the work I felt a profound pity for all the shams and pretences struggling for a place in the sun—for all of them, including myself.

I looked at nothing else whatever and went out even without trying to see Mr John's drawing. I have been very powerfully affected; it was so much more than I expected—and yet you know my opinion of him. C'est un artiste hors ligne, affirming himself as such in his very promise. And now my expectations shall be boundless.

I must come up again to look my fill once more. In my present state I was not worthy. Art, and such art is an august thing and should be approached with a free mind since true appreciation lies just in the surrender of that freedom to the artist's triumphant power. It was terrible to get out into the street. Awful!

Our best love. Affectionately yours,

CONRAD.

I stayed for a time with Gilbert Murray and his wife, near Farnham. Lady Mary was a daughter of Lord Carlisle, and it annoyed her to hear me say that her father was

a link between the Impressionists and the Pre-Raphaelites.
For Lady Mary disapproved of the Impressionists. I liked
Lord Carlisle's paintings, which were admirable landscape
illustrations; they told one so much of any scene, or building,
or garden that interested him; for he had an accurate eye and
a charming mind, and the figures he put into his landscapes
always had distinction.

In Gilbert Murray I found a rare combination of scholarship and interest in life. He did not then know Conrad's
writing, or Hudson's, but at once recognised their genius.
'Conrad is indeed in bad luck', he wrote after I had
told him of Conrad's difficulties......'An old pupil of
mine, now a doctor and quasi-missionary at Chuide at the
mouth of the Zambesi, has just been to see me, & was saying
that Conrad was the only living writer of whom he wished
to read every word.'

When Hudson's *Green Mansions* appeared, he felt too the
charm of that rare book: 'I have just read *Green Mansions*.
It is a beautiful book, really beautiful. Thank you for telling
me of it'.

While the *Hippolytus* was being acted in London, Murray
wrote:

'As to Hippolytus, I think there are always two classes of
people to receive a poetical play—those who have not the
imagination to *read* it as a play, & only understand it when it
is acted; and those who form a conception of it in their own
imaginations & are consequently apt to be disappointed or
disgusted by the acting. I mostly belong to this second class
myself. But I thought the actors this time very good—most
of them; especially Phaedra & the Messenger.'

I, too, belonged to the second class. Hence I enjoyed the
romping revues at the Gaiety Theatre, which gave full scope
to the peculiar drollery in which English actors excel. I used
to say that the only theatre which deserved a national sub-
sidy was the Gaiety, and the Gaiety did not need one. When
Granville-Barker took the Court Theatre, and produced a
cycle of Shaw plays, I felt the same about the Court Theatre.

But a National Shakespeare Theatre! when scarcely an actor or actress can let half a dozen lines of blank verse run off the tongue. Yes, decidedly I found myself in Murray's second class.

During September (1903) there came a packet by book-post; no gift pleases me more than that of a book. I was not disappointed—it was *Man and Superman* which Shaw had sent to me. This I deemed to be the best play Shaw had hitherto written. Man is by nature an ungrateful animal; favours received are soon forgotten. But to one who paints a picture which stirs me, or who writes an inspiring book, my heart goes out in thankfulness. I still regard *Man and Superman* as Shaw's masterpiece. Coming as it did fresh from the mint, I enjoyed it the more.

Conder was this year commissioned by Edmund Davis, who was now filling his house with treasures, to paint a series of panels for one of his rooms. These paintings on silk are among the loveliest compositions conceived by an English artist. I have lately seen them again, and again fell under the spell of their beauty.

I heard recently from Anquetin, who wrote of the high opinion he, and other of Conder's Paris contemporaries, had of his genius; nay, more, that Conder had a marked influence on their own vision. Yet to-day, those who most laud the Frenchmen neglect Conder's achievement.

CHAPTER IX

A LETTER TO *THE TIMES*

DURING 1904 a few of us met together with a view to
starting a small society of draughtsmen, etchers, wood-
engravers and lithographers. Muirhead Bone was the leading spirit; the original members were Bone, Cameron,
Clausen, Conder, Gordon Craig, John, Legros, Sturge
Moore, Nicholson, Ricketts, Shannon and myself. We called
ourselves the Society of Twelve. Muirhead Bone worked
hard for the Society, whose exhibitions were very successful, expecially in bringing drawings before a wider public.
Bone showed his first prints at the New English Art Club
in 1899. These so impressed Legros that he bought one.
Then Bone himself came to London and shared rooms first
with his brother, James Bone, afterwards with Charles
Aitken, in the Temple. He began by making drawings for
the *Architectural Review*, and other papers; but his merits
as an etcher were soon apparent, and his drawings and
etchings of London streets and buildings found ready
purchasers. No wonder, for they were remarkable. And
Bone too was a remarkable person. He could work anywhere,
no matter how crowded or inconvenient the place he selected;
he would begin his drawing on any scrap of paper that was
handy, continuing on other scraps, which he fitted together
with consummate skill. He had the eye of a bird for detail,
and a remarkable sense of proportion; he drew buildings
with the skill and ease with which John drew his figures.
Whistler's influence as an etcher had been a doubtful one;
for as youngsters to-day copy the latest manner of Renoir

and Cézanne, so etchers then affected Whistler's later style, which tended to be slight and broken. Bone had studied Whistler's early Thames etchings; still more closely perhaps Meryon's plates, and he was now applying himself to recording Newgate, before and during its destruction, and St James's Hall.

Bone was the most generous of men. I had a passage of arms with him once, a small matter, a question of the election of Lucien Pissarro to the Society of Twelve—during which Bone was handicapped by his kind nature. Ricketts and Shannon for some reason opposed Pissarro's election. Bone was uncomfortable, but took his stand on the question of Pissarro's nationality. But I was tenacious, and many letters passed between Bone and myself, until Pissarro was admitted.

About this time Herbert Trench invited me to join a dining club of which he was the leading figure. He had got together a brilliant set of men who met monthly at the Pall Mall Restaurant in the Haymarket. At one of the dinners, which were men's dinners only, Herbert Trench introduced, without warning, the Duchess of Sutherland. I had never before met a Duchess, and was flattered to meet this gracious and beautiful lady, but I pretended to be indignant at our being, as it were, shown off—saying that great ladies could themselves invite whom they wished, but that surely Bohemian society should be left alone, and not invaded as a kind of spectacle. A right and proper sentiment no doubt. Then shortly after, Trench wrote that the Duchess had been particularly interested in meeting me, and wanted very much to see me again. Would I take tea with her on Tuesday? But what about my fine sentiments? I asked myself, and I replied vaguely. On the Tuesday I put on my smartest clothes and walked towards Stafford House, but being too early I turned into Carfax on the way. At Carfax I found MacColl, Tonks and Robbie Ross. I noticed that they too were smartly dressed, and that they appeared distrait and not very pleased to see me. A few minutes later we all found ourselves walking in the same direction, each

trying to separate himself from the others. Then we met on
the steps of Stafford House. Upstairs we found all the
writers and painters known to Trench! He had written a
similar letter to each of us, making each believe that the
Duchess was anxious to meet him above all others. However
I was soon grateful enough to Trench; for the parties at
Stafford House were not only the most splendid, but the
most delightful parties I ever went to. The Duchess, kind
and considerate to everyone, was an admirable hostess. Her
radiant beauty as she stood at the head of the great staircase
to welcome her guests is fresh in my memory.

I recollect two evenings at Stafford House more clearly
than others. One was some time after the settlement of the
Boer War; the Boer Generals were then in England, and the
Duchess gave a reception in their honour. General Botha
and his friends stood in the centre of one of the great rooms,
dressed in very provincial evening clothes, innocent of any
decoration; while round them pressed women with glittering
tiaras and necklaces, and men covered with stars and ribbons.
On the second occasion the Duchess had provided two
famous *apache* dancers, a man and a young woman. Somehow it shocked me to see the crude, sensual dances in this
great house, before a ring of great ladies seated on the ground
or standing in a circle round the dancers. There seemed something sinister and menacing in this invasion of *apaches* into
the great Whig stronghold; I left feeling that the end of an
epoch had come, that a society which admitted such dubious
entertainment was somehow doomed; had indeed sentenced
itself.

There were other ominous portents. My friend Kessler
was then much troubled about Anglo-German relations.
Personal intercourse between King Edward and the Kaiser
had become strained—if this continued, Kessler thought,
matters would go from bad to worse—did I know any relations of the King? something must be done to prevent the
misunderstanding going further. I did not move in Royal
circles; but I happened to know Countess Helena Gleichen,

the painter, who was cousin to King Edward. Kessler asked, could I arrange a meeting? So I invited Lady Helena to lunch. She agreed that something should be done to prevent the mischief growing. Subsequently Kessler asked me to find out whether, if twenty of the most distinguished German intellectuals published a letter insisting for their parts on the absence of hostile feelings, an equal number of Englishmen would respond. Kessler also consulted Emery Walker; and a letter was drafted—by whom I don't remember—to be signed by twenty Englishmen and sent to *The Times*. Copies of the letter were sent to a number of people; some of these were ready, others were unwilling, to sign the letter as it stood.

The objections made to parts of the letter seemed reasonable. Some of those concerned on our side were indeed very critical of the German attitude, notably Andrew Bradley, Villiers Stanford and Bernard Shaw. In the light of what happened nine years later, their suspicions were justified. It may not seem out of place to include a few of the letters.

Andrew Bradley wrote:

> *9 Edwardes Square,*
> *Kensington, W.*
> *Dec. 20. 1905.*

Dear Rothenstein,

Nobody can be in more complete sympathy than I am with the object of the letter, and therefore I am exceedingly sorry that I can't sign it. I know that one cannot expect to agree with everything in a letter to be signed by a number of people, and I should not boggle at some things: e.g. at the last paragraph but one, which I am afraid is not quite accurate (I mean that I think there is a good deal of resentment, not only at that telegram of the Kaiser which began the business here, but at the facility with which monstrous reports about the behaviour of our army in S. Africa were believed to be credited in Germany). But the letter suggests the idea that we share the fate of our German friends in having a foreign policy influenced by dynastic considerations & by a military class, and capable of being (if not actually being) quite out of harmony with the feelings & wishes of the electorate. I cannot think this is so. Of course the electorate cannot manage or dictate foreign policy (and personally I hope it will not try to), but steps like this Japanese Treaty or the 'entente', would never be taken without regard to the feelings of the nation, and we have nothing in our country corresponding to the power of the Kaiser in these matters. And the worst of it is that the idea suggested is not only, in my view, incorrect but implies a criticism on our political condition which seems to me unjust, and which also, I feel sure, wd. be generally denied, with a great deal of indignation, in England. It will be said, I think, 'these men of art & science are complimenting the Germans by telling them that we are as helpless as they are in matters of foreign policy' and then there will follow contemptuous expressions about the political backwardness of Germany which will do a lot of harm. What the Germans need telling on this head, I shd. say, is rather that their notion of our Foreign Office as a deep Machiavellian power with a secret & profound policy, is quite ludicrous; and also that our sensational press represents our Government as little as our people; and again that *no* newspaper with us can be taken to represent our Government.

You will see that, thinking as I do about this matter, I could not sign the letter. But I am exceedingly sorry, for I sympathise heartily not only with the object but with a great deal in the letter itself. I am going away tomorrow to c/o A. F. Warr, Clearwood, Mossley Hill, Liverpool, and I don't like not to give you my address: but this doesn't mean that I want to bother you to reply. Only I can't help saying I am unhappy not only at having to decline but because I foresee that the letter, so far as it implies that the nation either is or could be seriously out of harmony with the action of the Government, will be hotly repudiated at home, and that this may do more harm than the letter otherwise can do good. It will be protested, too, and I think rightly, that our Government has done nothing as regards Germany that is out of harmony with the feelings of the nation as a whole. Of course sometimes, as in the Boer War, the policy of our Government is out of harmony with the feelings of a part of the nation: but when it is so, this means that the nation itself is divided, & the Government represents the prevalent part, & if it does not, is quickly made to feel the fact.

Yours in great haste & much regret

A. C. BRADLEY.

Then came a letter from Villiers Stanford:

50 *Holland St.*
Kensington W.
Dec. 21. 1905.

Dear Mr Rothenstein,

I am (& long have been) one of those who deeply regret the state of feeling that exists in Germany against England, & which has been so forcibly expressed that the slow-to-grasp but equally slow-to-forget feelings of the average Britisher are beginning to reciprocate it. I would gladly sign anything in reason to help to mend matters. But I cannot sign the draft letter you send me, because it contains many points which I cannot subscribe to. I must say that I think in the event of printing such an important letter as this, the signatories should have a voice in the drafting or at any rate in amendments of the drafting, otherwise you may place many of our leading men, I am myself an instance, in the unenviable & unjust & unfair position of being identified with anti-German feeling when they have no sympathy with it. The whole matter wants touching on in a shorter form & with a lighter hand. The true cause of growing anti-British feeling in Germany is not touched on, perhaps had better not be: it is the teaching of an anti-British distorted view of England & English History in the schools. But if this is not touched on, it is as well not to insist too strongly upon far less real causes. I sincerely hope that some means will be

74

found of drafting a letter which is sufficiently broad & dignified in its lines for anyone to sign without difficulty.

Yrs very truly,

C. V. STANFORD.

Others, too, to whom the letter had been sent made objections or suggestions, and the form of the letter was altered.
Then George Prothero, now Editor of the *Quarterly Review*,
made fresh objections:

24 *Bedford Square*
11 *Jan.* '06.

My dear Rothenstein,

I have given my best consideration to the question of
signing the letter, but, on the whole, have reluctantly come to
the conclusion that I would rather not put my name to it. In
its latter form, it is certainly free from some of the objections
to which it seemed to me to be open before; but it does not
seem adequate to the occasion, & the German letter strikes
me as very superior. Apart from this, however, I am doubtful whether this is an opportune moment for such overtures.
The Morocco Conference *may* lead to very dangerous complications, & the chief danger appears to lie in a suspicion,
either in France or Germany or both, that this country is
likely to back out of her present relations with France. I do
not like to take part in anything at this moment which might
be used to give credence to such an idea.

Yours ever

G. W. PROTHERO.

Bernard Shaw would not sign the altered letter. 'I think
you will find it quite useless to conciliate your second hand —
and the rest by alterations & additions. The popular tendency
is to deny our own Ministers credit for anything deeper than
the merest opportunism, whilst imagining that every foreign
Chancellor is a Machiavelli pursuing a secret and subtle
design for the subjugation of Europe. My objection is that
I will not be a party to a display of silly vanity by which the

three tailors of Architectooley Street will come forward to assure the public that all's well with Europe because they appreciate Strauss & Helmholtz, etc. etc.' But the two letters, the English and the German one, appeared together in *The Times*, and in Germany. Alas, it required something more than such vague expressions of amity to prevent the tragedy which the Fates were rehearsing beyond the clouds.

CHAPTER X

PARIS REVISITED

A BOUT this time we were shocked to hear of Irving's death. He died at Bradford suddenly, after a performance, away from all his friends. A doctor, who happened to be our family doctor, was sent for too late.

Irving had seemed to represent, in his person, the entire English theatre. He was one of the last of several symbolic figures. He was *the* actor as Ellen Terry was *the* actress, Sir Frederic Leighton *the* President of the Royal Academy, Gilbert and Sullivan *the* authors of Comic Opera, and as, in my early youth Mary Anderson was *the* beautiful woman, and Mrs Langtry *the* divorcée.

Irving had been to me a fascinating but alarming figure. I remember that once, after a visit to his flat in Grafton Street, he took me with him in his brougham, and insisted on my having the comfortable back seat while he sat on the narrow front one. I tried to resist; and of course I felt miserable, and thought him rather cruel, though Craig assured me, when I mentioned this many years later, that it was natural courtesy on Irving's part.

During 1905 I first went, with my brother Charles, to Italy. We visited Milan, Brescia and Bergamo and then went on to Padua, Verona and Venice, and from there to Florence, where we stayed for some time. Afterwards we walked through Certaldo and San Gimignano to Siena, finally going to Ravenna, and then to Arezzo, before returning to England. Who has ever visited Italy, and the cities I have mentioned, without being stirred to the depths?

77

Yet at first I was surprised by the almost casual appearance of the frescoes in the first churches we visited. The photographs I was familiar with had led me to look for a rich museum quality; and when I came across famous paintings in casual corners, or high up on the walls, almost like posters, there was at first a sense of disappointment, which presently changed to one of enthusiasm, as I realised more and more the quality, the profusion of the Italian genius, and how generally this genius was used, as to-day we use that of our engineers. Padua, with its arcaded streets, gave me a vivid idea of an old Italian city; while the Arena Chapel I thought the most perfect work of art I had ever seen. Here was Giotto at his greatest. What architectural unity, what noble form and composition! and what drama! I think I can *hear* the crack of Caiaphas's robe as he tears it asunder; and then the awed silence of the Last Supper! just the turning this way and that of the heads of the Disciples. What magnificent designs and what sumptuous illustrations! For illustrations, on a noble scale it is true, all these Italian fresco paintings are. They were made at a time when few men could read; and who could illustrate more clearly the moral tales the priests told their flocks, than skilful artists? The notion that these were great religious artists because all the painters and sculptors believed in the stories they were hired to illustrate, is a fallacy; indeed, the greater part of the subjects depicted dealt, not with the life of Christ, but with apocryphal stories of the Virgin Mary and saints, often local saints; and such local subjects allowed the artists to paint the streets and buildings of the towns in which they lived, the landscape outside the walls, and the many interesting characters—nobles, ecclesiastics, soldiers, burghers, beggars, and, too, the beautiful women, with a completeness achieved by no painters since. Compared with some of the quattrocentist painters, such men as Manet and Degas touched but little of contemporary life. For a great subject matter allows an artist to gather together all the threads of his experience and observation. How I rejoiced in the variety of the life depicted in Mantegna's frescoes at Padua, Masaccio's at Florence, and Piero della Francesca's at Arezzo, and in how many others! And then the marvels of Venice. But after the quiet, and the very Italian atmosphere of Padua and Verona, Venice, noble and impressive as she is, depressed me somewhat. There were too many touts and parasites in Venice, too many cosmopolitan tourists and too many idle and unwholesome-looking people. I must return at leisure, I said to myself, and live quietly in Venice, and get to know her more intimate beauties. In Florence we had the Berensons to guide us, and their house at Settignano to rest in when our minds were glutted with emotions. How different my painting would be, I believed, after studying the Florentine galleries and churches, the Palazzo Pubblico at Siena, where I saw *The Good and Bad Government* by the Lorenzetti; perhaps the greatest secular paintings, it seemed to me, ever painted. Yet when I returned home, my work remained much as before. And though I felt that something new had come into my life when I saw the great Virgin at Torcello, and the San Vitale Mosaics at Ravenna, I noticed that seeing great works is like making good resolutions or reading great books—we find we have, each of us, as it were, our natural horizon line, which dictates the perspective of our lives.

I went over to Paris during 1906; Conder was having a show of his pictures at Durand-Ruel's Galleries, the last he was destined to hold. I noticed, while sitting with Conder and his wife, he would grow suddenly irritable; but this is no unusual thing between husband and wife, and Conder seemed to be enjoying Paris as of old. We went together to the Théâtre des Capucines, a tiny theatre on the Boulevard, which held no more than a hundred people—and very select people they were—to see *The Judgment of Paris*, a daring play, with daring dress—or undress, a delightfully witty trifle, such as one sees nowhere else but in Paris.

Soon after Conder's return to London, Mrs Conder came to me, in great distress. Conder had been very queer; he had long periods of weakness and she feared his health might be permanently affected. I was anxious, knowing how reckless with his strength he had been; and his letters had something sad, though eager as ever. He wrote from Cornwall, telling of plans for future work:

> *Eothen,*
> *Newquay,*
> *Cornwall.*
> 5 *Sept.* 1906

My dear Will,

I was delighted to get your postcard, and I envy your pilgrimage to Courbet's home—when I was in Paris his work attracted me I think more than anyone else's after Fragonard's and Watteau's. The horrible *obvious* pomposity of the so-called *great* masters is too much for me—I confess. I don't believe I ever saw a place that would in my humble opinion suit you better than this one. I think you would be delighted with it, and there is a most lovely beach and one sees such charming sights of a kind of strange picturesque people who are always on the beach. If I only had more realistic power like you I could do some splendid things of the children of 4 and 5 years of age; they are perfectly marvellous and you sit on the verandah, or in our summer house, and can draw them. It takes two minutes to go down to the beach, and there are some rocks and islands that surround us that are wonderful in their noble lines and have much more form than the familiar cliff of Sussex which doesn't interest one—I think half as much. The stone of these cliffs is of a grey blue; sometimes portions of it are rusted yellow, a most beautiful tint. This is all to persuade you to come down later on with your wife; they say that the flowers all bloom in November and even December—the weather never changes much in Newquay.

I heard yesterday from James the painter, he is some distance off us and very difficult to get at. I believe it takes two days to get to Instow from here by coach. I hope he will come down all the same later on, he is a very nice man I think.

My wife tells me that you spoke so affectionately of me when you heard I was ill—I was so delighted that you do

care for me and in my heart I always hoped that it was so—
It is impossible for two men who *must* always have their
own way to get on like turtle doves, they can be most sympathetic, and yet have rows. The only people alas that one
really gets angry with are those we really care for—'n'est-ce
pas vrai, vieux philosophe?'

How much I enjoyed seeing you in Paris and going to the
'Judgment of Paris' and the Musée Guimet—I have often
thought since of the beautiful *Thaïs*; and I feel sure that dead
figure inspired 'France' to write his charming book. I am
thinking of doing some lithographs of Mlle de Maupin. I
know you love the book. I would love to do the picture of
'Theodore and her little groom' and also when she dons the
costume of Rosalind—I have already done a sketch of this.
I was ill the other day after banging my head against the top
of a very old beam in the summer house—and was quite ill
afterwards. But the doctor has sent me a nurse—as this blow
on the top of my head upset me and put me back a little. But
I think if I am careful I shall soon get well again—the
medicine has made me cross in my manners and the doctor
told me that it was the medicine!!! but I think if I may say so
that the two months in bed did my brain a great deal of
good in this way, that I feel a great interest in my friends and
regard life with more love and interest. I went through a
most severe cure at the last place I was at, and there were
times when I thought I couldn't stand it, but they say I have
a good constitution.

Do try and come down dear Will and we should get on
like a house on fire. There is about 300 yards of beach without any holes and very shallow and people go on bathing
even in October.

I wish I was well enough to bathe but sea water doesn't
seem to suit me. I expect to be here nearly all the winter and
our house is most delightful. This is the first long letter I
have written for 3 months or more—writing as you may
understand is more difficult to me than painting—so I hope
you will be able to read this. I am sending you some draw-

ings as a little present; they aren't very wonderful but you may like to have them as they are rather different to my old ones. I do a great many drawings with Wolff's 'Creta Levis' pencils and add colour afterwards. They are so convenient to carry about as they have a little grease in them they take in a most agreeable way to the paper. Newman sells most lovely blocks and books—beautifully bound and made of *Landseer* paper, at least the books are but the blocks are yellow, and remind you of the paper Watteau drew on. Write a nice long letter when you have the time and do your very best to come down; it will get you up.

Thank your wife for her very kind letter. Love from us both to you both,

Your affectionate friend

CHARLES CONDER.

At Newquay, in spite of illness, Conder painted some sea-pieces, enchanting as ever in colour. He refers in his letter to a visit my wife and I, with my brother Charles, paid to Courbet's birthplace. Everywhere at Ornans we were reminded of Courbet's landscapes; here were the rocks he loved to paint and nearby were the forests; while the village itself was beautiful, with old half-timbered houses standing above the river which he painted, too, so often. We called at the painter's house and found his sister, now a very old lady, still living there. She was glad, I think, of our homage, and showed us over the house.

I heard from John also; no letters delighted me more than his:

Calvados.

My dear Will—

How pleased I was to hear from you & how I should have liked to see the Courbets with you. I hope some day I shall spend a summer in the open as you are—I feel envious at times of the joyful devotees of Phoebus following the Golden Car with hymns & dances and feel myself partly reptile by contrast & dark visioned, lying in caves with jewelled toads

& crocodiles & stealing out at night to seek strange company half bestial half divine and talk of ancient days and the forgotten Gods. I am vowed to nudity & spirit haunted stones & still pools & elder trees, and foreign fowls. I fancy I've been damnably lazy this summer but am happily un-repentant. I fancy idleness ends by bearing rarer fruit than industry. I started by being industrious and lost all self respect—but by now have recovered some dignity & comfort by dint of listening to the most private intimations of the Soul and contemning all busy-body thoughts that come buzzing & fussing & messing in one's brain. It is sad about Conder. I hope he is still capable of work.

I look forward to a studio again. I wish I could petrify my children and so become the greatest of sculptors. I seem to see Alice reclining with ample and olympic indolence motor-car disdaining, a noble & radiant shape!

Au revoir

Ever yrs

JOHN.

John had now left Liverpool; his place was taken there by Gerard Chowne, who, with his gracious and beautiful wife, was popular in university circles. The University School of Art had been lately taken over by the Municipality. Meanwhile John had joined Orpen in starting a school in Chelsea; which, proving successful, was to be taken over by some other painter; they were to be paid £200 for the good will on condition that they continued to teach. Scarcely was the agreement signed, when John was again sounded about Liverpool, where there was talk of Lever founding a new University chair of Art. John consulted me; 'An excellent proposal, dear John', I said, 'but aren't you bound by your recent agreement?'—'Only morally,' was John's laconic reply.

John was wise to look to his painting for a living. The closer he kept to his easel, the better for himself and others; yet he was paid but little for his paintings. Even *The*

Smiling Woman found no purchaser for some time; and then the price for this masterpiece was only £60! Nature intended John to be a great improviser. To repaint did not suit his superb lyrical gifts, which were best expressed through swift and happy lines, and the fresh bloom of an inspired brush. The neglect of John's copious inventiveness, so perfectly adapted for the decoration of a theatre or concert hall, irked me. I pleaded with Beerbohm Tree to get John to decorate His Majesty's Theatre; who better than John understood the genius of Marlowe and Shakespeare? The cost would not then have been great; and how great the loss! We think only of preservation, of acquisition—yet to employ John would be a more fruitful form of preservation and acquisition than the purchase of a new canvas for Trafalgar Square, or some early treasure for South Kensington. But we artists are largely to blame; we should not allow such unnatural conditions to continue without energetic protest.

Formerly there were no museums; but through the fruitful use of artists and craftsmen, the people were familiar with the arts. To-day we turn a deaf ear to living song, while we provide, as it were, golden cages for stuffed birds. We have removed images from our churches, to bend the knee and burn incense before them in our museums. By all means let us treasure the works of the great creators; above all, artists are grateful for the inspiration they get from such. Certainly it is the first duty of each country to look after its own inheritance, and a museum provides safe keeping for treasures which, otherwise, might be ill-cared for or even destroyed; herein it performs a national service. Further, it offers, for our inspiration and information, a selection of masterpieces illustrating man's past. But the greed, the scramble and rivalry among collectors and directors of museums for mere possession, has become an ugly, an unnatural thing. I read lately of a drawing by Dürer, which Germany desired to retain; but we gloried in outbidding the Germans, paying for it an absurd price which we could as ill afford as they. Would not a good photograph have sufficed for the use of our scholars? Moreover, how many would notice the addition or absence of a single drawing from among the riches we already possess? Our museums are as vast as public cemeteries, compared with the old church-yards, veritable cities of monuments. Each addition becomes more costly, more wearying and confusing to the visitor, and a further encouragement to restlessness and haste, where peace and leisure are needed.

What, I wonder, will future critics of our civilisation say to this disproportion between the claims of the living spirit, and the preservation of her past garments? For a new Titian, much repainted, £120,000 was lately paid—an annual rental of £6000 for a few feet of wall space! Such a sum, well spent, would enable many living artists and crafts-men to add to the national wealth. The museums, whose function was to improve taste and active craftsmanship, have created a lust for antiques and for that pleasing quality which time gives to the work of men's hands. The growth of 'antique' shops is a disquieting sign of the times; our best craftsmen, who should be supplying the needs of the many who desire to have good modern furniture, silver and table ware, are retained to make forgeries or copies of past styles.

It is true that much bad decoration would result from public patronage; but from quantity comes quality. Not from villages but from crowded cities hails the superfluous energy which generates art; there was much indifferent painting and carving in medieval Europe, so general it was; but without a great demand few glorious works would have been achieved.

CHAPTER XI

EPSTEIN AND ERIC GILL

DURING a visit to Paris in 1907, I saw for the first time some sculpture by Maillol. I must have said something to Kessler about this, for I find him writing:

18. II. 07.

Dear Rothenstein,

Your letter about Maillol is perfect and will be remembered, some day. Allow me to send you a book about Gauguin, who was the great influence that started Maillol on his way. It consists mostly of letters and extracts, and as the life of the man was very extraordinary, I think you will find the book not uninteresting. I have been reading Hudson, and reading him with growing delight. Much as I admire Conrad, Yeats, Hardy and some others, *he* is to me the greatest living master of noble English. In his simplicity, directness and grace he reminds me of the great Attic writers of prose narrative, Lysias, etc.; his phrase flows with the same exquisite limpidity, every image surging up in its right place and perfect in proportion. Everybody else's style sounds affected in comparison; *he* does not seem to care how he writes, but to be, like the Greeks, naturally perfect. How can it be, that a chapter like 'The Plains of Patagonia' is not celebrated, and ten years passed since it was first published? You have added one more to the many things I have to thank you for, and I feel I must tell you.

Yours sincerely,
KESSLER.

How quick Kessler was to appreciate true talent! There

were few, at this time, who could praise, with such certainty, Hudson's prose.

I told Rodin how much I liked Maillol's sculpture. He said at once that, had he seen Maillol's work earlier, his own ideas of form would have been changed; generous terms in which to speak of one so much his junior. I was soon to find English sculptors to be more grudging in their recognition of fresh talent.

About this time a stranger came to see me, bringing a letter from Bernard Shaw. Epstein was a young sculptor with a powerful head and frame, determined looking, enthusiastic. His people were Russians who lived in New York, he told me. He wanted to work in Europe, but had no means. Shaw couldn't help him; he thought his drawings mad, like burnt furze-bushes, he wrote; but Epstein deemed I would think otherwise; so Shaw sent him to me. He showed me his drawings, illustrations to Walt Whitman, which were intense in feeling, if somewhat thin and tenuous. Judging from the style of the drawings I believed he would find more sympathy in Paris or Berlin than in London. But Epstein replied he had reasons for wishing to work in London. For the moment he must go back to New York, but must somehow get back to England again. A friend of Epstein told me that his parents would not hear of his being an artist; if he remained in New York they would ruin his career. Perhaps if I wrote to them they might be persuaded. There was a brother too, who might help. Of course I would write, but would a letter from me be of any use? Somehow Epstein did manage to return from New York. I approached a Jewish society and persuaded them to assist him; and with further small contributions, Epstein was just able to live and work for two years. With a small shed for a studio, he began to model Rodinesque figures, wanting in form, I thought, but with a strange and uncouth power. 'What you say about my work is true'; Epstein said; '*but* do not think that I am satisfied with what I have done myself; I know its faults & if a regard for perfect form makes an artist a classicist I am a classicist of classicists.' To bring a work of sculpture to perfection needs, more than anything else, time; also peace of mind in which to work out and perfect what one is doing. Neither of these conditions had, as yet, been realised by Epstein. He regarded what he had done as unfinished and only craved the time and opportunity in which to work on them to better them.

Epstein never complained of having to live on a very small sum, but worked ceaselessly. Then came Adams and Holden, those paragons among architects, who were planning a new building for the British Medical Council. They at once realised Epstein's power and proposed he should fill certain spaces on the façade of their building with symbolic figures.

Directly Adams and Holden were able to assure him that the matter would go through, he took a suitable studio and set to work. It was a big undertaking to carve 16 figures; but Epstein was full of courage. He found the work, as is usual with sculptors, more costly than he had bargained for. I took Count Kessler to see Epstein's work, hoping he might be interested; but it failed to move him. Epstein met with many difficulties while carrying out the work. To carve life-size figures was no easy matter; but when the figures, depicting the birth and death of man, were uncovered, there was an uproar. Here was a sculptor who actually attempted to say, through his work, what he meant. This was not to be tolerated. For two centuries at least sculptors in England had been saying what they did not mean with such skill, that mere empty gesture had crystallised into a tradition. Mischievous people complained to the police, and there was talk of action being taken against Epstein.

After fourteen months' work on his figures Epstein complained bitterly that, on the score of indecency, secret malice and enmity seem likely to bring about the destruction of his conceptions. 'To have laboured, conceived & brought forth, to embody & make conceptions evident & then to have them destroyed & mutilated would be damnable.'

Besides the architects, John, McEvoy and myself wrote strong letters to the authorities defending Epstein, and finally

88

the work was left undisturbed: 'My Dear Friend Rothenstein', Epstein wrote, 'I am overjoyed at the splendid result
of the meeting on Wed. & I will go on now quietly to the
end. Your letter made me very happy & this great wave of
sympathy from everyone has filled me with happiness.' And,
as usually happens after all the fuss no further objection has
ever been made, and the building with its figures remains one
of the most significant examples of modern architecture in
London.[1] Epstein was now free to do other work; he made
some admirable busts, of Mrs Epstein, of Mrs McEvoy and
Mrs Lamb; Lord Howard de Walden commissioned him to
model his child; Lady Ottoline Morrell a garden piece; his
worst difficulties were now over.

Meanwhile another figure appeared who was destined,
though no one suspected it then, to stand high among
English sculptors. This was Eric Gill, who was not yet a
sculptor, however, when I got to know him.

I had recently painted a portrait for Magdalen College,
Oxford, of George Edward Baker—their Bursar. A Latin
inscription was to be added. I was no letterer, but my friend
Noel Rooke told me of Gill who had recently painted their
shop-sign in Paris for Messrs W. H. Smith. Gill had been
trained as an architect, after which he came under Lethaby's
influence. He liked to think of himself as a working craftsman,
his work anonymous as a blackbird's song; and he charged
so much an hour for his work. His ideal at this time was to
change the lettering of London street names, an aim which
was realised later. He now painted the inscription I needed.

I was charmed by Gill's blithe temper and we became
great friends. When we went to Vattetot in the summer, he
joined us there. He was delighted with the barns, the carts,
the flails still in use, and the reaping hooks; he played
charmingly on the penny-whistle, and astonished the visitors
at Etretat, whenever we went there, with his sandals, his red
beard and his hatless head.

[1] It has recently been acquired by the New Zealand Government;
a sure sign of its sanity!

I was beginning to tire of panelled rooms, and after four years we found a house near the Heath, with large, plain Victorian rooms, and a large garden. The landlord was willing to do it up completely. An old lady had lived there for years; there were portentous chandeliers and grates, and the ceilings were heavily ornamented with rosettes. New grates were put in, the ceilings shorn of plaster-work and, above all, the top of the house made into a studio. How remote these days seem, when landlords put their hands deeply into their pockets to oblige their tenants!

The Johns were then living in Paris; Ida was expecting another baby. Suddenly there came a telegram, saying that she was dangerously ill. My wife too was expecting a baby; she could not have gone. But I should have hastened to Paris on receipt of the telegram, even though we were on the eve of moving, and there were other circumstances that made me hesitate, before it was too late. I never forgave myself for this hesitation; in my heart I knew I should have gone at once, as McEvoy did, to whom John also telegraphed. I loved no woman more than Ida; and I knew John to be in the deepest trouble. I was never to see Ida again; her beauty and her light were gone.

Before we left Church Row I met Alfred Harmsworth, through Charles Furse. Furse had just finished painting Lady Harmsworth when he fell ill. It was his last illness; he struggled manfully against his old enemy, and held out to the end. His death was a grief to us all. To Sargent especially Furse's death came as a blow, for the two cared deeply for one another. Any portraits Furse had left unfinished Sargent at once offered to complete; he was afraid that otherwise some of Furse's clients might reject their portraits. Before he died, Furse had told Harmsworth to get me to paint his portrait; I was to do this at Sutton Court, the Harmsworths' house near Guildford. My fortune, said my friends, was as good as made. I, who believed in my artistic star but not in my commercial one, doubted this; but I started well enough, and Northcliffe began by sitting well. But Sutton Court was always full of people: admirals, generals, statesmen, financiers; and I was surprised how they all flattered Northcliffe. I had not yet realised the power of a great newspaper proprietor. 'People say success spoils a man', said Northcliffe (he had lately been made a Peer), 'do you think it has spoilt me?' I did not think so; but his wealth and reputed influence had an evil effect on everyone round him, and this I told him. Northcliffe's directness, one of his engaging qualities, invited directness. The impression he made on me was not so much that of a cynic who gave the public whatever it wanted, as that of a man who believed in the excellence of his wares. He had a quite sincere bad taste, and a certain naïvety, and what he liked he believed to be good. For my part, I saw in him little of the unscrupulous dictator he was reckoned to be; but rather I found him a touching, misguided man, whom everyone was conspiring to deceive, to spoil and to flatter. He inevitably succumbed to this poisonous atmosphere; as a journalist however he was not deceived. He rated C. P. Scott, Henley, Charles Whibley, Max Beerbohm and Alfred Spender at their true worth; and he so respected George Steevens, that he had his portrait painted by John Collier, and hung in a prominent place at Sutton Court. Furse had encouraged him to form a collection of modern pictures, which should challenge, by its quality, the Chantrey Bequest. Now he chose me in Furse's place. For I got on well with Northcliffe, rather to my surprise, though I did not get on with the portrait; for after I had been to Sutton Court for two or three week-ends, he proposed I should go on with the painting at his house at Broadstairs, where the lighting was of course different, and, again, at his house in Berkeley Square. Work under these conditions was hopeless; I could neither do justice to Northcliffe nor to myself, and so I gave up the attempt. He wanted the portrait as it was, but I kept it from him. When he asked for it again, the canvas could not be found; it had disappeared during the move from Church Row to Oak Hill Park.

I was now painting the last but one of my Jewish subjects.

This was shown at Agnew's, at an exhibition of 'Independent Painters' arranged by Croal Thomson, to which Steer, John, Orpen, Nicholson, Pryde and others contributed. Owing to MacColl's attack on the administration of the Chantrey Bequest, exhibitions other than the Academy were now visited, for the purpose of the Bequest, by members of the Royal Academy Council, and my canvas, a study of three Jews in a synagogue, was recommended by Clausen for purchase. This was, I think, the first work thus proposed outside the Academy. Clausen was keen his selection should be accepted. He wrote:

> 61 *Carlton Hill,*
> *N.W.*
> *May* 3. 06.

My dear Rothenstein,

Thank you so much for your letter the other day—it was just what I felt you would write. To-day is the fateful day, when the Council makes its decision—I think there are at least 16 works proposed—& there may be more, as members of Council may propose, as well as this committee. Sargent is a 'brick'—& is trying all he can for the kind of work we like—but of course there are differences of view—Swan liked your picture much, and so did Crofts.... Well, we'll see the result to-morrow!

. . . . . .

I hope I may be able to congratulate you to-morrow—very sincerely yours

GEORGE CLAUSEN.

But the picture was not accepted by the Council. One of my models had a maimed finger, and Poynter (so Clausen told me) pointed to the hand as a piece of bad drawing. Clausen was then buying for Australia, and under the terms of the Fenton Bequest he bought my painting for the National Gallery of Melbourne. Clausen bought other things for the Melbourne Gallery:

'I called in to see Bone & his work, and (you may know that I have got his drawing of *Underground Construction* for Melbourne) he raised the question of copyright, as he wanted to make an etching of it. It struck me "all of a heap" that I had not thought of this matter in any of the purchases I made; so I knocked at your door. I suppose you would have no objection to the copyright going with your picture? I'm afraid we were both forgetful—but perhaps, like me, your copyrights have never brought you a penny piece & are therefore a negligible quantity! I *think* the law on the matter is that unless the copyright is stipulated for at the time of purchase it ceases to exist—and the owner of the picture can do as he pleases in giving access to it. (I have always in selling a picture given the copyright when asked)—

Would you care to say that you give the copyright, or to let the matter remain as it is?

Since seeing you I have bought three fine drawings by Havard Thomas, studies for his bas-relief of *Weaving*. But oh! it's difficult to get *real good* things! I've been through the R.A. & New Gallery dozens of times—into dealers—2 hours in the N.E.A.C. Many things I like measurably, but it is difficult to say absolutely yes to them. A propos of the N.E.A.C. I can't help feeling—and I hope you won't mind my saying, that I thought much there should not have been shown—& the show wd. have gained: for it is overcrowded (like the R.A.) Your picture and Steer's landscape I like the best of all there. Then the other Steers. He's beautiful in colour; is it wicked to feel unhappy about his drawing? Brown's landscape is good, and Tonks's nice colour: and I like John and dislike, at the same time, almost as much, the wilful badness of parts. And I can't like the Conders. I suppose though—if one may make a comparison between the bad things at the N.E.A.C. and the bad things at the R.A.—that the N.E.A.C. things show as a rule some aim at a pictorial motive, which is generally absent in the bad things of the R.A.

Ever yours sincerely

GEORGE CLAUSEN.'

Clausen and the N.E.A.C.

George Clausen, as a young man one of the founders of the New English Art Club, had been an active assailant of the Royal Academy. Sir Frederic Leighton brought him into the fold; and Clausen thereafter was a reformer within, instead of without, the Academy. Most of my friends, Frederick Brown especially, for Brown was a grim Ironside, a sort of Fifth Monarchy man, held the narrow door of the New English Art Club to be the only gate to Heaven. But Clausen's character was as honourable, and withal as independent, as his painting; and if he was loyal to the body he joined, he was equally loyal to the art he pursued, and to artists whom he admired, like Steer and Havard Thomas; though he was unable to convince his Academy colleagues of Thomas's merits. Clausen was always generous to me; indeed, a kinder man never lived. Perhaps on account of his kindness he would sometimes defend indifferent work. Resolute opinions make enemies, and Clausen had no enemies.

I took Sargent's advice, and found a studio at the back of a house in Church Row, which belonged to two pupils of Whistler, doctrinaire disciples, who tried to paint like Whistler, and to live, think, eat, sleep and talk like him too. But I was glad of the studio; I need no longer bicycle to Whitechapel every day, for my Jewish models were now willing to come to Hampstead.

CHAPTER XII

HAMPSTEAD DAYS

IT was indeed a relief to be in an ordinary house after spending four years in a museum piece. Here I could hang pictures or do what I wished with the walls, which had no panelling to impose its will upon mine. Behind the house the ground fell away, so from the drawing-room window we had a fine view over London; and there was a balcony, with steps down to the garden. And what a garden! full of rose trees, with a broad, old-fashioned English cottage-border, and a big lawn for the children to play on.

Another amenity of Hampstead was the fair; caravans appeared and settled down, with their horses, women and children, on the Heath, while tents, gay with striped canvas, shooting-booths and merry-go-rounds sprang up over night. Then for a few days Hampstead and the roundabouts brought back memories of old fairs I knew as a boy, of which the Nottingham Goose-Fair was the most glorious. Then there were not only roundabouts and shooting-galleries and coco-nut-shies, but 'exhibitions' of fat women, of giants, of acrobats, of dwarfs and monstrosities (I remember paying 1d. to see a dog with wings!); and the booths were glorious with gold and paintings. Indeed, the fair is the debased but legitimate descendant of the medieval church and palace. The paintings on the booths, on the merry-go-rounds, on the ice-cream barrows are the last links with early painting, more genuine than those that have since been consciously revived by our neo-naïfs and primitives. The great fairs in the past must have been glittering places. Indeed, to our fancy, all life in those days seems rich in interest. I have thought, sometimes, that men like Titian and Raphael may have felt, as they walked through the streets, how much they were missing through having to paint so many religious and classical subjects; did they feel sometimes a longing to paint more scenes from contemporary life? For local dress, and local customs must have charmed painters then, during *festas* especially, as they charm us still, in Hungary and elsewhere. And to the great fairs came strangers from far countries, merchants and scholars too, in strange dresses.

I remember walking to the horse-fair at Barnet with Augustus John, when he picked out some gypsy women to whom he spoke in Romany. But they didn't respond, and gave him hard looks. John was proud of his Romany; no wonder, he knew it better than most scholars. Watts-Dunton, too, prided himself on this knowledge; but once, when I spoke of Watts-Dunton's deafness, John said tersely, 'he was deaf enough when I talked Romany to him'. John could sometimes be very dour; his own careless gaiety had become more fitful; he was proud, and felt the unresponsiveness of the English public. He was now less in London. He took a house in the country, at Matching Green. Later he went to live near Boulogne, where I joined him for a time. He made some lovely drawings there of the young fisher-girls. Like most English artists, he loved France. He spent much time in Paris too; I wondered often that the French painters were not more struck with his work. But he had a patron in John Quinn, a rich Irish lawyer who lived in America. Lady Ottoline Morrell bought some of his drawings, and got others to buy his work. At her house, Lady Ottoline invited young artists to meet men of the world—each, she believed, would be of use to the other—and though she was not herself wealthy, no one was more generous to artists, poets and writers. Many young men owe their start in life to Lady Ottoline; and once they won her friendship, they could count on it always. Another remarkable woman, an artist herself, was Mrs Herringham; I had met her some years before. Mrs Herringham had a dominating personality. Endowed with rare integrity of character, she expected much from her friends, both as artists, if they were artists, and as men and women facing the perplexing problems of life. There was something imperious in her nature, which at once commanded respect; and when she singled me out, insisting I had more to say in my work than other painters, I found it hard to maintain the standard she expected. Having gained a rare knowledge through copying—her copies were unique —she looked, in contemporary painting, for that combination of intense observation of particular form coupled with a worthy subject matter, which was the glory of Florentine artists. If I fell short of one or other quality she was sternly critical. 'Why, that is only *genre* painting, which many artists can produce'; and since she was one of the few who encouraged me in my aims, and who understood them, Mrs Herringham's friendship was an asset in my life. On the other hand, MacColl, as critic, was too much attracted by a happy quality of paint, and by charm of colour. Fry cared for something more than this, for gravity of design, and a dramatic interpretation of life. Steer and Tonks talked daily with George Moore in Ebury Street of Manet, though Tonks had predilections, also, for the Pre-Raphaelites. Mrs Herringham recognised Steer's great gifts as a landscape painter; being something of a feminist, she was critical of the pretty girls he chose to paint. But an exhibition he held at the Goupil Gallery showed Steer once and for all as a great painter. Only John could stand beside him, I thought; only John with his superb drawing and his dramatic imagination, could surpass him. Orpen who had a touch of Hogarth's frolic, and much of Zoffany's skill, was now entirely taken up with commissions for portraits, and McEvoy as well was being drawn more and more to portraiture: 'Half hours with the best sitters!' I chaffed him, when I found his studio full of charming, tentative studies.

I was tired of painting the greasy clothes and shawls of East-End Jews. During the next four years I devoted myself chiefly to painting pictures of my wife and children. Mother and children; here was a subject that appealed to me. I could never make much use of casual models: I seemed to need some definite subject on which to concentrate. I have noticed that good composition comes naturally from an inspiring subject; nay more, a searching observation and a right reading of the human drama lead to good form and good design. Bad psychology, shallow and insincere interpretation of life, invariably tend to make bad design. It was here I felt a separation between my 'New English' friends—between Steer and Tonks and myself especially; Conder was, in his peculiar way, a subtle interpreter of life. In Tonks and Steer was a certain indifference to the profounder emotions, an indifference which was reflected, I thought, in their work—in Tonks's especially. For Steer's painting, as I said before, was inspired, in a measure, by the wisdom of his brush; in his best landscapes there was certainly dignity of design. But few of my 'New English' contemporaries cared for the more massive and sculpturesque side of nature, which appealed to me. John, fortunate person! had both the magic of charm, and a sense of the grandeur of form, marred now and then by a tendency to pastiche. And the methods of Rembrandt, Watteau and Puvis de Chavannes, were three ingredients which would not always mix in his mould. But John seemed to me then, as he does still, the most gifted artist in Europe.

Steer was now selling nearly all that he painted. A wealthy member of the great Butler family had become his constant patron. Cyril Butler, on Steer's advice, had purchased one of my 'interiors', and lately he had offered to take my Yorkshire Quarry and my portrait of John. But the price he offered, £150 for the two, seemed to me too small, considering how long I had worked on each canvas; and my brother Charles said on no account should I part with the paintings for so small a sum. He himself bought the Quarry for £200, and a little later the portrait of John was purchased by subscription at Liverpool, and presented to the Walker Art Gallery. But Steer and Tonks deemed me unwise to refuse

Butler, a collector. They were right, I am sure, for Butler never looked again at my work; though my brother became a loyal patron, and but for him things would have gone ill with me. For except in that of my brother, I was represented in none of the collections of pictures painted by men with whom I was closely associated; nor since that time have I been more fortunate. I was, however, early represented in the Tate Gallery. One of my paintings of Whitechapel 'Jews Mourning', at Canon Barnett's instigation, was offered to the Trustees of the National Gallery, who then administered the Millbank as well as the Trafalgar Collections. Oddly enough, my friend, D. S. MacColl, then Curator at Millbank, opposed its acceptance, but not so Lord Carlisle and the other Trustees, I was told. But I have not found that representation in public collections helps one to sell one's work; but rather that those works are coveted which are seen and admired in private collections.

CHAPTER XIII

ST SEINE L'ABBAYE

WE had not been long at Oak Hill Park when H. G. Wells came to live at Church Row. The Wells's proved admirable neighbours. In the two Wells boys our three children found resourceful playmates. Both H. G. and Mrs Wells were as hospitable to people as they were to ideas. Room was always found at their table for visitors, and table-talk was free, adventurous and gay; indeed Wells was the jolliest host imaginable.

We started, too, a 'Sunday Tramps' of our own. Friends would come up to Hampstead, some breakfasting with the Wells, others with us, when we would take tram or train to some place outside London and walk all day. John Galsworthy, E. S. P. Haynes, Hugh Walpole, Hester and Maitland Radford, were the most constant tramps.

I found Wells difficult to draw; his features were round and rather commonplace I thought, and didn't show his genius. But once when Shaw and Granville-Barker came to fetch me to a meeting in the Hampstead Town Hall, and took me with them on to the platform, I caught sight of Wells in the body of the Hall and noticed, for the first time, how striking were his eyes. I remember that meeting for another reason: Barker was to speak while Shaw took the chair. But Shaw in introducing Barker spoke so long and so brilliantly, he took the wind out of Barker's sails. I thought this selfish, and unworthy of Shaw.

Wells had lately published *Anne Veronica*, closely followed by *The New Machiavelli*, and was not very popular in consequence. He had something on his mind that made him resentful at times, and he complained of old friends who had turned against him. But this was a passing mood only. He could always be gaily vituperative, but he was rarely bitter. There was something frank and unashamed in Wells, a vigorous enjoyment of life, that disarmed criticism. He was perhaps a little greedy in his zest for life, I thought; as some are greedy over the pleasures of the table. Yes, Wells was greedy, but how much better appetite is than apathy! It was this lusty appetite for every phase of life, for work and for play as well, which I liked so much in Wells. And when he played, he played to win. Badminton was a favourite game with both of us, and Wells had tricky little strokes: he couldn't resist them—he couldn't bear not to win. Yet he was quite aware of his weakness, for in one of his books, I remember, he commented on this kind of play.

But Wells's weaknesses give him an uncanny insight into other people's minds, and, what is more, a forgiving understanding. He does not want to change people so much as to tidy up their surroundings. There is in Wells the writer, together with his genial understanding of human nature, an undeviating idealism which, in Wells the man, is often hidden behind a cloud of laughter. There is a good deal of the research-student left in him from the time when his ideal of a world was a perfectly-ordered laboratory, and everything about him must therefore be clean, tidy and ready for use; and with a grasp of detail, he has retained the scientist's habit of generalising from single facts.

I think of Wells as a great literary cartoonist, who depicts what is happening in the world, and in men's minds, and when I re-read his books, many things I had forgotten come back to me. And what a teeming brain he has! Ideas pass through his head as coins pass through a banker's fingers, to be invested at once so as to bring in the highest possible interest: and such amusing ideas too, with which Wells plays delightfully. His idealism he keeps for his books; there is little of it in his talk; nor, indeed, does his temper encourage idealism in anyone else; his response to it in others is rather a teasing facetiousness; though this may well be because Wells likes to think things out for himself; or that his sense of fun is uppermost. Although the Hammonds lived at Hampstead, they never came into close contact with Wells. For Bennett, I remember, they showed marked enthusiasm. Hammond was then a Civil Service Commissioner. He had relinquished his editorship of the *Speaker* when it became the *Nation*; but so used was he to expressing his opinions, which were strong, that he threw up his safe appointment, preferring his critical independence to silence on public affairs, which, as a Civil Servant he must preserve. In this he had the support of his wife, whose courage equalled his own. Their researches into social grievances were to result in the remarkable studies which began with *The Village Labourer*.

Rodin recommended me, for the summer's painting during 1906, to go to Thiers; he had been greatly struck with this little hill-town. But searching round my old Burgundian haunts, I found St Seine instead, not far from Dijon, a village with a beautiful Abbey Church. Where one finds one good subject for a painting, one is sure to discover others.

That summer was, I think, one of the finest I have ever known. We found rooms in an 18th-century château, the grounds of which had once been part of the Abbey. The family to whom it formerly belonged had emigrated during the revolution, or perhaps had been beheaded, and the château was sold for a song. The new owner's son became a medical man at a time when the water-cure was the latest craze. There were springs in the old Abbey garden; he suddenly discovered that the water of St Seine had curative qualities; so why not a thermal establishment in his own grounds? He had baths installed in the old monks' cells of the Abbey, had a swimming-bath made, and shower-baths everywhere, showers that came down on the patients' heads, and showers that shot up from the ground, and foot-baths, leg-baths, heart-baths, liver-baths, were provided for the prospective patients. The Empress

A deserted château

Eugénie came to St Seine with all her ladies, and St Seine was crowded with rank and fashion. Then suddenly water ceased to be the Imperial remedy; the visitors dwindled and finally no more came: some other sovereign cure for human ailments had been discovered. The doctor died, ruined and heart-broken, leaving nothing to his only daughter except a large château, a park and a decayed hydropathic establishment, in the deserted rooms of which lay scattered the rusting relics of better days. The daughter, now our landlady, had married a minor railway official, to whom she had brought the property as her *dot*. Here the two lived, a sad and childless couple, in a corner of the château. They were glad enough to let us have rooms, but we must fend for ourselves since they had no servant, and but little furniture. The châtelaine was of an astonishing naïvety. One night when I met her in the garden there was a full moon. 'Have you the moon, too, in England?' she asked. Another time, when I was painting and she passed with her husband, I remarked on the beauty of the clouds. At this she looked up and said, '*En effet*, I have never noticed the clouds before'. The beautiful Abbey Church abutting on to the garden, the garden itself large, wild and neglected, the cloisters, the deserted baths and buildings, the forlorn château, and the little railwayman and his wife: what could Max not have made of such a subject?

CHAPTER XIV

RODIN AND SHAW

URING 1906 Charles Holroyd was made Director of the National Gallery. He was succeeded by MacColl at the Tate, at which the Academicians were not displeased, for as Curator of the Tate Gallery MacColl became an official and must now give up his free-lance writing in the *Saturday Review*. Fry, too, had lately been asked by the Trustees of the Metropolitan Museum in New York to take charge of their Department of Paintings; but he put them off as long as he could, hoping to be appointed to the National Gallery. But the time came when he had to say yes or no to the New York Trustees, and he decided to accept. Just before sailing for New York he told me he had been offered the Directorship of the National Gallery, but the offer came too late.

Fry, master of an American purse, was now courted and cajoled by collectors and dealers. It seemed strange to me that the once shy and retiring Fry should now be swimming in such dangerous waters. I saw what his difficulties were, when Fry asked me to accompany him to Paris, to see an important collection of paintings which was in the market. For though I was no expert, Fry respected my judgment. A fashionably dressed and attractive-looking lady showed us over the collection. While Fry was occupied, the lady joined me. What taste and knowledge Monsieur showed; was Monsieur alone in Paris? Perhaps Monsieur was married, though he looked so young—had even children? No doubt Monsieur found life expensive, and so forth. I wondered at her interest in a stranger, before I realised that since Fry consulted me over various pictures, she thought my influence of importance: and was hinting at a bribe! I did encourage Fry to acquire a beautiful Renoir, about which he was hesitating. Renoir had not then his present reputation. It is only of late years that his exquisite art has been fully appreciated. Manet, Degas, Monet and Puvis de Chavannes were then the painters' artists. Still Renoir had a few ardent supporters, among them Durand-Ruel, who had a notable private collection of Renoir's pictures. And I saw a number of admirable ones too, at Rouart's house. I recollect that during an exhibition of Renoir's work at Durand-Ruel's in the early nineties, one of the loveliest exhibitions I had ever seen, I found myself the only person in the gallery; but there was Renoir sitting disconsolately on a red velvet sofa in the middle of the room. I remember too speaking of this to Whistler, who shrugged his shoulders; he was indifferent about Renoir's work. I am told that in Paris Renoir has taken Cézanne's place and is now the painter's idol.

This year Strang was elected an Associate of the Royal Academy. I was somewhat surprised, as Strang had long been hostile to the Academy, and in writing to congratulate him, I regretted his leaving the independent artists with whom he had hitherto been associated. Strang replied:

'*Danehurst*'
Westgate on Sea.
13*th Jany* 1906

My dear Rothenstein,

Thanks very much for your kind and sympathetic letter, and I quite see your point and see the cause for regret. One reason people go into the Academy is, not that they agree wholly with it, but that they are not satisfied with the conditions outside. If we were agreed and harmonious there would be fewer desertions, for the number of Societies who won't speak to one another constitutes the strength of the Academy. I am not defending myself but only trying to find a reason, and hope you will take these things into account in your judgment of me. For instance, I might have been better treated by the International, for it is cliquey, and the division between it and the New English is to be regretted as being a source of weakness.

However in the matters of conduct as in art, one must to an extent be a law to oneself, and do the best one can, and I hope I will do work that some approve of.

I am yours sincerely,

WM. STRANG.

I hope you won't think I was underhand in trying to get into the Academy, for I hardly knew my name was up and only on Saturday did Tuke tell me I had a chance, and have not sent to the Academy for quite 15 years, nor have been to the exhibition even. Also being the first original engraver ever elected I did not think there was the remotest chance of it coming about.

As a matter of fact all young men speak harshly of academies. They naturally begin by being of the opposition. Furse, Clausen, John, Orpen, and how many others! talked as Strang did, yet they finally allowed their names to be submitted for election, and when elected, they no doubt felt awkward at first. But I have known no good man spoilt nor bad painter improved, by being in the Academy. Whistler, who always held the Academy up to ridicule, would gladly have accepted election. Steer was sounded on the subject some 25 years ago. He did not want to join the Academy; yet he was pleased at being approached. But what would Brown and Tonks have said, and George Moore and Mac-Coll! It was MacColl who drafted Steer's letter of refusal.

I recall when I was invited to dine at the Academy Club, I was among those called upon to speak. I said what was obvious, that there were sound painters like Legros who had remained outside official bodies, and those who studied under Legros first showed their work at the New Gallery or the New English Art Club, and it was natural that they should continue to do so. The great saints, I added, were sometimes outside the Church; but the Church needed them for its own welfare, and usually managed to include them in its hierarchy! Clausen wrote to me afterwards, in his usual sympathetic manner:

My dear Rothenstein,

It is most kind of you to write, and I am very glad you think well of my things, but Oh Lord! how I wish they were better; and I'll try to do it this year. I'm afraid I'm rather remiss in many ways and leave things unsaid; but your letter gives me the opportunity, and jogs my elbow—to make me tell you what an excellent impression your little speech made the other night at the R.A. dinner.

I don't mean so much that *you* made an excellent impression by it, although you did; but that you put forward very nicely and clearly a point of view that had not occurred to many of your hosts: and I think convinced them of its soundness.

Kindest regards to you all

ever sincerely yours,

GEORGE CLAUSEN

Later, I too, was to be faced with the problem, whether to accept or refuse the Associateship.

Meanwhile I was asked to paint a portrait for St Paul's School of the High Master, Walker, who was then retiring. Oddly enough I painted this portrait in Watts's old studio. Walker's son had bought Little Holland House; but how its glory had departed! Little Holland House which, while Watts lived there, I had known so rich and so splendid, was now empty, chill and dour. The walls of Watts's old studio were distempered a hot terracotta; and through the high windows (there were neither curtains nor blinds) a cruel light poured in on my sitter. Walker was a powerful-looking man, but with too material a mind, I thought, for a great schoolmaster. I was glad enough of the commission, for few portraits have come my way. I used to chaff Orpen, saying that I was the real professional, since I drew and painted portraits when nobody wanted them, whereas he painted to satisfy incessant demands.

While Walker was sitting to me, Bernard Shaw was posing for Rodin. I was surprised that Shaw should have the means to employ Rodin. Rodin had never heard of Shaw; but Rainer Maria Rilke, who was acting as Rodin's Secretary, being a writer and a German, of course knew who Shaw was, and Shaw was received at Meudon as a great man.

Rilke wrote while the bust was in progress:

182, *Rue de l'Université*,
Cher Monsieur, 26 *Avril* 1906

Monsieur Rodin, enfoncé dans son travail, me prie de vous remercier de votre lettre si chaleureusement amicale, ce que je fais avec autant plus de joie, que je n'ai pas pu vous exprimer suffisamment combien j'ai été heureux de vous rencontrer ici chez notre grand ami.

Le Maître et moi nous avons toujours espéré de vous voir passer encore une fois à Meudon avant votre retour en Angleterre; vous auriez dû venir partager encore quelques jours notre vie paisible, et Rodin aurait été ravi de pouvoir vous montrer le buste de Shaw qui s'avance merveilleusement déjà, vibrant de vie et de caractère; ce que ne serait point accessible, si Mr Shaw n'était pas ce modèle extraordinaire qui pose avec la même énergie et sincérité qui font sa gloire d'écrivain.

M. et Mme Shaw viennent tous les jours à Meudon, puisque Rodin évite autant que possible Paris et son atelier froid et humide dans ce temps-ci.

Vous nous avez manqué samedi dernier à l'inauguration. Le Maître était très content de cette fête qui se tenait dans des limites presque familières, sans trop de bruit. Et *Le Penseur* trône admirablement sur sa place définitive. La grande porte du Panthéon s'ouvre derrière lui comme dans un noir inconnu, dont il médite la profondeur.

The judgment of time

Rodin vous remercie du souvenir que vous gardez de
Meudon et de son printemps, et je n'ai pas besoin de vous
dire, combien il est heureux, que la 'tête' vous plaît et vous
contente. C'est une vrai récompense pour lui que de savoir
ces œuvres chez des amis, entourées de cette tendresse per-
petuelle, qui, témoignée à elles, revient à lui.

I believe Shaw tells the story that Rodin made his bust
without knowing anything about him: Rilke's letter shows
that Rodin was aware of Shaw's 'gloire d'écrivain'.

The inauguration to which Rilke refers was, of course,
the unveiling of *Le Penseur* in front of the Panthéon.

Rodin's messages were apt to be flattering. He himself
gravely accepted exaggerated adulation. His fame at this
time was wider, perhaps, than that of any living artist. It
is easy to deride the passing of figure after figure in and
out of the limelight. But there is much to be said in favour of
the fashion which each succeeding generation creates; for it
is through this that the flavour of an artist's work is enjoyed.
A work of art needs the co-operation of the spectator, and
without fashion the connoisseurs would be as mariners without a compass, and a picture as a wit with an inattentive
listener. One can imagine sayings, which have become
current throughout the world, passing when first said, unnoticed. Likewise things which at first repel or are ignored,
seem, when the moment is ripe, the perfect lilies of art.
Then, maybe, to the next generation, they become the 'lilies
that fester'. Yet men's final judgments are sound enough,
and Rodin, Manet, Whistler, Degas, Renoir, Gauguin,
Cézanne will, in due course, find their places; so will
Rossetti, Watts, Madox Brown, Holman Hunt and Burne-
Jones. Time alone, said Leonardo, is just. We may hazard
guesses; but a study of contemporary opinions during the
18th and 19th centuries should make us pause. I have often
felt that, as an athlete or an acrobat trains from his earliest
youth and continues to train to keep himself in condition, so
an artist should prepare for the meannesses, attacks, and

neglect that are likely to be his portion; and prepare too for the more subtle attacks of flattery and excessive praise, which, if he reach ripe years, he is bound to suffer. But against these last he would prefer perhaps to be unarmed.

Another great man who was subject to flattery was Anatole France. We had made France a member of our Oxford Rabelais Club, and he had asked me to come and see him sometime when I was in Paris. At the Villa Saïd I received a warm welcome. I found Anatole France, like Edmond de Goncourt, to be an inveterate collector; classical and medieval sculpture was his prey. His house was like a museum, while he himself, in a flowered dressing-gown, with kerchief tied round his head, seemed like a figure from the past. His face, long and bearded, with its twinkling eyes, large nose and pale, heavy cheeks, had a Rabelaisian look. Like most subjects of flattery, Anatole France was an unashamed flatterer, but his compliments were spiced with irony. Such an attitude to the young from a senior is embarrassing; from Anatole France it was especially so, for he had with him a young secretary, and one or two young Frenchmen, and these, while he treated me with extravagant politeness, he chaffed unmercifully; moreover, he exaggerated the import of everything I said, pretending to find wit and wisdom in my stumbling remarks, to the detriment of anything his disciples said. Like Meredith, he talked as he wrote, though I was reminded more of his urbanity and naughtiness than of his large humanity. When many years later the young man who had been his Secretary wrote *Anatole France en Pantoufles*, I understood why he had drawn so cruel a portrait.

CHAPTER XV

MICHAEL FIELD

In the following year, 1907, Coles, who was Headmaster of the Winchester School of Art—the Coles who joined Brown and Steer in their painting every summer—asked me to address his students. I had never yet spoken in public, but I read a short address. This was reported in the local paper, which someone, it seems, sent to Lady Burne-Jones; for there came a letter—might she get my address printed by Emery Walker, at her expense? Thus began for me a precious friendship; for Lady Burne-Jones had moral strength combined with graciousness. To a shrewd estimation of character she added the true woman's gift of getting the best they had to give from her friends. She was wise and gentle; yet a fire burned within her, and when made aware of selfishness and injustice, she could get angry enough. And she lived, too, in the present. I had expected to find her, as the wife of her husband, and the friend of his friends—of Rossetti, Morris and Holman Hunt—engrossed in the past; yet no one was more keenly concerned with what was now most vital in art, literature and politics. And she had the gift of allowing one to be one's self in her company; a rare gift, one of the best a rich nature can offer.

The Michael Fields too had this gift and a like zest for life. Now my friendship with them was renewed. They took a great fancy to my wife, for whom they invented a charming name—Noli me tangere. They wrote to me:

Court House,
Rottingdean,
Nr Brighton.

Jan. 20th 1907.

Dear...

But I cannot call you anything formal, can I, now *we* have given you our real names to call *us* by? What is to be done?

A name should be written on the forehead of every new friendship. It is only these name-friendships that weather the storms of life. It is only a name that really seals.

Our fresh friend—your wife—we call to each other *Noli*—and why? Because she shoots out her words like a stalwart balsam shooting out its seeds—they forthright things, completely of her character...yet, all the while she is a balsam, a delicious, loveable *Noli me tangere*. Will she have her new name confirmed to her? And you...do not be jealous, we have caught no name for you yet! Can you aid? Ricketts did in one of his names. How glad we are, after the dark defiles and darker forests we have wandered, that you see us tossing our lit faggots at the top of the mountain. It exhilarates that you have seen this sight. To us it is almost pathetically strange to find in you one who not only talks from his own thoughts but is so freely human. Alas, we who translate life for the Gods, so often get severed from the life we translate and lose much of our humanity—we encounter so much hatred, because we are not contented with the mother-tongue of Fact, we grow aloof and strange ourselves. You and dear Noli are both amazingly human and simple—John[1] too is an excellent example of humanity and simplicity. I have been ill—we think with influenza; as after the asthma and acute internal pains dizzy craters have opened in the head, down wh: consciousness tumbles. If we can make arrangements for comfort we may stay on here till February 4th to get restored. If the asthma will yield we hope for Hampstead after that—but if it is still too early for us to trust ourselves to a northern hill and heath, you must first

[1] Our son John.

come and spend a day with us. Do not let our ill-health discourage you, friends, or make you think us backward. It is a constant hindrance in the winter, but with kindness soon loses importance. If you have the photo by you, do send it here, as we may have another fortnight. We are beginning to 'work' on the infinite plane of the Downs. One evening they were firm as only land can be that has a moon behind it.

Our love to you all. One so resents the marriage of a friend, chosen when unmarried—force is brought upon one of another's choice; but a friendship with the married a double-flower elected for its richer doubleness, is one of the good things of life.

FIELD

Say to John,[1] if Nelson had promised a post-card to a lady, he would not have kept her waiting. He would have gone forth in the snow, with guns being fired at him all round, and a lion growling in front to choose that post-card, Say, I am quite sure of this.

M.

The ugly dog (Binyon told me, too late, that he was not a dog at all, but a lion!) that guards the Chinese Heaven I suggested as a name for myself, and henceforth, for the Michael Fields, I was ever *The Heavenly Dog*.

1, *The Paragon,*
Richmond,
Surrey,
Wednesday.

Heavenly Dog,

Can you and Noli come to dine with us on Saturday—coming also, if fine, to 'tea' with us and to see November pour her silver regally into the stream under lights and smiles of a strange benevolence? It is so unbelievably beautiful.

Do come!

[1] Our son John.

And we want to hear if you have made Bernhard[1] a Professor or a Faun—if the blue that has left his eyes visited your brush and will make us remember what was so fugitive.

Come to see us—no lamb-dog-thing, but the real Dog of monstrous and vital contemplation the good Jap sees before he reaches heaven. This month of the dead has rather taxed us. Come and bark us into heavenly-mindedness—and golden Noli come to join our Chorus of merriment!

FIELD

No one ever sent more delightful invitations than these two ladies; here are two more, chosen from many:

Come—you and dear Noli—come and represent the kingdoms of this world—and their power, and splendour, and beauty and temptation! Come, and make us Renaissance fair. They are breaking stones on the road, and the fog, and the wind—full of black salt!!

Dine with us on Saturday, or on Monday. Possibly we shall be going away next Wednesday to whence there is music.

Come on Saturday. Bring with you beautiful pictures. Let Noli dress in gold.

M.

1, *Paragon,*
Richmond,
Surrey.

Dear Friends

Our garden begs for eyes to look at it with us. Do come both as you did before tea and early supper this Sunday and then we will settle the anticipated visit to you.

We shall expect you unless you wire. It will be charming to meet again and among roses and lilies—that fade so fast this year. Do come—

In haste—but in the leisure of friendship in the heart.

FIELD
joined by MICHAEL.

[1] Bernhard Berenson.

114

The Paragon, the Michael Fields' house at Richmond, was an 18th-century house, with a garden running down to the river. In the living-rooms the furniture was of satinwood, chosen by Ricketts, and on the walls hung Shannon's lithographs, and prints by Ricketts and Sturge Moore, exquisitely mounted. Ricketts and Shannon gave to mounting and framing the care which only Eastern artists give as a rule. There were always choice flowers, lovingly arranged, and in a large cage cooed a pair of doves. Field, wan, a little drooping, with her large eyes, clear forehead and sensitive lips looked the poet she was; Michael, stout, with a high colour, masterful, protecting, was the active, managing spirit of the Paragon. Field again looked the poet in any dress she wore; but a dress, like everything else, must for long be discussed and pondered and finally ordered from the modiste with elaborate directions. But most important were the hats. Once a year a visit was paid to Kate Riley, a Dover Street milliner, and imperial hats were chosen; purple, with superb feathers, that drooped over Field's small ear, and waved proudly above Michael's head. But these poetesses were fiery ladies. There were grass borders in the gardens of their minds on which one must never tread. For they were both ardent converts to Roman Catholicism, and they gave all the wealth of their imaginations, their entire obedience, and somewhat, I fancy, of their worldly wealth to what was for them the only true church. And what a rich fantasy was theirs; what lightning play of mind, and how they valued the same in others! They knew but few people, but from these few they expected—everything, all they had to give. They were imperious ladies, these exquisite poets, Michael especially. They knew the value of their friendship; if they gave it, it must be with both hands; but those to whom they gave must be worthy of their trust every moment, whether in their company, or out of sight and hearing. None was more sensible of beauty, of the fine shades of life, or wittier than Michael and Field; to re-read their letters is to evoke their lovely spirited and spiritual souls. Knowing such women, one can understand the age of chivalry. Our age is not such; contemptuous of ceremony, it believes in stark nakedness of mind, and of body, too, it would seem. Truly, there is the light of the moon and the light of the sun—each succeeds the other; and we of this generation lean towards the poetry of sunlight. But even so, there are moments when the softer and mysterious radiance of the paler planet, its more solemn lights and shadows, move us more profoundly than the franker passion of the sunlight. We now so love the mid-day sun, however, that we doubt the worth of sunrise and sunset; fearful of sentiment we avert our eyes at the brief moment of blossoming; as though there were degrees of value, and high summer were truer than the spring. Whistler would have it that between dawn and evening, nature was too raw for the artist's use; now our painters migrate each summer to the south of France, to paint cactuses at mid-day. We are so made, indeed, that only the appearance upon which we concentrate is real to us. Each generation has a blind and a seeing eye, like a man who looks through a telescope; that with which we are immediately occupied seems true, while that which occupied our fathers appears not only false, but ridiculous.

CHAPTER XVI

A VISIT TO ITALY

UNDER MacColl's direction the Tate Gallery was becoming a fine gallery of British art. Charles Aitken was later to continue MacColl's enlightened policy, thereby to make the collection of nineteenth century paintings at Millbank one of the best in Europe. MacColl saw to it that Alfred Stevens was adequately represented, and that works by artists unlikely to come under the notice of the Council of the Royal Academy were added to those acquired through the Chantrey Fund. I mentioned earlier that one of my paintings, "Jews mourning in a Synagogue", was, during 1906, presented to the Tate Gallery. MacColl sent me word when it was hung:

National Gallery of
British Art,
Millbank,
London, S.W.
Feb. 20 1907.

My dear Rothenstein,

It was a good day's work. Besides your picture I got through twenty-one pictures & drawings, viz. a Potter, a Legros head, seven Brabazon & twelve Stevenses, so things begin to move. Keep this to yourself till the announcement appears in the 'Times'. I'll let you know when your picture is hung and ask you to come down & bring Mrs Rothenstein. And you might come back with us & dine after.

Yours in haste
D. S. MACCOLL.

I thought your picture at Whitechapel looked so well—extraordinarily sunny.

I believe I was the first member of the New English Art Club to have a picture at Millbank, and much was made of the event. So with the Print Room at the British Museum; for, some time before, MacColl had written:

'Colvin would like to have a drawing of yours for the Print Room if you saw your way to giving it. They can't buy living men. He felt the delicacy of asking directly, & I said I would sound you. Also one of John's. Perhaps you would sound him.'

Since then many pictures by the younger men have been hung at Millbank, and on Campbell Dodgson's wise initiative, prints and drawings by living men are acquired through subscription and gift, for the Print Room of the British Museum.

During the autumn Bernhard Berenson asked me to come out to Florence to paint his portrait. I was glad of another chance of going to Italy and of seeing Florence again.

On my way there I went through Germany, and saw for the first time some of the south German cities. Hitherto I had been somewhat prejudiced against German art; I had lived so much in France, that I thought nothing could equal French architecture and sculpture. But when I saw Nürnberg and Naumburg, Rothenburg and Bamberg, I became aware of something Gargantuan in their great market places round which stood huge, rollicking, drunken-looking gabled houses, uproariously arm in arm as it were. Vischer's fountains in Nürnberg especially delighted me. Yes, these south German cities were as truly Rabelaisian as any I had seen in France.

Perhaps I had been prejudiced against mediaeval art by the English arts and crafts revival; now I saw, as I had never yet seen, the swift, nervous vitality of medieval forms; a fertility of inventiveness, together with a fierce strength, which even the Greeks had never shown. The

Greeks gave a breadth, a freedom, a dignified radiance to their figures, since unsurpassed. But those tall, swaying figures with their smiling faces bending over the Infant Christ, or symbolic of Faith, Hope, Justice or Charity, their long clinging draperies so exquisitely designed, so energetically yet sensitively carved, had about them an unexampled vitality. And what gravity, what austerity, in the faces and figures of the Kings, Bishops and Knights! No wonder the Church made full use of artists, who could give such beauty, such conviction to its dogmas.

Only in the stained glass of Morris, Rossetti, Madox Brown and Burne-Jones has the modern church shown anything real to its Sunday congregations; otherwise our torpid ecclesiasticism, bloodless, pale and feeble, has nothing in common, save perhaps in its music, with the full blooded vigour of the medieval church. But German memories soon faded when I found myself in Florence again.

I Tatti, the Berensons' house at Settignano, was a delightful place to stay at; and the landscape round Settignano was magnificent. I would go out before breakfast and walk up through the woods to a bare rocky scene that recalled Mantegna and Cosimo Tura. Someone must surely have written of the satisfaction of mere *recognition*; to see with our own eyes that which we have seen depicted, or of which we have read, is an unfailing pleasure. Here was the landscape, here were the Tuscan farms, the cypresses, the bare hills, I had seen in so many Tuscan paintings. The little church at Settignano with its belfry and campanile reminding one of Giorgione, touched my heart; so did the likeness of the old German towns, which I passed through on my way to Italy, to those in Dürer's drawings; while the mountains and forests put me in mind of Altdorfer.

During my stay, Berenson was asked by the Italian Government to examine the state of Ghirlandajo's frescoes in the Church of Santa Maria Novella. A scaffolding had been raised round them, by means of which I was able to study the frescoes closely, and see how the finer work, the drawing of the features, and the jewels, had been added *a secco* by Ghirlandajo's own hand.

I spoke earlier of the somewhat casual impression which the first frescoes made on me, an impression which returned when I saw, in a dark side chapel of the Church of the Carmine, the famous Masaccio frescoes. How much smaller they seemed, and, at first, less dramatic, the Adam and Eve especially, than photographs had led me to believe. But gradually the concentrated intensity of the designs, the modest splendour of the form and colour, and the inner power of these great paintings grew on me. How superb were the sleeping sentry, the man shivering by the river, the seated mendicant, the woman holding her child, and the dandies walking in the street. These same dandies, I thought, now so indifferent to the labour of love before them, would to-morrow be struck down with the plague, or be murdered by some jealous rivals—who knows?

Much nonsense is talked about mural decoration. I could find no difference, in conception or treatment, between the wall paintings and the painted panels of the Italian masters. I was reminded of the prevalent conception of 'decorative' painting only when I saw clumsy black lines traced round Giotto's paintings at the church of Santa Croce, where happily the lovely Salome dancing before Herod has been more reverently left, unrestored.

The Italian painters did not aim to keep the impression of a flat wall; on the contrary, they wished to deceive the eye, to give a similar reality and depth to their frescoes, to that which they gave to their panels. Painting on plaster tends to flatten colours; but so far from desiring this flatness the Italian painters did their best to counter it by perspective, by the imitation of mouldings and their shadows.

At the Uffizi and Pitti galleries, I again felt the extraordinary vitality of the early painters. Giotto's great brooding Mother and Child moved me strangely. Perugino, whom I had regarded as a delicate painter, in his composition of Christ taken from the Cross, showed the energy of a

Rubens. Signorelli's crucifixion, a marvellous conception and design, was new to me; the group around the thief on the hill-top and the impassioned beauty and gesture of the young girl at the foot of the cross, I thought superb. How was it I had hitherto seen no reproduction of this painting? Truth to tell, I had never admired, either at the National Gallery or at the Louvre, Leonardo's *Virgin of the Rocks* so much as I had pretended; the landscape beyond is beautiful, but the figures always appeared to me to be overmodelled, to be somehow 'sticky'. But at the Uffizi, standing before the figures of his *Annunciation* I understood why Leonardo was considered a perfect painter. The profile of the kneeling angel is drawn and painted with a purity which equals that of Fra Angelico, but with an added complexity which does not, however, take away from its final simplicity.

Botticelli's *Primavera* I had assumed to be his masterpiece. Lovely as it is, it has darkened sadly, and now shows little of the radiance of his *Venus*. But no, the composition of the *Venus* is more perfect; surely it is one of the most satisfying pictures in the world. Here is indeed a new birth of one of art's most favoured children. Not far from the *Venus* hangs the great painting of Van der Goes, with its pale pinched women, its chill landscape, and bare wintry trees, a masterpiece too, which put me in mind of Erasmus's itch to get away from Flanders and England to the warm, free Italian air, and to sun himself in the atmosphere of easygoing enlightenment to be found in Rome alone; and how civilised Florence, with her streets of stone palaces, and her churches like rich ivory caskets, must have appeared to a traveller from London, who knew only the half-timbered houses and stone gothic churches of the City! So too, the Italian landscape, with its terraced hills, on which the vines and olives are so lovingly tended, put me in mind of Horace and Virgil. The craftsmen and artists have gone from the scene, but the peasant remains, true artist of that most ancient of all crafts—the care of the soil; while up and down the *salitas* the women, carrying their burdens upon their heads, walk straight and strong as the figures of Andrea del Castagna and Piero della Francesca.

On my visits to the churches and galleries of Florence I had as my companion Geoffrey Scott, who had lately won the Newdigate, and the English Essay prize at Oxford. Dark-eyed and pale, he looked strikingly like a Botticelli portrait; indeed, he was more Italian than English in appearance. Scott had come to stay at I Tatti for a week; but after several months he was still there, and no wonder; he was the most inspiring and entertaining of guests. I for my part have met no one, not himself a painter, who appreciated painting more than did Scott. A wonderful talker, his talk at the Berensons' was something to be remembered. Berenson, too, with his astonishing intellect, delighted in the play of ideas; he could illuminate regions, however remote, not of art only, but also of literature, philosophy, politics, history, ethics and psychology. And sometimes we gossiped; for there were armed camps and fierce rivalries in Florence then, as in past times; but the fighting was far less bloody, concerned as it was with attributions rather than with Ducal thrones. Berenson, Horne, Loeser, Vernon Lee, Maud Crutwell, all had their mercenaries—and their artillery. As a non-combatant I could pass freely among them; and safely too, for these warriors and amazons fought with words only. I was sometimes amused, more often vexed by the clamour; but I could always avoid it at Settignano, and there was other company to be enjoyed, away from the cognoscenti, notably that of Janet Ross.

It was said of Janet Ross that she hated or loved at sight. She happened not to hate me; and her beautiful villa, when I was surfeited with galleries, became a haven. Janet Ross might have walked from the pages of Meredith; she had in fact been the model, I discovered, for one of Meredith's heroines. A proud manner distinguished her, and courage, wit and wide experience of the world. And how handsome she still was! and what a splendid villa was hers!—the same it was said as that wherein Boccaccio had placed his company of fine ladies and courteous gallants. And what a garden, and what a table she kept! Then there were the Laboucheres; they too lived on a grand scale. Labouchere was nearly eighty; yet he complained that his doctor had warned him that he must soon be careful about his diet! Good Heavens, the dishes he could face! What stuff those early Victorians were made of! Whistler had told me many stories of Labouchere; he was one of the people in whom Whistler delighted. I remembered his account of the young Labouchere laying down the law in a London club, on any and every subject, to the indignation of an old gentleman, who exploded: 'Young man; I knew your grandmother', to which Labouchere, rising and bowing replied: 'Perhaps, sir, I have the honour of addressing my grandfather'.

The cognoscenti in Florence had just discovered Cézanne; Loeser had bought several of his smaller landscapes; but there was already a large collection of Cézanne's work in Florence, that of Signor Fabbri. It was through Anquetin in the early nineties, that I first became acquainted with Cézanne's paintings; one could see them at Vollard's, and at one or two other picture-dealers. But it never occurred to me, nor to anyone else at the time, that Cézanne would become an idol to be worshipped. I thought him a puzzling and provocative artist; his pictures seemed awkward, but yet had a strange and powerful honesty, so that despite his lack of skill, they had an intensity which was denied to the pictures of men of greater natural capacity. What impressed me, too, was the way he scorned to hide his defects; what mattered defects, when his aim was so far ahead of what he, or any painter, could ever achieve? But to assert that he did what he wished to do, that he was in fact, a great master, is—it appears to me—to miss Cézanne's importance as a painter. Cézanne, like Whistler, was a great amateur, and like Whistler he proved that it is far better to be an inspired amateur than an uninspired professional. It is for his integrity, his dogged tenacity in the pursuit of the grandeur he saw, but despaired of representing adequately, that he is to be admired, tenacity in attempting again and again, despite failure, the unattainable. Whistler was the more sensitive, Cézanne the more powerful artist; but each was the product of an age when true mastery, the perfect craftsmanship of men like Ingres and Millet, was no more. It is comforting, no doubt, for us who were born at a time of further decline, to find men of genius doing incomplete work; it excuses our own incompetence. But though beside Rubens, Velasquez and Rembrandt, Whistler and Cézanne are but fumblers, they put something of beauty into the world, which gives them an important place in European art. Fumblers before the Lord, they were, and, like Francis of Assisi, regarded first as heretics, then as saints. The gold of Whistler's halo is already wearing thin; will that of Cézanne's prove everlasting?

The cognoscenti are inclined to believe that the picture they see is the one the artist consciously aimed to paint. Yet a painter may start out intending to paint with the finish of a Van Eyck, and in fact achieve something very different. I do not believe Cézanne intended his paintings to be such as they became. For we are told he was a great traditionalist, that he spent many hours each week at the Louvre, and wanted to paint like the old masters. His large sense of design, his powerful colour, his frustrated impulse to draw and construct as he wished, give an interest to his paintings which appeal strongly to this generation, intelligent enough to see that Cézanne was a rare artist, but misled in believing that his qualities depend on his incompleteness.

I forget what it was that Loeser admired so much in Cézanne, not I think the third dimension or volumes, for these had not yet been invented. Still, I was thankful to see anything so fresh and vital as a Cézanne painting in an Anglo-American-Italian interior. The palatial rooms in which the scholar-aesthetes lived, their massive Italian furniture, their primitives, bronzes, wood-carvings and Venetian stuffs which one was expected to appraise, wearied me. Everyone lived among these princely things which, for all their beauty, seemed as misplaced as an enamelled and bewigged mistress in the house of a young man. The atmosphere in these vast apartments seemed heavy with past intrigue. It was a relief to turn from such acquisitive people, to Gordon Craig who dreamed of creating wealth. I would find him maybe at a small underground *trattoria*, or sitting outside a café, or searching for rare books at the antiquarian shops. A fine figure Teddy looked as he walked through the streets and squares of Florence, in a wide-brimmed hat, with a great cloak swinging from his shoulders; like some Old Testament herdsman-prophet, I thought, with his shepherds and handmaidens; though alas! he had no flocks of fat kine to water at the well. For Teddy was as poor in goods as he was rich in ideas. He was working out his latest experiments in his *villino*—of course he had found a perfect treasure of a house—and had in his work-room an exquisite model theatre, fitted with lights, which threw grand and mysterious shadows upon his miniature stage, on which he tried his scenes. Craig had discovered too an actual theatre, long deserted, where he wanted to produce his plays, after the manner of the old *Commedia dell' Arte*. He hoped Berenson might help him; but Craig, who impressed many people, failed to impress Berenson. Perhaps Berenson thought it was a pity that the disciples who ministered to Craig neglected to mend the holes in his pockets, through which coins disappeared with alarming rapidity.

While I was in Florence I heard from Steer, a gossiping letter such as he often wrote. The reference to Druce, I suppose, refers in some esoteric way to Druce's claim to be the Duke of Portland.

109, *Cheyne Walk*,
S.W.

My dear Rothenstein,

I was very glad to get your letter. Florence has evidently a cheering and inspiriting influence and I gather that you are having a real good time. It was very naughty of you not to leave anything to be sent to the New Eng., needless to say you are very much missed there. I had the unique sensation of seeing the exhibition all hung and in order as of course I could not serve. It seems a very decent show although not one of our strongest. Sargent has three brilliant pictures, one view of Mont Blanc which I like best. Orpen also sent three; I am sorry to say Peter[1] sends nothing. I don't think there is anything of any special merit from outside. Sickert has sent some very good drawings, he and Moore spent an evening with me which as usual was very pleasant, we talked a great deal about hawking which is the sport that G.M. is especially interested in at present. I tell him he ought to begin to make friends with Druce before it is too late. The Baker St. Bazaar wd. be an excellent address. Mancini is also in town in tow of Lane; he wants a studio to paint portraits in. I hope soon to get to work again although at present I feel somewhat languid and disinclined. Please remember me very kindly to Berenson & I shall look forward to seeing his portrait.

Yours very sincerely,

P. W. STEER.

On my return I sent a photograph of the portrait I painted of Bernhard Berenson to the Michael Fields; Field acknowledged it by one of her charming letters:

1, *The Paragon*,
Richmond,
Surrey.
Dec. 27th, 1907

My dear Heavenly Dog,

The vigilant brows you have in your celestial effigies must be quite unbearably threatening to such sinners as we are. To receive that beautiful photograph that really gives hint of the sky you have dimpled & mottled in weird sensitiveness round Bernhard...well!—cease frowning—we have been condemned, there is no condemnation any more to be dealt. So glad we are you set Bernhard against the spaces

[1] L. A. Harrison.

of Tuscany—the width & austereness. A sad Bernhard—
the record of much nerve-suffering in the face, with such
sensitive chequer of clouds about it. Thank you, painter of
the picture & giver of the memorial of the picture!
We have been nearly dead with the warmth—not of the
weather & now freeze! Work is impossible. We sent you
wild bees to prepare your hearts for 'Wild Honey' which
will be given to the world sometime in January.
We are wondering if you progress in the new labours, or
if you are back with your brush & your Jews. And Noli?—
How fares the corn-gold Noli? Our dear love to her. We
send John a luck-pig. May he be the most fortunate boy who
ever lived.
Affectionate thanks to you, kind Heavenly Dog!

M — FIELD.

The Michael Fields hoped that one at least of our children
would belong to the true church. They took a fancy to our
youngest child, who was born this year (1908), about whose
precarious spiritual state they wrote a sonnet:

To W.M.R.

A Babe, still, rosy from the cherubim
Set solid by his Mother on my knee!
O lovelier the Vision that I see
The oscillating light that sits with him!
O fresh as the first fig-leaf Eden sprung,
Warm as the Egg that from the dove we part,
Something thou lackest—drops of chrism clung
About thee, and God's charms wrapt round thy heart.
O hidden Sacrament! O second Birth,
O honey-breeding secret in the hive,
Stealing as Ver by inches through the earth,
Spurring each instinct mightily alive
Shall they deprive thee of this lovely thing?
O Babe, weep with me for thy Christening!

M. F.

Had they lived they would have taken comfort from the
fact that one of my sons became a Roman Catholic; but not
he to whom they dedicated the poem.

CHAPTER XVII

CARVING AND MODELLING

I HAD finished the last of my synagogue pictures and now I began a painting of my three children in fancy dresses; these dresses were elaborately patterned, so I had little papier-mâché half-figures made on stands of the size of two of the children, upon which I put the dresses. An Italian would have brushed in these dresses largely in monochrome, and have later applied the colour by glazing, and superimposed the pattern on the fabric. Being a modern, untrained in such a method, I attempted the impossible, painting the rich dresses in solid colour.

While I was at work on this picture, a youth from Whitechapel came to see me, young Gertler. He longed to be a painter, but his people were too poor to help him, and without some support he could not study. He had applied to the society which had helped Epstein; but Solomon J. Solomon, after seeing his work, reported unfavourably. So he had brought his work to me. This showed promise, and I wrote to the society recommending young Gertler, and to Gertler's parents, praising his paintings. When later, I called on Gertler's parents, I found they had actually had my letter framed and hung on the wall! Gertler went to the Slade School, where he made rapid progress. He professed an ardent admiration for my painting, and for long he consulted me about everything he did. Then he was taken up by the most advanced circles, and I neither saw him, nor heard from him more.

Epstein, too, had chosen to quarrel with me, in a way I

resented at first, but not for long. Epstein followed the tradition of the man of genius, a good tradition, which allows of an uncompromising attitude to the world, and freedom from social complications.

I admired much of Epstein's work, most of all when it was not too forceful. He has a tendency, common among contemporary artists, to give more power to his forms than they can comfortably carry—as though one pumped more air into a tyre than it needed. But when Epstein is at his best, as for instance, in the *Lilian Shelley* in the Tate Gallery, where head and figure are beautifully designed, there is no modelling in England to compare with his.

But Epstein seems to me essentially a great portraitist. So much was said, both for and against his *Rima*, and the carvings on the British Medical Association building, that in the din of controversy no sane voice could be heard. Indeed, no sane man could comfortably speak either for or against a man, and his work, so immoderately attacked, so uncritically praised. Epstein is by nature a modeller, rather than a stone carver. There is no magic in carving; makers of tomb-stones have never ceased to carve. Nor is there anything derogatory in modelling in clay. Yet for the moment it would seem as though modelling were something inferior, and only carving were worthy of sculptors. Ruskin has written more wisely than anyone else about sculpture; he realised perfectly that roughness is necessary for work which is to be seen at a distance; a roughness which, from a distance, looks smooth. But Epstein's stone carvings look neither rough nor smooth; I doubt whether he would have modelled his figures thus, had he been working for bronze.

An artist is the God of his own creations. It is his business, as creator, to give these strength, sanity and health; if he makes them either too feeble, or too inflated, they are unlikely to survive. A disciplined ecstasy is the finest gift of the Gods to man; it is likewise the best an artist can give to the work of his hands.

CHAPTER XVIII

BIRMINGHAM, GRACEDIEU AND ROTTINGDEAN

ABOUT this time I was asked to paint a portrait of Professor Alfred Marshall, who was now retiring from the chair of Political Economy at Cambridge. Marshall I was told had a broad outlook on economic subjects, but on other subjects his views were angular, his opinions all corners. In talking with Marshall one had need to be circumspect. For everything one said he took literally and met with the full weight of his pedantry the most casual remarks. I tried to speak cautiously, to be conciliatory, to be thoroughly non-committal, but in vain; no gleam of humour lightened his talk. Fortunately, he also took sitting seriously, for he was vain, and vain men make the best sitters. Hence I regard vanity as both the most useful and harmless of human weaknesses. I made a drawing of Professor Verrall, too, for Miss Jane Harrison, who had now forgiven me, it seemed, for my early portrait of MacColl. But I drew little at this time—perhaps the excellence of John's drawings put me off—and the drawings I made were by no means good.

But in painting I was feeling my way towards a new method. I was becoming more conscious of the solidity of form, and of the radiant light which solid form reflects back. The use of mediums, glazes, every method except that of gradually building up a mosaic of values so closely related to one another that their effect becomes one of unity, took away, I found, from the sense of a solid and reflected radiance. A heavy impasto was the result; but I did not seek to produce this rough surface, which came through the constant repainting necessary to achieve the values and the form I aimed at. Steer, too, was fascinated by light and his sense of colour was impeccable, but he was less interested in form. I wanted the impossible, perhaps; a fusion of the three; and not this alone, but, as I said before, a fusion of the three combined with a less accidental, a less trivial subject matter, than that with which my friends seemed satisfied. I felt form in landscape to be as important as form in the painting of a figure; and I aimed, in my landscape work, at the solid, permanent qualities of sculpture. Hence the architectural side of landscape, cliffs, quarries and stone buildings, appealed to me most strongly; subjects depending less on passing effects than the more lyrical landscape motives, of which Steer was a master.

This was before people talked of volumes and the third dimension; and I found little understanding of that which I was attempting. But this new interest, which applied to my figure as well as to my landscape painting, was an absorbing one, and gave a new incentive to work. I remember a discussion between MacColl, Fry and myself, when I told MacColl that he wanted to build with air, I with bronze. Fry was a warm supporter; but Fry wished the quality of my paint to be other than it was; for he was then anxious to revive the precious surface achieved by the earlier painters, 'If I could only have your pictures to work on after you have done with them!' he said.

Soon after I had painted the portrait of Marshall, I received a visit from a lady who at once won my heart, Mrs Charles Booth. She wished me to paint her husband; he was not very strong, so would I come to Gracedieu, near Leicester, and paint him there? I had long admired Charles Booth, and my friend George Duckworth, who worked with him on his great work, *Life and Labour of the People in London*, often spoke of him. When I met him I was not disappointed. He was the ideal type of the man of commerce, courageous, adventurous, far-seeing, large-minded; and above all, a man of vision. He had a head like a Van Dyck, with finely modelled features, and his figure was slight and alert. His father, he told me, who had owned a few small ships, when he died, left a small sum of money to himself and his brother. Should they invest it or else, risking all, buy a ship? They decided to do this last; and proving successful, bought another ship, and trade along the Amazon river prospered; so the Booth Line became a great enterprise. Then came a challenge from Ballin, the formidable German ship-owner. The Booth Line must either share the Amazon trade with his company, or he would drive their ships from the river. Charles Booth weighed the risk and decided to fight; the whole of his fortune was in his ships; and he dropped nearly a quarter of a million before Ballin gave in.

In Charles Booth there was much of the Elizabethan temper. Intensely patriotic, he wanted England to keep the leadership her genius for government had brought her; but never at the expense of justice, of the spirit of *noblesse oblige*. Charles Booth shared my regret at the decay of local culture in England, and listened with sympathy to my views for enticing more able men into the provinces. If I could have put my views before Chamberlain, he said, he would have responded; but he feared there was no one now who would care. During his early years in Liverpool, Charles Booth lived in lodgings, among clerks and such like workers, and managed to keep his identity secret, an experience which prompted the idea of his *Life and Labour of the People in London*.

Booth was generous with his time, and gave me the sittings I needed. When I finished his portrait, he asked me to paint his wife as a companion picture. It was a privilege indeed to do this; for Mrs Booth, marvellously well-read and well-informed, as became a niece of Macaulay, was an astonishingly vital person. Indeed, the Booths were a great clan; to dine with one of them meant meeting other Booths, or members of the families, Macaulays, Ritchies, Trevelyans, Macnaghtens, Meinertzhagens, with all of whom they were connected.

A farmhouse at Througham

The summer of 1908, during which I was painting Mr and Mrs Charles Booth, I had taken a farmhouse at Througham, near Bisley in Gloucestershire, where I joined my wife and children from time to time. From Througham we drove over to Sapperton, when we first met the Barnsleys and Ernest Gimson. They had come there from Pinbury, where they had leased a house that belonged to Lord Bathurst. Lord Bathurst had lately married, and his young wife had fallen in love with Pinbury, and Gimson and the Barnsleys were persuaded to give up their place there, Lord Bathurst offering in return to build them houses at Sapperton. So they chose the sites and designed the houses; for they had been trained as architects, though they were then, and thereafter, better known as designers and makers of furniture. I little thought that a few years later I was to be a near neighbour of these men, and to become closely associated with them.

While at Througham, I was struck by the distinguished bearing of our landlady, and by a certain harshness in her manner. Later I was to discover the unexpected tragedy in which she had played a part. This was after we had settled at Oakridge, close to the scene of the tragedy.

The woman's father was a small farmer of powerful build and passionate character. He had an invalid wife, and a son and daughter living at the farm; but he had brought another woman to live at his house, which led to his daughter, who resented the presence of this other woman, being illtreated by him. Again and again the son threatened to kill his father, and one day he took a gun and shot him dead before his sister's eyes. The son was hanged at Gloucester; and the daughter, our landlady, lived on with this dark secret in her heart. I told this story to Masefield, who afterwards wrote a poem based on it—*The Cold Cotswolds*, he called it.

Througham was merely a hamlet, consisting of three Tudor farmhouses, and a few labourers' cottages. I longed to paint there, but had to return to Gracedieu to finish my portraits. At Gracedieu, in the early morning, I heard a maid singing. Being by nature unmusical I am touched by the unconscious grace of a young voice where a trained singer's leaves me cold. Perhaps it is the words, too, which move me, for in folk songs, tune and words together seem perfect. I could well understand how Hudson fell in love with a voice: only beauty makes life intelligible. I could imagine Hardy creating a character who would become enamoured of a voice, and marry a servant-girl and become miserably disillusioned. Nature uses beauty for the continuance of her creatures; man but follows her example when he interprets life in terms of beauty. Art is fruitful, and deceptive, as nature. Men will march towards death to the roll of drum and the sound of pipes. Stories of heroism, untrue, maybe, in fact, but true in their beauty, make men heroic.

I had the use of a pony at Gracedieu, and usually rode before breakfast. The Leicestershire country is gentle and undulating, with the pensive quality that far distance gives to a landscape. Early one morning, a young woman, good-looking but somewhat haggard, standing at a cottage door, pressed me eagerly to join her within. There was something sinister in this appeal to a passing stranger, which haunted me for long afterwards.

In 1908 I was invited to give the annual address at the Birmingham School of Art, following on all sorts of distinguished people, among whom was William Morris. These annual addresses were printed and circulated. I was now often asked to speak in public—a thing I disliked doing. My views were tending towards socialism; the private patron, I foresaw, on whom artists now depended, would slowly disappear, and therefore the State must learn to take his place. Moreover, I felt increasingly the need of a dignified subject matter. I held it to be the artist's business to make clear what men see and feel but vaguely; I was also unhappy about the nature of the pictures shown at the New English. Something less trivial, I felt, was needed to take the place of the made-up Academy picture, and it was for the State and the Municipalities to employ artists, to bring life and colour into our public buildings. Inspiration among painters has always been rare; but the imposition of a definite task serves to rouse imaginative faculties which, without it, may lie fallow. Creation was neglected; attention was given only to preservation; the museum and picture gallery seemed to be the be-all, and the end-all, of public duty to the arts.

Through my friendship with Robert Steele and Miss Morris, I met many of William Morris's friends, among them Emery Walker and Sydney Cockerell—Cockerell had been Ruskin's, then Morris's, secretary, and was later in partnership with Emery Walker. They looked on me as a link between Impressionism and Pre-Raphaelitism; and Walker knew that Lady Burne-Jones approved of my opinions. Cockerell was friendly with Neville Lytton, and thought it would be a good thing if Lytton, who knew few painters, saw something of me. Lytton was then working independently, doing drawings and paintings which were based on the methods and manner of various masters. The Lyttons were an enlightened pair; Mrs Lytton, a true daughter of Wilfrid Blunt, was all for the freedom of subject races; while Neville was a devotee of Tolstoy. A handsome couple to look on, they would both come down to dinner dressed in splendid Arab clothes. What dignity such clothes give to men and women! We speak of the noble bearing of men of the East; how much, I wonder, is due to their dress? When wearing ours, they seem scarcely superior in mien to ourselves.

We went more than once to stay with the Lyttons at Crabbet Park. Mrs Lytton would meet us at Three Bridges, driving four beautiful white Arab horses. At Crabbet Park life was of the simplest, the food was vegetarian, swans'-down was banished from the beds; but Lytton had his own private tennis court, with a professional to play against him. I had never seen the true royal game of tennis, and marvelled at Lytton's skill at this difficult game. He held the Amateur Tennis Championship of England, but was anxious not to be taken for an amateur artist. He was very productive; I envied him his facility, though I was somewhat critical of his methods. For Lytton, like Legros and Ricketts, was convinced that one could best learn one's trade by following the practice of proved masters. I must have written to him on the subject, for I find him answering from Crabbet Park:

Dear Rothenstein,

Thank you 1000 times for your excellent letter. As always you are much too indulgent and tender-hearted. I don't want to try and defend myself from your complaint of too much research of style. Who knows what *our* language really is? If I painted otherwise than as I do I should not be following my instinct as to what is beautiful. I don't make an effort to resuscitate traditional methods out of intellectuality as Fry does. If I make a definite aim at a definite technique it is because that kind of painting tickles me down the spinal cord, and is an animal impulse that I can't resist. What is more I am sure I am not a solitary struggling in a wilderness of opposition. For instance take that new set of flats in Sloane Square (built by Thackeray Turner, I think) or the house at the bottom of St James's St. I am sure that my pictures wld look more of a period hung in those buildings than say the paintings of Besnard. Heaven knows that I don't want style to interfere with the spirit of life which is the one and only really essential thing to art. I worship it even in the art of an anarchic artist like John. In fact I think John's daring and talent is an excellent example for us & shows us in which direction it is expedient for us to throw our bonnets over the windmills. But at the same time I think that John ought to be able to gain something from our sanity and love of form.

I like very much what you say of Geoffrey's[1] things. If he is not a man of noble emotions I don't know who is. He loves style perhaps more than I do, but that is truly French.

As to the critics they have been much more indulgent this time than ever before and we have been criticised at much

---

[1] Geoffroi de Chaume, a young French painter who was working in Sussex, with whom Lytton was now showing his work.

greater length & with greater promptness than ever before. It is true that there has been a great deal of 'irreverence', which is peculiar to English critics. I have never seen the like of it in France. But it is right and proper that the public here shld be unconscious of the meaning of art. It always has been so in England. We have had great painters but never a great public, & I am not sure it is not best so.

I had an excellent conversation with Webb the other night and he told me many intimate anecdotes of Rossetti, Ford Madox Brown, & Morris.

Yours ever,
NEVILLE LYTTON.

Webb was Philip Webb, the architect, William Morris's life-long friend. He lived close to Crabbet Park, in a cottage where he fended for himself, though he was well over seventy. He didn't hold with having a servant: like other people I have known who believed firmly in some things, he disbelieved obstinately in other things. He disapproved of capital and interest. He had saved enough money to allow of his living simply after he gave up work, so he thought. Unhappily, or I should say happily, his conjecture as to the number of years he was likely to live fell short of the mark, and now his savings were giving out, and he had to sell his Kelmscott Press books (including a copy of the Chaucer) given him by Morris.

Webb had the courteous manners of the older generation, though he held, as I said, strong views about politics and art, views he had shared with William Morris. Webb was distressed, of course, by the ways of architects. Building for him must be structural building, and all this make-believe, this dressing-up of steel girders in fancy-dress stone was the destruction of architecture, as he understood it; and drawing and painting seemed to be going the same way.

He had been a Pre-Raphaelite all his life, and it was too late for him to change—hence he shrank from judging contemporary art. When my Birmingham address was printed, my wife sent a copy to Philip Webb, who was cautious in expressing an opinion. He wrote:

`24 April '09`

...'Of course, such serious effects as Rothenstein's in the way of leading the coming-on generation in following the arts—visible and literary—also in a *serious* way, that everything he writes calls for like thoughtfulness of attention; and I am rather slow witted, and like to read honest work more than once or twice before saying anything about it. Old age has so touched me now, that I am hardly capable of saying anything worth thinking about, for the backbone of intelligence—human memory to wit, is now in me so much a minus quantity, that putting my thoughts on paper has become so hopelessly tiresome, that I "shirk" the effort till all spontaneity vanishes: that is why I have not written direct to Rothenstein, preferring to wait till he looks in upon me here, as he has promised.'

Indeed, I did not want these elders of ours, who had done such significant work, to be other than they were. I respected their scrupulous characters, and their outlook and opinions. Period minds are as interesting as period furniture; and looking back on all these men of an earlier generation—Sir Henry Acland, Holman Hunt, William Rossetti, Burne-Jones, Cobden-Sanderson, T. M. Rooke and Philip Webb, I liked them as they were, such a flavour their views held, such courtesy and charm they possessed. I have not met their like since. With William Rossetti and his family I remained on terms of warm friendship. One day I painted a head of William Rossetti, which won more praise from the family than it deserved. It was always a pleasure to visit the Rossettis, to look, again and again, at the pictures on the walls, to hear each time something fresh about Dante Gabriel, Madox Brown, Millais, Ruskin, Whistler or Holman Hunt. William Rossetti never said a cruel thing, nor ever an unwise one. In his comments on life he had something of the gentle pessimism of Thomas Hardy; he did not share his sister Christina's faith. Yet his own sweetness and rich humanity gave me an added belief in men, as talent or beauty of character never fail to do.

Unlike Webb, Masefield wrote in no uncertain terms of my Birmingham address.

30 *Maida Hill West*,
W.
June 3rd, 1908.

My dear Rothenstein,

Your address came last night, & I read it through twice before going to bed, & hope to read it through twice again to-night. It is a most splendid thing: the most eloquent thing ever said about art. A great artist so seldom leaves anything but his work to tell posterity of the faith that moved him; & the young man, generally undisciplined, & without finely trained sympathies, can only understand the work imperfectly. He needs to repeat the creed of a great artist daily, as well as to brood upon great work. I cannot tell you what a help & inspiration such words as those on pp. 8, 9 & 10 would have been to me, had I but heard them in my student years. Well, Ronsard started French literature with a pamphlet, & Sidney, English literature with an essay. I wish I might live to see all the great ripples of beauty which your words will send across the world.

Believe me,
Yours always,
JOHN MASEFIELD.

Alas, my poor words were as ineffective as words, and not deeds, usually are. But Masefield was always heartening and warm in support of any large project. He wrote again soon afterwards:

30 *Maida Hill West*,
W.
July 3, 1908

My dear Rothenstein,

You said last night that you wanted a subject for a picture. A picture which I should like to see you paint would be a symposium of all those of our time who have worked un-flinchingly for beauty, sitting about your table, as in the old pictures of Ambassadors.

It was a great pleasure having you here last night.

With kind regards,

Yours ever,

JOHN MASEFIELD.

I would have liked to paint such a picture, but the difficulty of getting so many people to sit was too great; I must be content to do drawings. Though my sitters may not have known it, I am stirred by some such feeling as Masefield's letter suggests and when I ask for sittings, it is to pay secret homage to men and women whom I admire.

My visit to Birmingham gave me the chance of seeing the Fairfax Murray collection at the Art Gallery. Here were some of the noblest of Rossetti's drawings, including the head of Fanny, the study for *Found* of which I spoke earlier. Why, I wondered, should we value Continental opinion so highly, when it shows such deplorable ignorance of a great European school. The superb designs by Burne-Jones impressed me too; Burne-Jones is here seen as an artist of outstanding power, of hand and of mind. My opinion of him was reinforced when I saw the vigour of his earlier drawings. Both he and Rossetti in their later painting got entangled in the toils of facial loveliness, and lost some of their vitality; but in the fullness of their powers their handling of brush and pencil was vigorous and sensitive. Whistler, in some respects, was more of an amateur than either Rossetti or Burne-Jones. What power there is in *How They met Themselves* and *Dr Johnson at the Mitre*, which I saw in William Holliday's house, where I stayed while in Birmingham.

A few months before speaking at Birmingham Lady Burne-Jones wrote:

'A copy of your Winchester Address has found its way into the hands of the Headmaster of the Brighton School of Art, and in consequence he wishes to know whether you would be willing to give an address to *his* students, next month, at the Annual Distribution of Prizes.

'This morning he brought me a note from the friend who handed on the address, asking how he should "approach" you on the subject, and I offered to ask you directly, as I now do, in order to save time.... Please, nothing more than yes or no, which shall be forwarded to my friend at once.'

I went to Brighton, and later stayed at the Burne-Jones's beautiful home at Rottingdean. I felt Burne-Jones's presence in every room; besides studies hanging on the walls, there was a small fresco by his hand in the nursery, which the children could look at when sent to 'stand in the corner'. And there was a lovely angel painted in the night-nursery, and a piano, the case of which was decorated, outside and within the keyboard, by Burne-Jones. There were some delightful toys kept in a cupboard, with which my children, when at Rottingdean, wanted to play; but they were stuck to the shelves; a wise precaution, for the old traditional English penny toys I had collected in rivalry with Gordon Craig (who produced a book on the subject) were demolished by my son John.

Rottingdean, with the sea below and the downs above, with the old church, a windmill, and pleasant houses, was a favourite holiday place of my family. William Nicholson had a house there, and our children made friends with his children.

'I am so glad you like the Nicholson troupe,' (wrote Max) 'they are somehow more like a troupe than a family—Nancy standing with one spangled foot on Nicholson's head, Ben and Tonie branching out on tip-toe from his straddled legs, Mabel herself standing at the wings, holding the overcoats. I said there was no news, but I forgot that the Italian fleet—or a great deal of it—was here yesterday. Is that nothing to you? The population of Rapallo went quite mad with joy, in a quiet way, and didn't at all seem to mind the heavy taxation by which alone such a spectacle is compassed.'

The Kiplings too had lived at Rottingdean ('Can you tell me where Mr. Kipling lies?' an American lady had asked Lady Burne-Jones in the street), and these great names were a danger, for they helped to draw the notice of the jerry-builder to an unspoiled village. In summer Rottingdean was invaded from every side; moreover the builder had his eye on a place so near Brighton. Lady Burne-Jones writes:

'How wise you have been not to come here this month if you want quiet. Our village is *very* full, and what the pressure upon indoor accommodation must be I fear to think. It is pleasant to think, however, that you may return to it at a quieter time and I shall welcome you gladly. You must be prepared for a change in the valley to the north of the village. Just as the downs rise again from the right of the road there is being built a very large "Institution". Its exact name and nature are unknown to me, but I have heard it described as a "Reformatory". Opposite to it on the left side of the road two small and unattractive houses now stand. How well I remember the last time we were down here together, fourteen years ago, what my husband said about that row of cottages (Klondyke) which had just been built at right angles from the road: "They have ruined the place—they have dwarfed the valley." I have long thought that in building a house of any kind an architect must have to reckon with the whole landscape around if in the country, or with all the houses about, if in town. You will be fortunate if you are able to secure a cottage which was built in the happy time of *instinct*, which used to seem an unfailing guide to the builders of humble dwellings.'

In the letter in which Max described the Nicholson family, he wrote of having finished *Zuleika Dobson*.

'Zuleika will be with you anon. The proofs are flowing in, and the book will be out not later, I hope, than the first week in October. I am really very glad I found it impossible to go on writing the book in London years ago. I have developed since then; and the book wouldn't have had the quality it has now. It really is rather a beautiful piece of work—though it may be a dead failure in point of "sales"—and on the other hand might sell quite well: just a toss up. Heinemann evidently believes in it from his point of view, for he pays me £400 in advance of royalties and a good many copies have to be sold therefore before *he* can begin to profit. If the binders and paper-makers don't play me false, the book will *look* nice; not like a beastly *novel*, more like a book of essays, self-respecting and sober and ample.'

Zuleika Dobson was for long the least liked of Max's books, for reasons I could never understand.

CHAPTER XIX

THE DARWIN CENTENARY

HUGH LANE was doing his best to get Dublin interested in Irish art. Besides Dermod O'Brien and Yeats, Orpen, too, was helping Lane to acquire pictures. Lane had infected him with some of his enthusiasm for Ireland. I noticed in answering something I had written about a self-portrait, Orpen replied:

8, *South Bolton Gardens*.

My dear Rothenstein—it was indeed good of you to write about my picture—and your letter gave me great pleasure—there is no use saying that I admired yours now—but I did. I think Master John is splendid—I must bring Mary in to see him. My picture is not English *it's Irish* and we grow ptarmigans in the West—but I suppose that is foreign enough. Will you come and dine at the Savile some night?

Yours—WILLIAM ORPEN.

I hadn't associated ptarmigans with Ireland, but Orpen showed his patriotism not only by painting this native bird, but by going to Dublin every month to teach in the School of Art there; a generous move, I thought, for he was now much beset by people clamouring for portraits. Lane had commissioned Orpen to paint portraits of distinguished Irishmen, and he wanted John to decorate one or more of the public buildings in Dublin. I find a letter from Yeats, asking me to help:

18 *Woburn Buildings,*
W.C.
7th January 1908

Dear Rothenstein
Will you be in town any day this week, except Saturday,

when I shall be back in Dublin? Lane has asked me to try and get some people to write up the opening of his gallery, which is at 4 o'clock on January the 20th, and I would like your advice. I shall be desperately busy, or I would go out to you on the chance. I hear it takes three quarters of an hour getting out. I don't want to bring you in specially, but if you were coming in about something else, would like to see you. It is very important to get enough notice taken of the opening of this gallery to make the corporation believe in Lane, for if they do, they will leave him free, and if they don't, they will sooner or later annoy him in the interest of some bad patriotic painter. He has so many enemies in Dublin that all the help we can get from outside is necessary. He ought to be over here himself, but cannot come as he is busy hanging the pictures. I wish there were any chance of you yourself going over. I would like to show you Augustus John's portrait of me. A beautiful etching, and I understand what he means in it, and admire the meaning, but it is useless for my special purpose. Robert Gregory agrees in this, and has recommended me to show it to you. If you are not likely to be in town, please let me know and I will try and get out to you.

Yours,

W. B. YEATS

Yeats did not think John's etching did justice to his looks. I thought it admirable. He had made one, a year or two earlier, of myself, and pulled a single proof from the copper. Then he dropped some acid on the plate and ruined it. No one was more careless with his materials; yet the best of his plates seem to me to be above all contemporary etchings. John, indeed, is the last of the great improvisers; he was made to throw off his fancies at white heat; and he alone is able to draw nudes in any position, at any angle, as Tiepolo could. I said earlier that I wanted Tree to get John to decorate His Majesty's Theatre. But no one has yet asked John to decorate any public building; instead they have importuned him to paint their portraits. What a waste of a copious mind, of a great national asset! The State to-day is like the mistress of a great house, but with neither the knowledge nor the character to control her servants; for if a mistress herself knows not what tasks to assign them, what tasks will be done?

We miss what is due to art, what is due to the people. We think to prove our artistic worth through possessions. It began in Hogarth's day; Hogarth's satire on the Cognoscenti holds true to-day. We are obsessed with the notion that to possess great works of art is more important than to produce them. Hence nation vies with nation, millionaire with millionaire, until the price of a fine work of art reaches Bedlam figures.

During 1908 my friend Francis Darwin was chosen to be President of the British Association, which was to meet this year in Dublin. Darwin's opening address, modest and direct like his own character, dealt with the movements of plants, and how much consciousness can be attributed to them. He wrote from Ireland:

Dear Rothenstein,

I have been very slow in answering your kind letter. I put off everything till I could get peace—which we are now having in this lovely place with H. Butcher. It was very good of you to write & cheer me; I wanted it as I felt all the time that I was a failure. I daresay I was wrong, but there was the feeling, & a few letters like yours were the pleasantest part of the thing.

This is a very foreign land, I expect you will hear from Frances abt the women with their shawls over their heads that she wants you to paint. The whole thing is much Irisher than one could have hoped. On Monday we go to the other end of the world, Donegal, to stay with the Arthur Cloughs & I am to have some fishing which I used to love in old days.

Yrs ever

F. DARWIN.

A scientist's distress

Another letter from William Bateson, who had gone to Dublin with Darwin, describes his adventures on arriving in London:

'If Little Stafford House[1] had been more central you would have perhaps seen me burst in at some a.m. hour on Wednesday. Returning from Dublin at 11.30 p.m. on Tuesday I had a unique experience. The hotel I wired to was full. They sent me to Liverpool Street. That was full. Till about 1.30 a.m. I tried all hotels which I could find. All full. So at last I gave up hope & tramped the streets. It is a queer feeling not to be allowed to sit down when tired out. No hotel would let me have even a chair—"nothing of the kind permitted by the management" was the regular reply. Had the night been cold and death from exposure occurred, the police would have found a £5 note in my pocket with some gold, silver & bronze coins besides. Isn't that a hard case? I am ready to subscribe for another seat on the Embankment. Near 3 a.m. I got a place on a sofa in the Midland where I am known, and at 5.30 a.m. took train here. They say this has gone on for weeks. Every few minutes people were being turned away from the Midland while I was there.

'I seriously thought of giving myself up at Judd Street Police Station in order to get a few minutes rest.'

I too had an odd experience one night when I went out late to post a letter, without my latch key, and unable to make anyone hear bell or doorknocker, went in search of a bed, first at *Jack Straw's Castle*, then at *The Bull and Bush*. Being hatless and without luggage, no one would take me in. Finally, I had to take a cab to Morley's Hotel at Trafalgar Square, where I was known, to get a bed.

The Calderons, whom I saw next day, upbraided me for not knocking at their door; George always worked late. He and I went for long walks over the Heath, discussing art, ethics, literature, politics, religion, folk-lore—there was nothing about which Calderon could not theorise brilliantly.

[1] I used to call our house Little Stafford House on account of the size of the rooms.

To reconcile the desire for perfection, the still small voice, with the false values of daily life is a problem that faces many persons. The desire to cut the knot of our difficulties by retiring from the world, to obtain by literal obedience to the dictates of religion the peace that passes understanding, lies deep within us. Men like Tolstoy seemed to offer a way through the entanglements of civilisation, as a woodman cuts his way through the dog roses and thorns that choke the young trees in a copse; but the small voice is never stilled whatever the way of life we tread. A man may be truthful and honest whether he be Catholic, Anglican, Nonconformist or agnostic, and under any social system, Republican or Monarchical, and may be dishonest as an ascetic, or under monastic rule. Which is the better life, that of householder or monk, is the subject of one of the oldest of Indian writings. The followers of Confucius and Lao Tse discussed the same problem, which Marcus Aurelius attempted to answer in Europe. But Tolstoy's pamphlets still troubled me; Calderon, who admired Tolstoy's novels—no one without knowledge of Russian could appreciate the force and splendour of Tolstoy's prose, he would say—did not approve his later writings. He foresaw the disintegrating menace of revolutionary tendencies everywhere at work. A settled authority was needed, we agreed, that we might be free to do our work; work suffers when men become too political. A similar argument justifies established religion. I had lately read Baron von Hügel's preface to his *Life of St Catherine of Genoa*. A fruit garden needs four walls, partly to enclose it, in part to catch all the light and warmth of the sun. First the raising of walls, and then their destruction, has been the chief activity of mankind. We are uncertain whether we are creating or destroying. During a coal strike Calderon, who wished young university men to carry on needed labour, was an ardent supporter of William James's plea for social, instead of military conscription. This, with his antagonism to woman's suffrage, got Calderon into bad odour with his Liberal friends. They misinterpreted his gallant nature. For my part, commerce with many men has taught me to respect character more than principles.

Max came with me to one of the Calderons' enchanting parties at the Vale of Health. Calderon had lately written a novel, *Dwala*, which I was praising to Mrs Calderon. Mrs Calderon turned to Max, who in his sympathetic way expressed agreement, and she, delighted, plied him with questions, wishing to know which parts of the book he most admired; but alas, Max had *not* read *Dwala*! yet he managed to leave his hostess with her first impression unspoilt—a marvellous thing to have done, I thought; for mordant as Max can be with his pencil, he cannot bear to hurt anyone's feelings. So honeyed his tongue, so polished his manner, that beside him one feels oneself a clodhopper.

George Calderon and Laurence Binyon were now both turning to the Theatre. Calderon was busy with a comedy, *The Fountain*, which was later produced by the Stage Society. He sent one of his amusing letters to my wife:

Heathland Lodge,
(Vale of Health)
Hampstead Heath, N.W.

June 2nd.

Dear Mrs Rothenstein,

If you really don't dislike hearing plays read (and Rothenstein said so down the telephone) *do* come on Monday and let me read mine to you and Rothenstein together. I should be really delighted if you would come to hear it; I set the very highest value on your opinion, as you know. Besides, it is so friendly and sociable.

At any rate we both hope that you will come to dinner at 7; and if the idea of the play is painful to you, you could make some excuse when dinner is over and steal away. It would be a great blow to me, but I should understand.

If you will consent to hear the play, you will flatter me immensely by seeming to have some curiosity as to what my play is like.

Two plays

Dinner will be of two kinds, something very simple and harmless for Rothenstein; and something rich and harmful for you.

Yours,

GEORGE CALDERON

Calderon was himself an actor born, and to hear him read a play was a delight. I thought *The Fountain* a brilliant satire on the times: the central idea is that of a woman who wished to devote her life to the poor, yet unknown to herself, through her agent, she raises the rent of the tenements in which they live. *The Fountain* was acted in the provincial repertory theatres. Binyon was more fortunate. His play, *Attila*, was accepted by Oscar Asche, and was gorgeously produced at His Majesty's Theatre.

8 Sepr.

My dear Rothenstein,

Just a line to thank you with all my heart for your letter. It is indeed a great delight to feel one's work so warmly appreciated by so many friends. I only wish I had the play to do again. I could make it much better now. The weak points in it vex me, now I can see them clearly.

I am glad you & others of judgment liked the acting. I am rather angry with Max who tells me he is going to attack Asche tooth & nail. But really when one thinks what Tree or Alexander would be in the part...!

Thanks again to both of you for your good wishes. We are with the Calderons for Sunday, in a delicious country.

Always yours

LAURENCE BINYON

Attila had but a brief career. There was now little relish for high tragedy; yet Tree was ambitious to use his theatre for great spectacles. He now talked of producing *Macbeth*. Had Craig staged Binyon's *Attila* it would have been more effective. I had been reproving him for his improvident and uncompromising idealism; why not come to earth and work with others? He would willingly work with Tree, he assured me. I heard from Tree:

Dear Rothenstein,

I am greatly interested in your letter about Gordon Craig. Would it be possible for you to call here one day and we might then have a talk about him. I quite agree with you that his powers are remarkable but I have felt that he would refuse to work at any regular theatre and that it would be impossible for me to secure his services at any time. But from your letter I gather that I may have misunderstood him.

With kind regards,
Yours sincerely,
HERBERT BEERBOHM TREE.

Tree needed some persuasion before he made a definite offer to Craig. Teddie meanwhile was becoming impatient:
'I have seen Viola Tree & spent 2 days with her talking in the hope of hearing her say "I will"...but she said only "how beautiful"—"how fair a dream" & not "I will now go home and tell papa to be quick and invite you over".

I have also written to Whelen who is secretary to Tree, & who I hear is clever & quick.

But I have had no answer
So much for
England
my England—
But there must be something queerly nervous about London for other cities here have responded to me.

I have been asked to Berlin, Moscow—Warsaw and Budapest...possibly to St Petersburg....

So all being well I shall go on a swift & short tournée to each of these cities at once.

How nice it would be to call in on London & stay a while at the Carlton Hotel. We could make quite a little fête of it—& you should find no sorrow for a few days at any rate for you could put off your spectacles.'

Max was warm in his support, so also was Miss Constance Beerbohm, Tree's sister. I knew that Ellen Terry, who loved and was proud of her two gifted children, Teddie and Edie, wanted Ted to go on with his work in England. Triumphs abroad were well enough, but she was not a cosmopolitan, like Duse, and her interests were at home. She was delighted at the idea of Teddie joining Herbert Tree. What lovely designs Ted would do, surely then everyone would recognise his genius, and he would have his way and make the English Theatre the first in Europe. I loved going to Barkston Mansions, and later to King's Road, to sit at Miss Terry's feet. She was so impulsively alive, so witty and gracious and affectionate. While with her I adored; there was an atmosphere about this great woman, who radiated love, and accepted it, too, so naturally, that one wondered why one's relations with others could not be similarly beautiful. She again had the nosegay fragrance, that something modest—as of the cottage-border—that distinguishes, not English individuals only, but English china, furniture, manners, speech and dress.

Finally Craig came over to London, dissolved Tree's doubts, and at once set to work on designs for *Macbeth*. They were beautiful drawings. Tree was delighted, and for a time it looked as though we were to have a great interpretation of a Shakespearean play. Clouds gathered; suddenly Craig proposed that Tree should leave London and himself in charge of his theatre! Alas, it was Craig who left London; and Tree, and Craig and all of us were the poorer for missing a unique production, worthy of Shakespeare's *Macbeth*. Craig had fallen out, too, with Brahm in Berlin. But he got his chance with the Russians. The Russians! of course, they were just the people to appreciate Craig; and appreciate him they did. They thrust *Hamlet* into his arms, Hamlet, King, Queen, Polonius, Ophelia and all, and then argued about each of these characters day after day, night after night—for what is time to Russians? The play must wait until everything, down to the smallest detail, had been discussed to exhaustion. I got an enthusiastic letter from Craig:

Moscow. Métropole Hotel.

Dear Will—I am in Russia—& the theatre here has asked me to be their régisseur or stagemanager & for life!

God. dear Will this kind of thing takes ones breath away—it's like a leap year proposal—heavenly because so innocently new. & who knows if I won't be ever at the disposal of this theatre which has presented applause—by presenting its actors appearing to bow before the curtain—this vivid theatre which has dared to waste years in the production of one piece—this darling theatre which is so generous that it gives its audience a 3½ hours' show—bless its innocence—If I loved anything but a Theatre which must obliterate the Theatre I would stay here for ever & do my dull best—but *I* must do my gambling *worst*—& must risk all & again all to drag the soul of the theatre out of its cursed body & free it of all tricks & trappings—then—then—others!!

Tree—the charming fellow—I could murder him with *great pleasure.*

Here they are all so good—so true—so wildly believing in it & its trappings as moths the candle—their faith wins me back for one moment—makes me *miserable*—& them—terribly happy.

Am alone here...don't forget to write that open letter for the 'Mask'. Write as you feel—then you're wonderful—Those English idiots *can't* feel—not longer feel—have masked all feeling too long until—chalk cliffs!

I wish you were here—I have lived 2 days here & lived a year in each. 1st day three angelic creatures took me out at 11 o'clock at night & fêted me till 6 next day. Folk songs—dances—motors—flying from Volgas over Dons into Niepers—speeches—such as 'You are a splendid man, that I have seen in my life—Hoch!!!' One instantly leaps to his feet & dances a God's dance—nothing short of it....

A triumph for Craig

You'll be pleased to hear that the Mask has found a business manager who is raising its circulation to 10,000 copies per month.

My love to all your sweet pretty children & your wife who looks more lovely, young & gracious each time I see her.

E. G. C.

And *Hamlet*, when it was at last produced, was a triumph. Only we heard that Craig's simple cubes, against which the play was enacted, proved more costly than the gold and glitter of traditional scenery. But of course, one real pearl is more costly than a necklace of counterfeit.

Craig indignantly denied the truth of this report. Everyone at the Moscow Art Theatre had been warm in recognition of the practical adaptability of his invention. Rumours of Craig's success at the Moscow Art Theatre reached London; we naturally thought that what he had done for the Russian Theatre he could do for the English stage. Herbert Trench had lately become Manager of the Haymarket Theatre:

'You cannot be keener than I am on making use of Gordon Craig's gifts,' he wrote. 'The difficulty is to know how it is to be done, as I have too large a staff already, and have Directors to face. You may rely on my trying to bring it off in future, but I can make no promises at present.'

But Craig would at first have none of Trench.

Hôtel Métropole,
Moskau.

Dear Will—

I was writing to you when my old friend Martin Shaw sent me a letter telling me that you and other friends of mine were preparing to tell a certain Mr Trench that he should invite me back to London.

I have heard of this Mr Trench.... I feel sure that such a man would go about asking if I was *practical* or whether I am not *expensive*. Of course I am both! He'll have to swallow that to begin with.

154

And then—

If he should ask me to act as 'tinker to one of his old tin pot ideas' I quote a good phrase from a letter I have received from a well known actress in England, then I'm as *un*practical as the devil. If he wants to dress up some doll of his I cannot help him. *but* if he wants me—to give a soul—to some beauty on his stage
'whistle, & I'll come (to) you my lad'
I am in my first HOME here in Russia. . .
And England—
tears & tears & tears and awful pain & perhaps the dearest of all.
Craig. . . .

Trench was a poet, handsome, urbane, ambitious. He left the Board of Education to devote himself to writing; then he became interested in the theatre. I had never thought of the handsome, dilettantish Herbert Trench in connection with the dangerous world of the theatre; poetry I believed to be his true love. One Sunday I called on Lady Ritchie. As I entered the room that dear lady said: 'Oh, Mr Rothenstein, have you heard the dreadful news?' What was the news? 'Herbert Trench has committed suicide.' This was terrible; but somehow after a time we surmised that poor Trench had got involved in a world, of whose wiles he, so long an innocent Civil Servant, knew little; indeed, before I left Lady Ritchie we both seemed to think some such catastrophe had been wellnigh inevitable. I went on to the Savile Club full of the news. Fortunately, that day being Sunday, the Club was empty. The next morning came a telegram from Lady Ritchie, 'So sorry, Herbert Trench not dead'! She had made a mistake; it was not Trench who had killed himself. But I could never afterwards see handsome Herbert without an inward chuckle at the thought of Lady Ritchie's words.

Later, when Gordon Craig got to know Trench better, he liked him, as we all did. There was something beguiling about Trench, which disarmed criticism: he was so genuinely interested in others and in himself. His enthusiasm for art and letters was infectious. During his later years life gave him hard knocks, whereafter his vision broadened and he achieved a fine mental balance.

During 1909, Darwin's centenary was celebrated at Cambridge, and Francis Darwin invited my wife and myself to attend the many functions. That which impressed me most was the scene outside the Senate House, where representatives from universities throughout the world come together to receive honorary degrees, walked in procession, wearing their robes, under a red awning, a subject, I thought, for a great mural decoration; I was reminded of the processional paintings I had seen in Venice. The doctor's robe, which gives to a figure weight and dignity, is one of the few survivals of medieval dress. At the garden parties, too, there were groups of men in variously coloured gowns, which outshone the dresses of the ladies.

Mrs Huxley, Thomas Huxley's widow, and Sir Joseph Hooker, both well over eighty, were staying with the Darwins. Were old world manners and charm, I wondered, more common in the past, or do they come with mature years? Mrs Huxley certainly had them, with a surprisingly alert mind. It was a touching sight to see old Sir Joseph Hooker with Francis Darwin's little grand-child in his arms. I thought what a wide period would be covered if the infant lived to the scientist's great age.

A great commemoration dinner, to which I was bidden, was given in the Hall at Trinity College, at which Mr Balfour presided. I had never heard Mr Balfour speak, and was somewhat disappointed, for his manner was halting, though his words were wise. The speech of the evening was made, I thought, by William Darwin. My wife looked on, with the Darwin ladies, from the balcony above, and heard the speeches. How proud Francis Darwin, and the other sons must have been, at the homage paid to their father.

I had, about now, a letter from Henry Newbolt. He

wanted my opinion on a book he was sending me. Why, he would tell me later. The book was called *Henry Brocken*, wherein the author had imagined the later lives of certain characters from fiction: a charming book; its author had obviously a beautiful nature. He was a young man, in the Standard Oil Company, Newbolt told me later, who could not bear office life—he had come to him for advice. Newbolt thought the work of high promise, but had hesitated to advise his friend to risk earning his living by his pen alone. Now he hesitated no longer, and the young writer decided to take the risk, to throw up his job, to devote himself to literature. For long he supported himself by reviewing, chiefly for *The Westminster Gazette* and *The Times Literary Supplement*, for poetry brings little pelf, though it brought steady recognition to de la Mare. De la Mare was endowed by the Gods with such natural goodness and charm that all who knew him loved him. What matter the world's goods when a man has personal magic? Natural charm is like radiant beauty—to him or to her that hath shall be given more. There is no more enviable quality. To Max Beerbohm this was given and to Walter Sickert; Oscar Wilde had it, but wasted it. Max Beerbohm, Sickert and Walter de la Mare have preserved their charm, and draw men and women to them with this potent magnet.

A strange thing is personality; there is also a counter-charm, a touch of aggressiveness, equally mysterious, which, be the heart never so kind, and the altruism never so ready, antagonises certain persons. Hudson, too, fascinated people; but while no one could be more charming when he wished, Conrad had an aggressive side, which his friends overlooked, because of his obvious genius. Yet Conrad was nervous and sensitive, and he could be very irritable. I mentioned earlier how prejudiced he was against Masefield's work. He was still more hostile to Shaw; and once when I told him that Max did not like Proust, he burst out against Max; yet, another time I heard him judge Proust harshly. But when he liked people he would admit no faults; indeed, he was inclined to flatter—perhaps this was a Polish trait—both in speaking and writing. Poor Conrad; he suffered much from gout, which racked his nerves and depressed his spirits. At times it took all one's energy to pump life and hope into him; for he was cheered by his friends' faith in his work. Not that he lacked faith in himself; measuring himself against his contemporaries, he knew his own power. But he strained after an unattainable standard of perfection, and the effort to reach it often exhausted him.

His letters show his anxiety regarding his future, and how much he had to struggle against ill health.

17 *Dec.* 1909   *Aldington,*
                                                 Nr. Hythe,
                                                 Kent.

Dearest Will

Don't you think that if I could possibly spare the time I wouldn't rather take a day and come and see you and yours to whom my heart goes out many times a week? Here I've been 2 years writing a novel which is not yet finished. Two years! of which surely one half has been illness complicated by a terrible moral stress. Imagine yourself painting with the Devil jogging your elbow *all the time*. But you who are one of the most intelligent men I know, or know of, and a stylist also (because you are—I've been looking at your Goya only the other day), you will know what a torture that sort of thing is when the effort and hindrance are mental. It is to make you realise how really unfit I am for what I call casual intercourse of mankind. And the truth also is, my dear Will, that we live here now in such conditions—crowded into four tiny rooms in half of a cottage, that I really don't like to receive strangers even the most admiring and the best disposed. You must not charge me with littleness of mind; we must take the world as it is; and indeed there is some concern for the dignity of letters in my reluctance.

I speak to you here as to a second self and thus I cannot

conceive you taking it ill. Perhaps I am unreasonable. But to-day in the second week of my 52nd year, a failure from the worldly point of view and knowing well that there can be no change—that this must go on usque ad finem—I may perhaps be allowed a little unreason.—Well, no more just now. I will only mention that I haven't seen you for more than a year, Galsworthy for nine months, that I have been in town for about six hours in March last and not since. Voilà. And if you think that I am indulging in a capricious savagery of disposition you are mistaken. Our dear love to you all

Yours ever
J. CONRAD.

And again:

Aldington,
Hythe,
Kent.
20 *May.* '10

Dearest Will—

I can just, just hobble over 50 yards or so of smooth ground but am too tottery and generally shaky to venture on the pavements of Babylon. Also one wrist is dead lame.

The mind is not much better. Can't concentrate for more than $\frac{1}{2}$ hour at a time. How to write long and short stories under this disability I don't know. But they must be written and shall be. It'll be, no doubt, very delightful.

I can't go and see your pictures. It's exasperating. I am keeping a tight hand on myself for fear my nerves go to pieces. I suppose I *have* been as ill as they tell me. At the time I was rather sceptical; now I begin to believe it.

To get away from this hole here is my ardent wish. We have found a house in the woods within $4\frac{1}{2}$ miles. It is picturesque and roomy. I *must* have space and silence— silence! I shall get that last there if anywhere outside the grave—which has no space.

You must come and see and approve, as soon as we get in.

I mean you two—for your approbation without your dear wife's would be worth nearly nothing.

Our dear love to all your house

Ever yours

J. CONRAD.

Hudson never worried about his work; he usually spoke with contempt of his own writing and for the writer's craft. Yet no one cared for good literature or respected good writing more. It pleased Hudson to assume indifference, while he really loved to talk of books and writers. And he was fastidious about his own prose. But after a few months in London he longed for open spaces; and he would go off to Hampshire, Devonshire or Cornwall, or to the East Coast.

We still spent our summers in France, usually at Vaucottes, where the Chownes and Frank Darwin and his daughter would join us. We would walk down from the inn to bathe, the children rushing into the sea without any clothes on, greatly to the disgust of the French ladies sitting on the beach, who thought it shocking that little girls but three and four years old should bathe thus. How much more conventional the French people are in fact than ourselves. Who in England would be shocked at seeing little girls without bathing dresses? More than once we tried unsuccessfully to get Hudson to join us. 'Many thanks for your kind letter and the invitation', he wrote. 'It must be a fascinating place and the green grasshoppers are a luxury one can't get anywhere. I wish I could go and visit you but 'tis impossible. We were at Deal awhile, and one day at Dover. I tried to drag Mrs Hudson to Calais, but she would not. I've never been in France and am quite sure I never shall now. The only place out of England I wish to go to (and hope to go before long) is New England —Maine and New Hampshire and Vermont where my mother's relations are. I've never seen any of them nor her native place and have a wish and desire—a kind of pious or superstitious feeling—to pay it a visit. It is the red man's feeling and I am a red man, or at all events a wild man of the woods. We are glad to know you are in such a delightful place and are all so well. Mrs Hudson is highly amused at your idea of being a strict vegetarian with rabbit and chicken on the table every day.

'Yesterday I was at the Mont Blanc to lunch and Hammond and some of the staff were there, all with a slight shadow on them, for alas, *The Speaker* is now about to change hands and we shall know it no more. The new people are going to "make it pay"—perhaps that means that it will cease to be an intellectual paper and be something different—God knows what. We were astonished at your news about the Conrads. No I have not seen him nor heard anything about him. I met C. Graham in the park a while ago and he says his wife is still very ill. Our united love to you all.'

'I am a red man.' This explains Hudson's forlorn feeling when he had to remain in London. He and his wife were at home on Wednesday afternoons, where we would meet the faithful—the Ranee of Sarawak, Edward Thomas, Edward Garnett, Cunninghame Graham, and sometimes Mrs J. R. Green, but Hudson didn't get on very well with Mrs Green. 'I think Mrs Green was not too well pleased with me for what I said about her wings, aigret and bird of paradise plumes, but I say what I think and shall do so till I die, even if it results in alienating the last friend I have on earth.' But what Hudson said alienated nobody; no man had more devoted friends.

He too loved his friends, though he willingly escaped from Westbourne Grove: 'My outings since I last heard from you have been within the British Isles, no further away than Derbyshire, the Peak, and the West of England. My object in life is to look after birds.' Watching birds was of course Hudson's passion, but he cared deeply for the English villages, and his letters are full of his wanderings in Cornwall, Norfolk and Derbyshire. It seemed he always chose villages with beautiful names. He wrote from the Lamb Inn, Hindon near Salisbury:

'This is a nice village, and there are others better near here, Fonthill Bishop, East Knoyle especially, I wonder if you will nurse the project of getting a place in the country? I'm enquiring here all the time, and yet I don't like the idea of settling down anywhere in the shadows of these gigantic human beech trees that kill anything under them, the Fonthill Abbey and Clouds and Longleat magnates. They kill the souls of the people and therefore my soul abhors them and I curse them in a book in a proper way. Oddly enough one likes these people well enough when you know them. It is not they but the system in which they were cradled. But why do I inflict all this on you? I wish I could see you instead of sending a wretched scrawl, however, I may be going up soon if I get round.'

He would often write thus bitterly, but when he met some of the 'Longleat magnates' or their relations at our house, he liked them. Indeed he would say worse things about Bernard Shaw, and the socialists, whom he disliked, than about 'magnates'. There was a strange Spanish pride in Hudson, who was attracted by people of principle and character, whatever their birth, and was sensitive to fine breeding. Were not Cunninghame Graham, Sir Edward Grey and the Ranee of Sarawak, his chosen friends?

Another time came a letter from Silchester:

'I found your letter at the Winchester post office yesterday morning and am very grateful to you for writing as you do. I wish I deserved the praise you give my work. I am doing some work here and will finish in a very few days, so shall most probably return to London at the end of this week. I hope to see you at Hampstead one day very soon. I had not made the acquaintance of some of the most interesting spots in Hampshire before, and yesterday from Winchester went to one—Cheriton, a small old-world spot, a village that calls itself a town, but is composed of a very few old cottages and houses and an ancient church. Another still more interesting spot is Bramdean, a village near—the battle of Cheriton in Cromwell's wars was fought close to this village. One of its chief glories is Woodcote House, a very beautiful Elizabethan manor house in a park. Here lives Sir Seymour Haden, the veteran etcher; he is, I believe, getting near ninety, and does no art work now, but is occupied in collecting all his original work he can get hold of. The house is full of it. He took me all over the place and could manage to get up and down the stairs very well in spite of his years.

You have not (I hope) a copy of *The Naturalist in La Plata* as I have one to take you when I go to see you. Dent has made a rather nice-looking book of it.'

Of course I knew Woodcote Manor; it was there I made my drawings of Seymour Haden, of which I wrote earlier. I do not know which book it was I praised, perhaps *Green Mansions*, which so few people cared for when first it appeared. It is now a kind of classic.

Among Hudson's closest friends were Edward Thomas and Edward Garnett. Thomas was shy and sensitive, but had a beautiful nature which made him loved by all who knew him; Hudson I know regarded him with deep affection. Garnett was the most selfless of men, and was among the first to recognise the genius of Conrad and Hudson. There was nothing he would not do for them, nor for any man whom he admired. On this account he was unfairly treated, for he thought and did so much for others, that his own claim to recognition as a discerning writer was overlooked. I think, too, that those who first befriend men who later become famous, feel as did the servants in the parable—that the late comers in friendship get as much as, nay often more than, those who give help and sympathy when it is most needed.

Galsworthy, too, was devoted to Hudson; indeed Hudson came next after Conrad, I think, in his esteem. Galsworthy was becoming a figure in the literary world. Conrad had at first spoken of his writing rather apologetically, as though it were the man who was most worthy of our acquaintance. But as often happens, it is not the master but the pupil to whom the greater success comes. Not that Galsworthy was in fact a pupil of Conrad; but he regarded Conrad as a master, and was modest about his own gifts. But through his epic picture of upper middle class life, he became a favourite among readers, both in England and abroad, before Conrad did. Tall, austere looking, with a Roman profile and tightly closed lips, always correctly dressed, Galsworthy would not have looked out of place in Downing Street. His manners were as severely correct as his dress; yet his calm patrician appearance was deceptive; he was by no means a friend to aristocrats. If there was a lame dog to be helped over a stile, one went straight to Galsworthy. 'Jack' was the name one heard most often during illness in the Conrad household. But fame was coming to Conrad too. The little Pent Farm was given up for a pleasant place near Bedford; then larger establishments were set up at Aldington and Bishopsbourne.

On Tuesdays Hudson often lunched at a little French Restaurant in Gerrard Street, the Mont Blanc, where he would meet, besides the faithful Edward Garnett, Hilaire Belloc, H. W. Nevinson, Conrad, J. L. Hammond, and others who dropped in. Hammond was now, together with his wife, exploring the less known tracks of social history—little known to me, at least, for their first book, *The Village Labourer*, gave me a new insight into village life. I sent a copy to Thomas Hardy, thinking it would have a special interest for him, as indeed it had. He acknowledged it from Max Gate:

'I have read with much interest a good deal of the book you kindly sent me. With details of the last peasant revolt I have, of course, been familiar from childhood, though it occurred earlier than my actual recollection carries me. My father knew a man who was hanged for saying to a farmer "It will be a light night"—(his ricks being set fire to before the morning). As a child I personally knew a boy who was starved to death in "the hungry forties" during my absence in London with my mother. He used to keep sheep near our house. However those times are happily over, and things are a little the other way now, for the farm-labourers are very comfortable, and better off than the London poor.'

Whether Hardy spoke of Hudson's books I do not remember; but Hudson admired Hardy's, especially *The Return of the Native*. Hardy himself cherished *The Well Beloved*, perhaps because it was less read than his other stories. Something I said made him refer to this book, and he spoke at length of the psychology of this unusual attraction of mother and daughter and grand-daughter for the same man. How unassuming Hardy was. He had much in common with painters like John Crome; indeed, Egdon Heath put me in mind of a landscape by Crome, and Hardy himself retained something of local quality and character about his person, a quality which some would consider provincial, but which I prefer to call true 'county'.

Steer, too, seemed to belong more to the country than to London. He had the quiet shrewdness of the countryman. His opinions, when offered, were homely and to the point. He bought his Chelsea figures, his prints and *chinoiseries* with the caution of a farmer buying a horse or a plough at a sale. He kept house like a well-to-do farmer; one was always sure of good beef, pudding and cheese at his table. His maid might have been a country maid, and Mrs Raines, formerly his mother's housekeeper, was 'a character', who looked after Steer as though he were still a boy.

Things were going well with Steer. The pictures he sent to market were no longer returned to him. He prospered quietly, saying little, painting in his drawing room, into which the sun would come, for it faced south. He now never worked in a studio; herein he was wise, for he got natural backgrounds for his figures. An old faded blue wall-paper, which was in the room when he bought his house, and which suited his models, was never renewed. And he kept to the same model as long as possible—usually until she married. Then Steer would grumble, and take a fresh one. She would be pretty rather than handsome, petite, nearer a girl than a woman, fair and Saxon; unlike John, he never cared for exotic or dramatic character; no gypsies for Steer.

John also was winning fortune, as well as fame. Besides Hugh Lane, John Quinn, an Irish-American lawyer, was acquiring numerous paintings and drawings from John. In his second wife, the matchless Dorelia, in her dazzling beauty, now lyrical, now dramatic, John found constant inspiration. Who, indeed, could approach John in the interpretation of a woman's sensuous charm? No wonder fair ladies besieged his studio, and his person, too; for John had other magic than that of his brush; no one so irresistible as he, nor with such looks, such brains, such romantic and reckless daring and indifference to public opinion. Tonks and Steer did not approve of romance. Tonks was richly endowed with the sterner virtues, which befit the bachelor. Young ladies of the best families were known to weep at Tonks's acid comments on their work; yet young ladies of the best families flocked to the Slade to throw themselves before Tonks's Jaganath progress through the life-rooms. There was a time when poor Tonks had to walk the streets, not daring to go home, lest ladies be found at his door, awaiting his arrival with drawings in their hands, whose easels had been passed by, and in whose hearts was despair.

There was one man who did not admire Hudson; this was Edmund Gosse, who was seldom well-disposed to writers whose merits he had not been among the first to recognise. Gosse was nervously anxious to be sympathetic to young people, but I was rarely at my ease with him. I went sometimes, in the nineties, to his Sunday afternoons, when Gosse would look round and pick out guests whom he retained for supper; and sometimes, if there were no great guns present, he would include me, and being vain, I somewhat resented being weighed in the balance. I would often meet Gosse at the Savile Club, but the slight discomfort of his bright, sing-song manner remained. Later, I found myself more at my ease in Gosse's society, enjoying his wit, and his passion for literature; and we had in common a friendship for Conrad. I was amused, too, at Gosse's pernicketty ways. When at the Leicester Gallery, I showed a drawing I had made of him and sent him a private view card, there came an indignant letter:

Dear W. Rothenstein,

I am told that your Exhibition is open, but I do not know where. I think you might have remembered your promise to send me a card of invitation to the Private View, or at least some intimation of the event.

I am much obliged to you for the interesting print of your portrait of Swinburne. You will forgive me if I say that I think the aspect of him which presented itself to you a very painful one. But of course it has a great interest.

If you had asked me to see your show, I should probably have wished to possess the portrait of Conrad. But most likely you have already parted with it to someone else.

Believe me, Very faithfully yours,

EDMUND GOSSE.

This was followed, the day after, by another letter:

My dear W. Rothenstein,

The mystery is explained. Messrs. Brown and P's card of invitation was delivered at my house last night! The envelope had an address so ingeniously and complicatedly false that the wonder is it ever reached me at all.

However, I went round to the Leicester Galleries yesterday, and was fortunate enough to secure the *Joseph Conrad*. It is a most magnificent drawing, and will be a great joy to me to possess. If I outlive Conrad, it is my intention to bequeath it to the National Portrait Gallery[1]. I went through the exhibition very carefully. You will not resent my saying that I think you experience the universal fate of portraitists,— that is to say you do not always succeed. But your successes far out-number your comparative failures. Unquestionable successes and of a very high order, are two (at least) of the Hardys, Newbolt, Stopford Brooke, Conrad, myself,

---

[1] Sir Edmund Gosse did in fact bequeath this drawing, and another of Maurice Hewlett, to the National Portrait Gallery.

'A.E.' and A. E. Housman. All these are superlatively good. I do not mean that these alone, or nearly alone, are good, but these excel.

I feel it a great compliment to be included in your gallery, and the 'Conrad' will be one of my treasures.

Very sincerely yours,

EDMUND GOSSE.

'Very faithfully', 'very sincerely', how like Gosse! and how quickly his natural generosity reasserts itself.

Later, my relations with Gosse became cordial; if a man have the talent to live beyond three score and ten years, his other talents seem to mature, to acquire bouquet. Gosse's nature ripened like a peach on a sunny wall, and during the last year of his life I saw much of him, and enjoyed the generous affection he extended to me. He was pleased with my praise of his daughter's painting, for at one time the modernity of her work had alarmed him. For Gosse, who responded so quickly to the work of young writers, remained a Pre-Raphaelite in his attitude towards painting.

Hence he was always delighted at my interest in the pictures on his walls; and since I had known Swinburne and Watts-Dunton he unburdened himself of some of his feeling towards them. Believing that Watts-Dunton had poisoned Swinburne's mind against him, it was the pre-Pines poet for whom he reserved his enthusiasm. He was interested in what I had heard from Major Charvot in the old Rat Mort days, about Maupassant's meeting with Swinburne at Étretat; and a fantastic story of a monkey, incredible to me, had some meaning for Gosse, who had heard a more accurate account from others. What credence should be given to tales one hears at second hand? Rodin once told me how, as a youth, he had known the old painter Gigoux. Gigoux, who in his day had been a great buck, and had associated freely with the great men of the thirties, told Rodin strange stories of his exploits. Had he ever known Balzac? Rodin asked him. Not known him exactly,

and the old man sniggered: but he had seen him once—
from behind a curtain in Mme de Hanska's bedroom. If there
be any truth in this story, the mysterious shadow across
Balzac's late marriage, hinted at in his letters, becomes
plainer. Rodin told me, too, that on going to Victor Hugo
for an early morning sitting, he stumbled against someone
lying outside the poet's door—it was the faithful Juliette
Drouet. Such stories strike the imagination, containing
elements of something more dramatic than mere gossip.

CHAPTER XX

DEATH OF CONDER

Mʀs Gʀᴇᴇɴ had been telling me about E. D. Morel. A great lunch was to be given him, together with a cheque (for Morel was poor it appears), in recognition for his services to the black races. I was not in a position to subscribe, but I offered to paint Morel's portrait. At the lunch (at which Lord Cromer presided), I sat next to Conan Doyle, who asked me to join his party at dinner that night. There I met a man whose name was to become notorious—Sir Roger Casement. I had heard something of Casement from Conrad. Conrad had known him in the Congo, and spoke highly of his gallantry and courage. He told how Casement would go off over the hill-side with a stick and a dog and disappear for months into the dark African forest. Then one morning Casement would reappear with his dog and his stick, as though he had been out for a walk. Black haired, dark-eyed, handsome in face and build, he was an impressive figure. I did not meet him again until some years afterwards, when he arrived at my studio with two young savages. He had brought them, he said, from Putumayo; their parents had been cruelly butchered and their kindred enslaved. He was full of their wrongs, and wanted to plead their case in England. Would I help? He wished me to paint the two youths, which I readily did. Their bodies were a rich golden colour, and their dress simple—but a few brilliant feathers strung together. Such models were rare.

While they sat, Casement would tell me stories of his adventures. He was full, too, of the wrongs of Ireland. 'As long as he only bothers about present conditions', said

Yeats, 'it doesn't matter; but Heaven help him if he fills his
head with Ireland's past wrongs.' I was uneasy about Casement; he was excitable and restless; and I was not surprised
when he wrote to me that his doctor had ordered him off to
Spain at once, lest he should have a breakdown. I thought of
this later, when Casement became so tragically involved.
I remember George Moore meeting him and Mrs Green
at dinner with us. George Moore and Casement got on
well together, but George Moore could not abide Mrs Green.
You never knew how George Moore would get on with
ladies, or what he would say to them. He had a silly itch to
shock them, but I recollect his once saying an amusing thing,
when he had been talking enthusiastically about *the Letters of
a Portuguese Nun*. Adrian Stokes and his wife were with us
and Mrs Stokes asked, 'were not these letters forged?'—
'Madam,' said Moore, 'can you forge a May morning?'

Poor Moore! Women reading his books, he complained, thought they had been through the experiences he
invented for his heroines. He got long letters asking for
sympathy and advice, and love-letters too. He was getting
them daily from some Viennese woman—long love-letters
full of psychology and passion. He read us his answers,
cautious answers, descriptive of his habits, of the pictures on
his walls, of his admiration for Monet and Degas—letters
which were a joy to Steer, and Tonks and myself. Writers
seem to invite confession. Wells, too, told me of letters
received from women who believed he would understand
their difficulties—difficulties of the heart. Painters invite no
such confidences; but I was fortunate in the intimate friendship of many women, whose letters were as blossom or as
fruit. Max Beerbohm always says that women, and not men,
are the true letter writers. They alone speak through their
pens, as it were in their natural voices.

One New Year's day I had sent the Michael Fields some
mohair, from my father's firm at Bradford; could a gift
bring a more enchanting reply?

A gift of mohair

1, *The Paragon,*
Richmond,
Surrey

O dear Heavenly Dog!—

A bale from Fairyland—so magic the generosity! Or is it what a Breviary hymn talks of as 'Eoa Munera'—the Epiphany tribute of a Mage? More distinctive than silk the webbed and shining mohair, and what elephant's ivory could surpass the tinct! it has gold in it—it has the grays of frankincense, the blond and austere suggestion of preciousness—the stuff has the drape of the myrrh-drenched shroud of a Queen or a Priest, very simple, and stiff with ceremonious resin. We are enchanted—we are enriched.

We believe the 'Heavenly Dog' has been robbing Heaven, instead of watching it; and we have that joy in an offence done for us that haunts woman's heart forever. Michael is going to write the blackest black kettle of Noli's dear gift.

How good you have been to us—trying to soften the rawness of a New Year with the suavity 'Eoa Munera' of the Wise.

Your thankful, smiling Field

'We are not going to Ireland till the "wise-open spring".'

Michael Field, Margaret Woods, Margaret Mackail, Frances Cornford, Christina Herringham, Fanny Prothero, such friends made me realise the ideal love of the Troubadours. The Michael Field's books are now little read; but what Field wrote of the shining stuff I sent her is true of their poetry— 'it has gold in it—it has the grays of frankincense, the blond and austere suggestion of preciousness'. Their poetry but sleeps; but not the sleep of death.

There were two American ladies of whom we saw much at this time; Mrs Chadbourne and Mrs Koehler, the last a remarkable artist, who made superb settings for noble jewels. Mrs Chadbourne had exquisite taste, with the means to satisfy it; and the two gathered round them a small but fastidious circle: Augustus John, the Herringhams, Percy

Grainger, the Baron de Meyer and Lady Ottoline Morrell. These ladies had travelled in China, Japan and India, and the many beautiful things they brought back gave an Eastern atmosphere to their apartment; an exotic atmosphere, for they lacked the tap-roots which allow the human plant to feed itself from limited, local sources.

Mrs Chadbourne, who knew Arthur B. Davies, the American painter, had some exquisite paintings by him of slim, white nude women, moving in a virginal landscape. She bought a self portrait I painted, which she gave to the Metropolitan Museum in New York, and she asked me to paint a portrait of Henry James for the same museum.

Henry James, massive in face and figure, slow and impressive in speech, had now become one of the great pundits, to whom ladies sat listening in adoration; pilgrimages were made to his house at Rye; his dicta, elaborate, wise and tortuous, were repeated in clubs and drawing rooms. A man must have great gifts to become a national figure; but above all others—the gift of years. If he but live long enough, bright fame will come to him, position, honours and authority. Until his sixties war may be waged against a writer or painter; once on his way to the seventies the silver trumpet sounds, and all is peace and kindness. The giants are dead, long live the giants. Meredith had just passed away; of the Pre-Raphaelite painters Holman Hunt was the only survivor. Thomas Hardy and Henry James were now come into their kingdoms. I wrote to James about Mrs Chadbourne's proposal, who replied:

Lamb House,
Rye, Sussex
January 6th 1900

My dear Rothenstein,

Your letter is interesting—your enquiry flattering; but I should have been glad to learn from you a little more the exact *conditions* of the project. You don't tell me who orders the picture—and that fact would have much to say to me (one way or the other,) as a sitter. And when you say 'to hang in the Metropolitan Museum', do you mean the Museum itself has ordered it? I don't quite understand—nor what mere amateur of the Fine Arts or of H.J. (or of Rothenstein) can *guarantee* that honourable situation. Pardon my putting these questions, but they immediately suggest themselves, and I shall be able to answer you better when I know a little more. I am not an exceptionally free or convenient sitter, and I have the last year or two sat copiously to two different painters, at their own earnest instance —and with not the happiest results. Likewise I am aged, infirm, unlovely, extremely occupied; and do little in London. But I will do what I can for you willingly—if you can give me a little more indispensable light. Believe me,

Sincerely yours,

HENRY JAMES.

Henry James was depressed about himself at this time. His heart was troubling him; he was like Hudson in this respect; he could not bear the idea of dying. He was not now in a mood to sit and he asked me to put off the portrait to a more propitious time. But this never came; his heart grew no stronger, gave out, indeed, some years later, but not before Sargent painted at the request of Henry James's admirers the vigorous head which is now in the National Portrait Gallery. But how undistinguished the clothes! no wonder, for the cut of men's coats, the dull shoulders and stove pipe sleeves, give no painter a chance. How ill these compare with the nervous folds and shapely sleeves in a portrait by Ingres.

I was now to find another woman friend. Max had spoken to me of a Miss Florence Kahn, whom he had lately met. She had come from America, where she had acted with Richard Mansfield; he must bring her to see us. Then I met a girlish figure with red hair, looking, I thought like Miss Siddall, but so shy and with a beauty so elusive that I wondered how she could dominate a stage. But my doubt was shortlived, for when I saw her as Rebecca West in

Rosmersholm, there was no shyness; the elusiveness remained, but her voice and her presence filled the stage, and so human, yet so spiritual was her acting, and so lovely her presence, that I thought it was indeed Miss Siddall come to life again, to act instead of to paint. For a time Florence Kahn lived near us at Hampstead, to the joy of our children, and when she became Mrs Max Beerbohm, Max was the richer; but the English stage the poorer.

Max was still writing on the theatre for *The Saturday Review*. 'Alas, I cannot come on Wednesday', he wrote to my wife, 'I have an engagement for that evening, which I must keep—unless, as is possible, I go to Paris to-morrow, to see *Chantecler* for *The Saturday Review*. This is an adventure which I rather funk, as I don't want to be drowned, and am not keen on typhoid—nor very particularly keen, for the matter of that, on Rostand. But the Editor implores me to go. And if the news from Paris to-morrow is good, I probably shall go. But, if I don't, I must not throw over the other engagement, which I accepted some time ago. Duty absolves, but pleasure doesn't—Thus you see that Will hasn't a monopoly of high principles!'

I used to chaff Max about the many telegrams he sent to put off engagements. 'Very many apologies for my absence the other night, and for the feverish telegram'—thus many of his letters would begin.

'I will cure myself of the telegram fever, if I can', he wrote. 'It is a deadly disease, to which all are liable who live in this fetid city. You must guard your son against it. Have his arm injected with the glue off a postage stamp. I am going to have mine done.' And by way of further excuse, there came a caricature of the family, accompanied by a letter:

48, *Upper Berkeley St. W.*
Jan. 13. '07.

Dearest Will,

Here are 'the Rothensteins at home'—a sort of pendant, though a very unworthy one, to Albert's delightful picture of them abroad. Rachel and Betty I have had to do from 'chic': they are probably much more charming than they appear here. And the three persons whom I *do* know well by sight suffer obviously under my pen. But there is in the whole design a sense of a *family*, I think—something spiritually real, though not up to the mark of our old friend Giotto—(I say *our* old friend, because I regard any friend of yours as a friend of mine.) What a dear little boy John is! So sunny and happy and always saying the pleasant thing to everybody: so *safe* and in that respect so unlike most other children—a great credit to you and Alice as bringers-up. At least, I hope it *is* a question of up-bringing. If his charm came naturally to him, I should be afraid he was a humbug! —such as you always accuse *me* of being.

Love to Alice,

Yours affectionately,

MAX.

I spent occasional week-ends in Bradford with my parents. The town seemed to change but little. Manningham Lane was the same straggling street, with the tram-lines I saw laid down as a boy still in use; the shops showed the same goods in the windows, Carter, the tobacconist, with cheap note paper and toys, cheap sweets, surprise packets and tops; then Cockroft, the stationer; and lower down the post-office, and the shabby old Theatre Royal, beyond which was a little wooden shop where oysters, crabs and ice cream could be consumed. Whether deservedly or not, this shabby little place, which, as school-boys, we were forbidden to enter, had a mysterious reputation. Then came the old Grammar School. In Darley Street was the Market, whose stalls, with their great barbaric sweets—humbug and rock—their old-fashioned toys, and bright carpets and stuffs, still attracted me by a strong local character. The plain stone warehouses further on in the town, also had a local character; my father's warehouse, erected about 1850, was solidly built throughout, and had dignity and style.

The prophet at home

When in Bradford I always visited my friend Ernest Sichel, whose sensitive studies, chiefly pastels, I admired as much as ever. But the collectors who bought canvases by La Thangue, Charles, Clausen and others, were not friendly to me. 'Nul n'est, dit on, prophète dans son pays,' Verlaine had written in a poem he sent to me; it was certainly true of my relations with Bradford. There was no work of mine in its art gallery, nor, except in my brother's, in any of the private collections. Not before 1910 was a painting acquired; and then not an important one, but a study for a larger picture merely. This is the only canvas of mine Bradford has ever purchased, which indifference saddened my parents. But my brother Charles, who was now prosperous, continued his support. But for him I should have fared ill.

Another Bradfordian was Humbert Wolfe, who had lately come to London from Oxford and who contributed occasional poems in *The Westminster Gazette* and was to make some show in the world.

While I was staying at Bradford there came a letter from Max, telling me the news of Conder's death. This, though not unexpected, was a blow no less. So much of my life had been bound up with his; we had loved and quarrelled, and parted and come together again. There were qualities of Conder's mind and art which no one, I thought, understood as I did. He felt this himself; and though we differed in many respects, a peculiar sympathy existed between us.

In some ways Conder was more adventurous than other painters; he was instinct with inventive powers, and could put down a complicated composition with extraordinary ability, giving life and beauty to his figures. His sense of the physical beauty of women, of the grace of their movements, of feminine radiance, was unique—in his period at least. To say that he belonged more to the eighteenth century than to his own, is too obvious. His art was based partly on his sense of style, of gesture, of artificial comedy, in a word, the comedy of Davenant, of Congreve, and of Watteau and Fragonard; and in large measure too, on his subtle observation of actual life. Each side of his nature helped the other. He had a great feeling for form, but because of an incomplete equipment, he was never able to express it, and thus he could never attain the disciplined art of Watteau, of Gainsborough and of Fragonard. Yet Conder has a place to himself in English art. He is one of the rare lyrical painters, singing now with the morning innocence of the lark, now with the more sinister note of the nightjar. His richly suggestive art is at present underrated; but its vitality, I am sure, when the moment comes, will blossom again in men's eyes.

CHAPTER XXI

INTRODUCES SOME YOUNG ARTISTS

LYTTON STRACHEY'S look in those early days was very unlike his later appearance. Long, slender, with a receding chin, that gave a look of weakness to his face, with a thin, cracked voice, I thought him typical of the Cambridge intellectual. Dining one night with Isabel Fry, I recollect saying that poetry, usually regarded as a vague and highfalutin art by many, was in fact the clearest expression of man's thoughts. Strachey replied acidly. Who, indeed, was I to talk of matters with which I was not concerned? And I thought that here was the cultured University man, who lies in wait, hoping one may say something foolish, or inaccurate, and then springs out to crush one, in high falsetto tones. But I was mistaken. Of course Lytton Strachey was much more than a cultured Cambridge man; he was to become a master of English prose; and with reputation came a beard, and long hair, and a cloak and sombrero, which gave weight and solemnity to an appearance previously not very noticeable. I think Lytton Strachey was of so nervous a temper, that he needed some defensive armour to cover his extreme sensitiveness, and a weapon with a sharp edge, with which to protect himself. He suffered fools less genially than Max, to their faces at least. Max used to say that after thirty, one should quarrel with no man.

I was friendly with two of his sisters, Marjorie, whose keen intellect I ever found provocative and stimulating, and Dorothy, who married Simon Bussy.

Lady Strachey, mother of many gifted children, was a

woman of great character and charm, whose friendship was flattering to my self-esteem, another Victorian, whose breeding and breadth of mind I admired. One day she asked me to her house in Belsize Park, to give an opinion on some studies by a nephew of hers, pastel portraits, which showed remarkable qualities; she need have no doubts I assured her regarding the young artist's gifts, or his future. I met her nephew, Duncan Grant, a shy, modest youth, every inch an artist.

Duncan Grant began, as did most young painters, by sending his pictures to the New English Art Club. They were not welcomed as they should have been—indeed, one or two of the best were rejected, as were others by Simon Bussy. I expressed myself somewhat strongly on the subject, to the jury, for the New English, I held, should welcome new men. Grant, who was modest about his work, in answer to a letter on the subject of his paintings, replied:

My dear Rothenstein,

I do not know how I am to thank you enough for your kind letter to me about my pictures at the Alpine Club. You accuse me of never showing you any of my work, but it has never been because I doubted your power of judgment, but that I considered there could be no two opinions about the many faults in my production.

It was therefore an extremely pleasant surprise to find that someone whose opinion I value as highly as I do yours should see some merit in my work or rather would consider that on the whole the merit exceeds the faults (in these particular ones).

You also cannot know how encouraging your criticism and sympathy are to me. I work, I feel, too much in the dark, so to speak, as regards getting opinions about my work, and I find yours both stimulating and illuminating.

I feel very strongly the need for simplicity, so that my failure to reach it is the more marked, but objects to me have a most deceptive way of *looking* simple, in spite of their details, and I only realise my mistake when I try to make them.

I hope you will not think me impertinent for telling you how much I enjoyed your exhibition at Goupil. I had seen many before but not since it was finished your portrait of yourself. It seems to me a very great success and extraordinarily interesting.

Yours very sincerely,

DUNCAN GRANT.

Another artist whose work I admired was Simon Bussy. I had known Simon Bussy for some time. He was a Frenchman who came to England in 1900 and took a studio close to us in Kensington. He had brought a letter of introduction from another French friend, Auguste Bréal, and we became close friends. He had a markedly personal vision, and an exquisite technique; his pastels were specially beautiful, and had considerable influence, if I am not mistaken, on the early ones of Duncan Grant which I saw at Lady Strachey's. Bussy had a struggle to keep himself going in London, and did not meet with much recognition from other artists, and to my disgust, as I said, more than one of his works was rejected by the New English Art Club. Frenchmen who are generous to foreign artists in France are apt to feel hurt at the lack of sympathy sometimes shown to them in England. Bussy once expressed his feelings on this subject:

La Souco
Cabbé Roquebrune
Alpes Maritimes
15 *Avril* 1907.

Cher ami,

C'est avec beaucoup de plaisir que j'ai lu votre aimable lettre pleine d'appréciations élogieuses—merci beaucoup.

Je me souviendrai toujours de l'accueil charmant que vous m'avez fait en arrivant à Londres et cette lettre spontanée montre une fois de plus vos sentiments bienveillants à mon égard. Je dois ajouter que votre sympathie m'est d'autant plus précieuse que je n'ai pas toujours eu à me louer des artistes anglais. Maintenant que je connais assez bien les anglais pour les aimer et pour apprécier leurs grandes qualités morales, il m'est pénible de penser que la plupart des peintres français ayant habité Londres au début de leur carrière aient conservé un si mauvais souvenir de leur séjour; pour en citer quelques-uns je dirai Carrière, Degas, Besnard. Et c'est triste d'entendre dire à Whistler à qui je parlais de l'hostilité que je rencontrais à Londres parmi les artistes *seulement* 'Si vous touchez à leur pain et à leur beurre!...' Aussi j'ai eu beaucoup de chance de vous avoir ainsi que cet excellent Roger Fry....

SIMON BUSSY.

Bussy, with his great respect for technical finish, deplored as I did the slipshod work which was being done in France. In a letter he wrote to me from Cortina, he refers to this:

27 *août* 1908

...J'ai été convaincu plus que jamais que le public français n'est pas disposé en ce moment à aimer la peinture sobre, grave et d'un métier savant. L'impressionisme a tout envahi; les bourgeois eux-mêmes ne regardent plus une peinture si elle est d'une bonne exécution. 'La peinture léchée est bien passeé de mode!', cette phrase prononcée dernièrement par la plus stupide femme que je connaisse est un signe des temps. Oui, mon cher ami, c'est ainsi, il n'y a rien à faire en France pour nous. Sans doute la réaction arrivera et elle est peut-être plus proche qu'on ne le pense mais en attendant c'est le triomphe de l'impressionisme. Les amateurs éclairés achètent les bons tableaux de cette école et les bourgeois achètent les mauvais. Pourtant je ne dois pas passer sous silence que j'ai eu quelques articles très élogieux par des critiques indépendants. Néanmoins nous sommes pris entre deux feux, la mitraille révolutionnaire et les gros canons—un peu démodés il est vrai—de l'INSTITUT. Je dis nous, parce que nous avons assez de points de ressemblance. Loin d'être

ému par l'indifférence et la haine, je m'efforce dans la solitude
de perfectionner mon art au point de vue matériel et vision-
naire. C'est vous dire mon cher ami que je vous conseille de
ne pas aborder le public parisien en ce moment, mais toute-
fois si vous pensez que j'exagère je suis tout à fait disposé à
vous faciliter une exposition chez un marchand de Paris.

He here speaks of impressionism, but we were shortly to
see what post-impressionism was to do for French painting.

From Bussy I got constant support and encouragement,
both for my painting and for my drawing. He urged me
above all, in spite of the fact that no one seemed to want my
drawings, to continue making portraits, which, he believed,
would one day be justified. So I still bothered my friends to
sit. Among others I wanted to draw Shaw again, and was
amused at the letter I got from him:

> 10 *Adelphi Terrace*
> *W.C.*
> *4th February*, 1908.

My dear Rothenstein,

I am afraid it is quite impossible. I am vainly trying to get
ahead with a new play in the intervals of an intolerable grind
at public and private business. Furthermore, I rashly told
John Collier last year that if I ever submitted to sitting again,
I would let him have a shot at me for a portrait in the style of
Holbein; and though this has not been commenced, and
does not seem likely ever to be commenced, he duns me
vigorously for sittings, and has cornered me so far that unless I give him first bite, I shall be treating him very badly.
Besides it will not be really worth your while to get me again
until the Rodin bust is out of date. You cannot get in on top
of that for two or three years to come. Meanwhile, your
older sketches must be ripening for use by Holbrook
Jackson as mementoes of a by-gone phase.

You will probably be generous enough not to remind me
that I am making the sittings I promised to Collier an excuse
for dodging the sittings I promised to you. But for some
entirely inexplicable reason, I feel morally reckless about you

and punctilious about John. Possibly I am influenced by the severity of the style of Holbein.

Shaw was also influenced by the style of Velasquez, for he sat to Neville Lytton in the dress of a Pope, and looked strikingly like Pope Innocent X in the Doria picture.

It was while criticising the students' compositions at Bolt Court that I singled out a drawing which showed unusual imagination. Its youthful author came up after the criticism, glowing with happy excitement. He was young Paul Nash. He would not get the training he needed at Bolt Court, I told him, and advised him to go to the Slade School. He wrote eager, enthusiastic letters:

> *Iver Heath*
> *Bucks.*
> *July.* 13. 1910.

Dear Mr Rothenstein,

I made an invasion upon you a few days ago bringing some new designs and many questions. I was met by the news you were away until September. I was very sick with myself, for if I had thought you were going away so soon I would have come before. But I have really waited until I had some new work because it is the fruits of your seeds of advice & criticism and I so much wanted to know what you thought of it. I hope you'll not have thought I was too slack to turn up—please don't. I have been trying to acquire a simpler way of expression and I have been taking much, much longer over the working out of designs. October sees me at the Slade, all being well, and at present I'm racking all my brains & tapping all the sources & raising all the wind to produce enough for the fees! You were very right about the feeling which comes—the desire to draw for the sake of drawing. I begin to feel it but as yet I am very uneasy & laborious. I wish I had not missed you the other day but I shall hope to see you if you'll have me after the holidays...

> Yrs sinc.
> PAUL NASH.

A painting approved

But the Nashes, it seemed, were not well off, and Paul must first earn his fees.

9, *Imperial Square,*
Cheltenham Glos.
23 *Sept.*

Dear Mr Rothenstein,

I was glad to have your note and feel I must write now and tell you I am away until the end of September with no chance of getting to see you. Directly I get back I shall come on the chance you have not started again, but I am rather sad about it. I have been for the last fortnight away in Normandy & Brittany seeing all those tremendous churches & cathedrals & drinking in, in long long pulls, the wonder of a first trip abroad. We saw twelve towns & incidentally a thousand beautiful things. I am chockfull of ideas & tho' I never had more than an hour & a half to sketch in there are a few useful drawings among the collection & I think I can make something of them. During the summer (save the mark!) I have been a good many times to see the show of pictures at the Japan Exhibition. Don't call me a prig but I think your painting of Talmud students—tremendous. I really love it. I was standing before it (it's in a devilish bad light) when an imposingly simple flock of country cousins ambled up— they were all related I'm sure & came from Balham or the wilds of Upper Tooting—and stood in uncomfortable attitudes about. One dear old lady seemed so fascinated that I officiously attacked her & insisted on telling her who had painted it, whereat she thanked me profusely & passed regretfully away saying she thought it very beautiful, which sentiment was echoed by each of her party. I've made £16 of my £21 for the Slade & hope to reach the goal before the end. I'm tremendously looking forward to getting to work there....

Yrs v sincerely,
PAUL NASH.

While at the Slade School Paul would bring me enchanting,

imaginative drawings, including some by his brother John, not poetical like Paul's own, but satirical comments on suburban life. Here were two artists who I believed would go far. How enthusiastic they were, and how pleasant their gratitude for one's interest and their regard for one's work! A few years go by; the youths become middle aged, and, belike, successful, forgetful that older men still value the sympathy of their juniors. Often while holding an exhibition, I have hoped in vain for some sign from men who have not found my praise unwelcome, nor neglected to ask for it when in need, nor failed to find me of use. It is a privilege, however, to praise. No one likes not liking. Nothing empties a man of vitality more than seeing unvital work, while contact with solid achievement and with early promise is invigorating and heartening. Tonks and Steer would sometimes tell me of promising students at the Slade, one of whom, Stanley Spencer, won my whole hearted admiration. His was a new and genuine note in English art, artless yet intellectual, simple yet rich in content. Then one day Charles Aitken asked me to come to the Tate to see a picture that he had been offered, showing a harvesting machine, boldly tackled, about which stood some naïvely painted figures, which I liked at once. The painter was Gilbert Spencer, a younger brother of Stanley. Henceforward I looked for great things from these brothers, the Spencers and the Nashes, and I was not disappointed.

One day there came a letter from Frances Darwin telling me of her great happiness; she was engaged, to Francis Cornford, a Fellow of Trinity College. He was staying with them at Lyme Regis; would I come and meet him? I must bring my small boy John with me, her father added. Who could be quite good enough for little Frances, I wondered, but whomever she chose must be nearly so, and I hastened down to Dorset. It was early spring; the country was at its loveliest. We would sit in the woods outside Lyme and sing songs— not I, who am voiceless—but the others. No one sang folk songs so movingly, to my mind, as Frances, and there was a song of Brahms that her father sang, I can still remember the jolly way in which he bumped out the words:

> Sitzt a schöns Vögerl auf 'm Dannabaum,
> Tut nix als singa und schrain;
> Was muss denn das für a Vögerl sain?
> Das muss a Nachtigall sain.

At Lyme my John developed a cold, was put to bed, when the doctor declared it was no cold, but measles. Horror! What a thing to have brought on one's hosts! I had put an end to the Darwins' holiday, and I must take all the rooms in the house, and get a nurse, who arrived from . . .'s Hospital, with a rich dressing bag out of which came silver brushes, hand mirrors and a manicure set: I had wished for a less magnificent nurse. Then I heard that Frances Darwin had caught measles too. If her father was annoyed, she was by no means sorry, for Cornford now came to see her every day; she even said she was grateful!

Frances used to send me her poems, for which I cared deeply, and believing that others would care as much, I urged that they must at all cost be printed. 'At all costs' was not a formidable phrase I assured Frank Darwin; there was a bookseller at Hampstead who was ready to print an edition for £30. So the poems duly appeared, to Darwin's delight. The little book was to become a rarity, it contained more than one poem which later appeared in most of the anthologies, the best known among them being *Oh why do you walk through the fields in gloves?* I sent copies of the poems to Hudson and to A. E. Housman, the latter replied in his usual grim manner; his praise usually had a sharp edge. His letter contained another version of the poem mentioned above, which ran as follows:

> O why do you walk through the fields in boots,
>   Missing so much and so much?
> O fat white woman whom nobody shoots,
> Why do you walk through the fields in boots,
> When the grass is soft as the breast of coots
>   And shivering-sweet to the touch?
> O why etc.

Frances wrote, in sending me a copy of the book of poems:

'Here at last is the immortal work. I haven't written in any inscription because I couldn't think of any one which would even indicate all the nice things I wanted to mean.

I think you are the fairy godfather of the book & that is its proudest distinction.

How nice & clean & proper & dignified it looks. I am proud of its appearance, only I long to put in a little notice at the beginning to say "The author means to do MUCH better than this" (much in red type).'

I knew that feeling well; each time I showed a painting I was ashamed of its weaknesses—the parts I would fain have carried out perfectly, but which I knew to be wanting would be especially noticeable. Yet when a picture was attacked, not for its faults but for its qualities, my natural aggressiveness would emerge and my shame be forgotten. Man is a queer mixture of modesty and vanity, but it is praise that brings forth his modesty. Yet at times a certain arrogance may not come amiss. I call to mind an occasion when Hugh Lane came to choose a painting in exchange for one he had acquired for the Dublin Municipal collection. He scarcely looked at the picture I offered, a self portrait (now in the Metropolitan Museum), but turned his back on it and began talking of bargains lately acquired. 'Lane, turn round and look at this picture' I insisted. Lane turned, but he did not love me the more. If a poet read his verses aloud he does not expect his listeners to gossip about other people's poetry the while; a picture upon which one has laboured long is worth half a minute's attention. When visiting galleries, in company with the learned, I have often squirmed inwardly at the flow of comparisons a picture calls up. There are persons who will interrupt the song of a nightingale to tell how they heard, on a time and in another place, a better songster.

CHAPTER·XXII

LETHABY AND THE CRAFTS

I GOT into touch with the Arts and Crafts movement through Eric Gill, who taught lettering on stone at the Central School of Arts and Crafts, of which Lethaby had been Principal. Lethaby had got together a remarkable group of teachers: Edward Johnston, Douglas Cockerell, Halsey Ricardo, George Jack and Henry Wilson. The school was formerly in Regent Street, housed in a less splendid way than later at Holborn. Not bricks and mortar, but men make a university. Lethaby was an admirable Head; a sensitive architect and a great medieval scholar, who had, without seeming to exercise it, a powerful influence on his staff.

These men were all practising craftsmen, and they gave to the school a part of their time only. I have always held that such teaching alone should be given; Lethaby saw that crafts could be well taught only by men who are themselves masters of their craft. At South Kensington, too, where Lethaby was Head of the School of Design, he had Edward Johnston to teach lettering, and George Jack in charge of the wood carving; but the Kensington system, under which the students learned something of everything and then, before they had mastered any one art, went out to teach for the rest of their lives, seemed detrimental alike to them as teachers (allowed no time to keep their practice alive), and to their students.

I was at once impressed by the atmosphere of good will and good workmanship at the Central School of Arts and Crafts; and there came to me a new interest and a new understanding for a side of art I had not yet appreciated.

I learned much from Lethaby, Eric Gill, Edward Johnston, Halsey Ricardo and from Alfred Powell, too, whom I had met at Cambridge, and whose skilful painting on pottery I greatly admired. I began to see that the collecting of antiques was detrimental to living work; that the normal course was to have things made for one's own use by contemporary workmen. Nothing else would keep invention and good workmanship alive; and my instinctive dislike for 'the man of taste' seemed justified, now that I saw how much easier it is to pick out pleasant things from an antique shop, than to have sufficient knowledge and judgment to get things made expressly for one's needs.

I once spent some days with Lethaby in Paris and at Chartres. It was a rich experience to go round Notre-Dame with him, and again to explore Chartres Cathedral. His knowledge was profound, but better than his knowledge was his tender and human feeling for building. He would doubtless have preferred to see Chartres before its interior was marred by later additions, but he would not hear of any of these being removed—a building is a live organism, to which things happen; it is a vital part of history, he would say: I remember, too, when, at the Victoria and Albert Museum Sir Cecil Smith spoke disparagingly of the Victorian chimney-piece in his room, Lethaby drily defended it: it was the natural expression of its time. Each age has its own probity. Lethaby's courage, hidden usually behind a gentle, almost self-deprecatory manner, was unqualified, and would declare itself on occasion in no measured terms. His character had, indeed, qualities of greatness. He was too proud to do anything but the best, and too conscious of the qualities and conditions needed for the best to crystallise itself, to get work as an architect. Hence he resigned practice for scholarship, and though his wisdom grew riper with the years, I felt sometimes that he lost something of the charity which the daily struggle for perfection, and failure to reach it, brings to the painter.

A follower of Morris, Lethaby resisted the pretensions of

painters and sculptors for a higher place than the working craftsman. He disliked Art with a big A, and his concentration on the great epochs of medieval art somewhat blunted his sympathy for modern work, save that of Morris, and of the Pre-Raphaelite and the Arts and Crafts movement.

I admired Lethaby's integrity and learning, but he was inclined, as were others connected with Morris, to say 'No' to life. Perhaps, among themselves, these men said 'Yes', but they made me feel that we painters were doubtful characters, with second wives hidden away somewhere, and an absinthe bottle in the studio cupboard. It seems strange that medieval art, full blooded and Gargantuan in spirit as it is, should have bred so much squeamishness and pedantry. However, my arts and crafts friends were indulgent enough towards me. I was even elected to the Committee of that admirable body, The Society for the Protection of Ancient Buildings, and a member of the Advisory Committee of one of the L.C.C. schools—Bolt Court, of which Emery Walker was Chairman. It happened that at a dinner in connection with this school, George Frampton said he had been meaning to tell me that some time ago, he, Sargent and John Swan had put down my name for the Associateship of the Royal Academy; he hoped I would allow it to remain. I was taken by surprise for I had not been consulted, but at the moment I felt it would be churlish to object to a generous gesture. But I was not comfortable at the prospect of joining the Academy; and in due time I wrote to withdraw my name, at which my parents were much upset; to them the three letters A.R.A. were magical ones. I hated to disappoint them, but I believed my place to be with Steer, Tonks, John, McEvoy, and other colleagues of the New English Art Club. But some of my friends, Mrs Herringham especially, were concerned when I told them what I had done; the Academy was constantly accused of narrowness and prejudice, yet now a generous move had been made towards me. Kind things were said about my influence for good; I was persuaded to ask for my name to be replaced. My parents were overjoyed.

But my discomfort persisted, and at the risk of being thought an absurd wobbler, which indeed I was, I again wrote to Frampton (who had behaved with consideration) telling him of my twice changed decision. I was then much happier; but that I had ever contemplated joining the Academy rankled in sound New English hearts.

I had always been averse to the 'dog in the manger' attitude towards the Academy; its faults were obvious; so far from being a true academy, it put up with some of the worst vices of painting and sculpture. But it had always included honourable men among its members, and the influence of men like Sargent and Clausen was the greater through their prestige as Academicians. This had been the temptation for one who, like myself, had something of a missionary spirit. I had always hoped that Prof. Brown would find some use for my services at the Slade School; but in this I was disappointed. Indeed, although I remained outside the Academy, I have had more generosity from its members than from either the Slade School or the New English circles.

It happened that some months before this I had been painting a lady who, though neither young nor old, yet had both charm and beauty. I had failed to do her justice, and seeing Sargent's painting of the Duchess of Connaught, I admired the way in which he had overcome the difficulties which floored me, and thereupon wrote to tell him so. I had forgotten this, until a friend said I should know that Tonks was saying that I had written a flattering letter to Sargent, with a view to being elected to the Academy. Such a suspicion, and one so unwarranted, upset me, and I wrote to Sargent, who replied:

> *Hôtel Pension Bellevue,*
> *Simplon-Kulm*
> 1e *Aug.* 26*th*

My dear Rothenstein,

I have only just read your letter which was enclosed in a budget from Tite Street, which I have been waiting for a rainy day to open. I regret the delay of my reply, as the report you mention is one that I could have promptly dispelled. You never wrote to me asking for my help for you to enter the Royal Academy, and I never said you did. I signed my name in support of your name as a candidate when Clausen asked me to do so. I supposed from the fact of his taking this step that you were willing to be proposed, though I never had had any intimation from you that you wished to become a member.

The only way in which I can account for a possible origin of this gossip, is that I remember having mentioned a long time ago, that you had written me a very kind and complimentary note about some picture I had exhibited. I was then told that you had resigned from the New English Art Club. Can this have been interpreted into an electioneering (illegible)? It is the only possible starting point that I can think of for this entirely unfounded rumour, which I by the way have never heard, and which I shall make a point of contradicting if I ever do.

I have nothing but regret for the fact that Chelsea to Hampstead are so far apart. Is it true that you are going to India? Please let me know by a line here, that you have got this letter. I am afraid that it may not catch you at Vattetot, as, owing to my bad habit of not always immediately opening my weekly London packet of letters, ten days have elapsed since you wrote from there.

Yours sincerely,

JOHN S. SARGENT

Herein lies the real evil of Academies; they encourage intrigues and suspicion, and such a suspicion I knew was unworthy of Tonks, and would not be lasting I thought. But I was to discover that ideas, if not bodies, have ghosts; and Tonks, haunted by such a ghost, allowed what had seemed a lasting friendship to change to a lasting hostility.

Sargent was touchingly devoted to Mancini, whose painting at this time he admired above all others. In his generous way he urged his own patrons to employ Mancini. In return Mancini took infinite pains with every portrait he painted. I greatly liked the one he did of Charles Hunter in a shooting cap, his arms crossed over a chair—the very spit of an Englishman; and a lovely portrait of a child, a grandchild of Mrs Hunter. There was a richness and radiance about Mancini's portraits which set them apart from most commissioned work. He was a purely visual painter, whose method of work—how he looked at his sitter through a net, while another net was fixed to his canvas—I have already described. Dürer, as I have said before, had a similar method, that of drawing his sitter by means of a squared glass fixed on to a frame. We modern painters have wrongly disdained such aids, thinking that mastery rules out a scientific method. There is evidence that Holbein, like Dürer, used glass for his portrait drawings. Probably the Dutch painters did likewise when painting figures and interiors, or when assembling the figures for their great portrait groups.

Mancini's art lost nothing through his reliance on accurate vision. His passion for work was untiring; he was a typical Continental artist, caring only for his art, and nothing for social life; hence his engaging candour. At a party Madame Marchesi gave, some game was served which she declared was too fresh. 'It doesn't matter,' said Mancini, vigorously plying his knife and fork, 'I have got strong wrists'.

CHAPTER XXIII

A STONE-CARVER'S DILEMMA

GILL was, from the beginning, more fortunate than Epstein. Up to 1906 he had carved only inscriptions; but one day he arrived at our house with two photographs, one of a figure of a mother and child, another of a spandrel-shaped carving of a young girl. He had cut these, he said, out of two odd pieces of stone which he had not been able to use for inscriptions—a sudden impulse; he had never thought of carving figures before.

I thought these first essays so remarkable that I acquired the *Mother and Child*, while Kessler, always interested in what was new and unusual, bought the other piece. I sent Gill down to Epstein, thinking he might work with him for a time, and the two became friends. And truth to tell, it was Gill who turned Epstein's attention to stone-carving again, as is shown by Epstein's Memorial to Oscar Wilde at Père-Lachaise; Gill was no modeller, therefore was not likely to be affected by Epstein's art.

Kessler wanted Gill to apprentice himself to Maillol. Gill, alive to the importance of Maillol's work, was tempted, but hesitated to place himself under an artist. He himself was a carver, a craftsman—not an artist, he said; what mattered was good workmanship.

I spoke earlier of Rodin's high opinion of Maillol as a sculptor. Rodin, who talked so much of the Greeks, was in fact little directly influenced by them. It was against the swellings and hollows which gave colour to Rodin's modelling that Maillol reacted. Maillol who heralded a new outlook and led the way towards a greater radiance and simplification of form, also helped the disease which was affecting French sculpture and painting. For in aiming too directly at the simplification of the figure, he neglected the attachments of the limbs. Later sculptors, like Dobson, exaggerate this boneless aspect; their figures seem as though squeezed from a tube into a mould; all articulation has gone. Maillol, moreover, was tempted by the charm of the sixth-century Greek sculptors, as was Albert Moore by the school of Phidias, to give a pseudo-Greek character to his charming French models. 'Plus ça change, plus c'est la même chose.'

No one has yet saved us from the Greeks and Romans; even Barye, the greatest of French sculptors, who, in his animals asserted his full independence, gave a Greek veneer to his human figures. But Maillol's study of the Greeks, combined with his own delicate temper, informed his figures with a virgin grace and a reticence which gives them a place apart. To work with such a man, Kessler believed, would be the making of Gill.

He was pressing, and Gill, half persuaded, went over to Marly to see Maillol, and, as Kessler hoped, to become his pupil. Suddenly Gill took fright and the first train back to London. He had decided not to work with any 'artist'. But Gill scarcely knew what to do, as Kessler had taken the lease of a house for him and his wife. He wanted my opinion:

> 16, *Old Buildings*
> *Lincoln's Inn,*
> *London, W.C.*
> 20 *Jan* 1910.

Dear Rothenstein

I wired to Kessler first thing this morning as follows: 'Re Marly lease please wait am writing.' This was because in the enthusiasm of his soul he had been so good as to say that as he was on the spot he would fix up the house for us and advance the 1st quarter's rent. He feared that the landlord not being over willing to let to a foreign artist I might have difficulty in working the thing by myself. He also wanted us to take the house for three years because otherwise we might not get it at all. We wanted to take it for one year only so as to give ourselves a chance of clearing out if we wanted to after one year. Well...at five o'clock this afternoon I got the following telegram from Kessler: 'Have signed and paid lease to-day, Kessler!' Now what on earth am I to do? It's really pretty devilish difficult. I don't want to bother you with my affairs but I'd be awfully grateful if you'd tell me if you think there's any way out of it. I thought Kessler might have paid the first rent—hence my wire. But it never occurred to me that he would go and sign the lease for us. I spent the best part of the morning composing a letter to him which is now useless. I'm at my wits' end.

I send you a copy of what I had proposed to say to Kessler. Meanwhile I'll wait. Only just time to catch post now. The worst of these energetic enthusiasts like Kessler is that they rush you so. What on earth will Kessler say or do? For really I don't think I can face it. I mean I don't think I can face the three years in France.

Yours A. E. R. GILL.

I haven't yet written to Kessler & won't till I hear from you. Do forgive me for bothering you so.

Two days later another letter came:

16, Old Buildings,
Lincoln's Inn,
London, W.C.
22 Jan 1910.

Dear Rothenstein

I got your letter last night. It was frightfully good of you to write so promptly and your letter was most helpful and to the point—to say nothing of its kindness. Well, yesterday morning I got a letter from Kessler, written before the receipt of my telegram to him, and there is one point of it that just clinches the matter. I think you will agree with me that it clinches the matter. I quote the paragraph in full. I had sent him two unfixed prints of the little statuette (as he had asked me to do as soon as I had got the thing into shape) & this is what he says: 'The statuette looks very interesting. I showed the photos to Maillol who liked them very well. He says they show great talent; but he rather deplores you do not work *in clay first*, as it is very difficult, or rather, impossible to correct mistakes in stone. He says you must learn to work in clay, if you want to develop your art. I transmit what he said as I think it may interest you.' (The underlinings are Kessler's.) It is rather a coincidence, isn't it, that Kessler should refer to the very point, or one of the very points, on which I had laid stress in my letter to him? I shall now send my letter off to him (I am glad you think it clear and right) with another to explain my delay.

Yours ever

A. E. R. GILL

This, and the letter following, show how early Gill foresaw the influence material was to have upon carving. The Greeks used the same model, probably a clay one, for marble as for bronze, but this practice, for so long accepted, was now to be challenged. Gill's medium is stone, and no one living better understands the possibilities and limitations of direct carving.

Copy   *Soper's, Ditchling, Sussex.*

Dear Count Kessler

I'm rather at a loss to know how to begin. I'm very much afraid after all you have done in the matter that I shall seem both rude and ungrateful. Under all my enthusiasm for the projected sojourn in Marly—(in such a beautiful place— starting afresh, as it were, free from the Arts & Crafts movement—and in the proximity of so splendid a mind as Maillol's—and in his friendship)—there were always misgivings—quite apart from the financial difficulty which you had in your generosity done so much to smoothe over and quite apart from the difficulty of freeing myself from the encumbrance of our house in Ditchling and quite apart from the dangers incidental to a so long absence from all the people I know in England and the loss of connection resulting therefrom—there were misgivings. These misgivings have now got the better of me. I can no longer face the prospect. The attractions which I have mentioned have ceased to weigh with me. Can you ever forgive me? I will try and explain what I mean if you will bear with me.

What was I going to Maillol for? Of course it was in order that I might benefit as a sculptor. And in return for the benefit received it was hoped that I should prove of some assistance to Maillol. Well then, in what way was I to benefit? In the first place technically and in the second artistically. But it has gradually been borne in upon me that, Maillol being more of a modeller than actually a stone-carver, technically I should learn nothing. Was it not even understood that I should learn 'pointing' before I went? I have come to the conclusion that I do not want to learn pointing—that I want to be a stone-carver—that I do not particularly want to know how to reproduce accurately and expeditiously in stone a clay model. I want to have only so much to do with modelling as is necessary for that kind of client who wants to know what he's going to get before he gets it. And even so I should refuse to guarantee a likeness between the model and the stone. The inspiration comes with the carving and is an entirely different inspiration from that which comes with the clay. You see I feel that splendid as Maillol is it is not the kind of splendid I can ever be or wish to be. Then you see, that, as a corollary of the foregoing that artistically it would be, to say the least, unsafe for me to work with or for Maillol. The similarity in our ideas, if I may so presume to speak, would be so seductive (Oh! this is an awfully difficult point!) that I should cease to oppose. And one *must* be in opposition. Maillol has a vision which I feel to be very largely *my* vision. Well then, if I am to achieve the expression of that vision I must achieve it for myself, through my own struggles, in my own battle with life. I do hope I am making myself clear to you. Well then, if these things are so, it is obvious that what I need to learn is about tools and the uses of tools—the chisel & hammer and what they are capable of doing. I cannot learn that from Maillol. Infinitely better would it be for me to go and apprentice myself to the most skilful & the most ordinary of monumental masons and learn to hack idiotic angels out of white marble. Then indeed I should be in opposition—and should find out what *I* meant and what *I* should do & say. Do you know I almost feel as if in that brief afternoon at Marly I got as much out of Maillol as I ever should get. I know this sounds horridly conceited. But what I mean is that, in a kind of way, I was allowed to see the vision—and that I cannot forget it. That if, from time to time, I were privileged to see Maillol and look at his work I should be more helped than by a continuous stay with him. I have tried to explain one or two points—and there are other aspects—such as my age for instance—which are also weighing with me but which I cannot go into now.

(After this I had written saying how much I hoped he had not yet consummated the lease and so forth. And then I got his telegram!)

I shall send the above letter in any case unless you think it's not the way out. You know Kessler better than I do and also you know better than I do the rights and wrongs of the matter. Anyway it is evident that Kessler has signed a three years' lease and paid the first rent! Can I possibly refuse it now? If you think I can—knowing him as you do—I will.

Yours A. E. R. G.

Gill did finally refuse the lease and remained in England. For a time a warm friendship grew up between him and Epstein. They infected one another with great plans, about which I heard from Gill:

Ditchling
Sussex
25 Sept. 1910.

Dear Rothenstein

I hope to be able to see you and talk about various things before you go away.

The fact of the matter is that Epstein & I have got a giant scheme of doing some colossal figures together (as a contribution to the world), a sort of twentieth-century Stonehenge, and we have been looking out for a piece of land for the purpose. We have now found such a place—about 4 miles south-east of Lewes—and are endeavouring to get it on a lease. It is a plot of about 6 acres, hidden away in a valley in the hills, with a decent sized house and farm buildings attached. Altogether so ideal a place for our purpose that I do not know what we shall do if we don't get it. We have applied to the owner (or at least *I* have) and can get it on a 14 years' lease. It is empty at present. We should have to do all repairs etc. But oh! if only we could buy the place outright! Then we should be free to do all we wanted without the fear of hurting anybody's feelings or the risk of being turned out at the end of the 14 years and our figures smashed up by some damned fools who didn't choose to like them. Of course 14 years is a long time and many things may happen before they're up, but I do feel that this is the grandest opportunity and it is increasingly evident that it is no use relying on architects & patrons and dealers. I wish you could come down and see the place. Is that quite impossible? Surely some millionaire could be persuaded to buy the place for us (we could pay him back by instalments).

Yours ever A. E. R. GILL.

Fortunately they did not take a 14 years' lease—they did not take a lease at all. Gill was too doctrinaire for Epstein, while for Gill modelling, as a preparation for sculpture, was a cardinal sin. So they parted, yet each had done something for the other. Epstein had brought something more human and more sensual to Gill's form, while from Gill Epstein got active encouragement for his stone-carving.

CHAPTER XXIV

SOME ENGLISH AND IRISH PLAYS

I WAS critical of the way in which Barker produced
Shaw's plays at the Court Theatre. In the stage scenes,
which represented commonplace rooms, there was none of
the fun of Shaw's dialogue; they were just unintelligently
dull. I told Barker what I felt: that irony should be shown
in scenes as it was in dialogue; that there were plenty of
young artists who could design scenes and dresses with
point and meaning, even for realistic plays. When Barker got
Frohman's support for a Repertory Theatre, he consulted
me about the staging—could I now find some young artists?
He was prepared to give them a trial. Whereupon I recommended Macdonald Gill who planned the scenes and staging
for Galsworthy's *Justice*, with which play the Repertory
Theatre opened. So pleased was Barker with the result that
he then asked me to design the scene and dresses for a
comedy by George Meredith, *The Sentimentalists*: Barrie,
he explained, had the MS. and would send me a typed copy.
I thought the play delightful. I made some rough drawings
for a formal garden, and for the dresses. Barker arranged
that Norman Wilkinson should work out a finished plan for
the scene, and he put me in touch with Nathan's, who
made the dresses from my designs. In Norman Wilkinson
I found a perfect collaborator; and Lillah MacCarthy who
played the chief part, was most helpful and understanding.
She looked radiant in her 1830 dress.

There was an enthusiastic first night. 'I think I saw your
hand at the Meredith play,' Masefield wrote, 'O, that enchanting, understanding mind. Was there ever such a
comedy on earth?' But the play was too slight, the dialogue

too Meredithian to be popular, it ran only for a few nights, when it was withdrawn. Barker however was again pleased with the success of the experiment. I heard from him after the performance:

> *Duke of York's Theatre,*
> *The Repertory Theatre,*
> *March 5. 1910*

My dear Rothenstein,

You really write me the most charming of letters and it makes me feel I haven't expressed to you all the thanks I feel. It would have been exceedingly difficult to make the Meredith go without a beautiful setting and dressing. As it is, most of the people who matter and care are delighted with it, and we owe much to you.

I should like to have a talk with you, as soon after the 9th as you will, for other plays will be coming along, and what had we better do, I wonder?

> Yours,
>
> H. G. BARKER

Barker was now convinced that what had been done for *Justice* and *The Sentimentalists* could be done for other plays. He engaged Norman Wilkinson and Keith Henderson to design the settings for the next production—*Madras House*.

Madras House, one of Barker's best plays, didn't meet with the reception it deserved, for I find Barker writing on April 13:

'... Candidly I am just a little bit angry at the attack on *Madras House*. It was so very important, not so much to me as to the repertory idea generally, that just at the start our good intentions should be allowed for. I never know quite how much one has the right to ask critics to allow for good intentions. Sometimes, I suppose, they should make great allowance and sometimes none at all. However that's all beside the point now. They have killed the blessed play for the moment and I remain angry at the material damage done, though honestly their opinion doesn't matter a dump to me—yours and that of some of the others does, your good opinion means much, very much to me.'

Barker, the sanest and most salutary personality connected with the contemporary theatre, had at least shown his metal, both as playwright and producer, and henceforth he never failed to use artists as fellow workers. Later, both Norman Wilkinson and my brother Albert did notable work for his Shakespearean productions.

During 1910 the Irish Players from the Abbey Theatre returned to London with a large repertory of Irish plays. Yeats had been the inspirer of the Irish Theatre; it was due to his energy and imagination that it came into being. It was Yeats again who foresaw Synge's genius, and who pressed him to write of Irish life and to use the rich talk of the Irish people. I had seen Yeats's *Cathleen Ni Houlihan* some years before beautifully acted by Irish players. Now I saw Synge's *Playboy of the Western World*. No play ever excited me more. Here was irony of a Gargantuan kind; a satire on man, on woman, on Ireland, if one chooses to take it as such, worthy of Swift, written with superb beauty of language, perfectly interpreted by the Abbey Company. These Irish men and women, recruited and trained by amateurs, brought into the theatre an artlessness which proved to be the highest form of art. I wanted to embrace Sara Allgood and Maire O'Neill, and to wring the hands of Kerrigan, Sinclair and O'Donovan. Instead I went round to congratulate Lady Gregory and Yeats in their box. *The Playboy* and *The Well of the Saints* are still, for me, the greatest comedies of our time.

Meanwhile Craig was still abroad. Some of us felt that the time had come to entice him back to England; we must show some mark of our sense of what the modern stage owed him. We decided to offer him a public dinner; Yeats was to have been in the chair; but at the last moment he shied at having to propose the King's health, and I had to take his place. It was a great gathering. I had Ellen Terry as my neighbour, and Mrs Patrick Campbell sat by Craig. It was touching to see Ellen Terry's pride in her son; tears were in her eyes during some of the speeches.

Craig, delighted with this public acknowledgment of his work for the theatre, wished to found a school for the theatre in London. A Committee was formed with this end in view; but after a time Craig returned to Italy, and when Lord Howard de Walden offered to finance an experimental theatre, it was in Florence and not in London that Craig undertook to run it. Here he gathered a band of young workers round him, and for a time all went well; but experimental theatres are expensive things, and finally insufficient support was forthcoming to allow Craig to carry on as he wished.

CHAPTER XXV

AN OFFER REFUSED

THE Duchess of Sutherland, knowing the views I held on the subject of local adventure, asked me down to Lilleshall. The Duke had offered to hand over Trentham, a great house nearby, with its grounds, to the Five Towns, but the County Council hesitated, fearing the upkeep would be too costly. But what a chance for a great trade-museum of pottery, a permanent exhibition of local products, historical and modern, which should make Trentham a focussing point for the china and pottery industry, whither buyers of home products, and foreign buyers, would come! The project had Frank Wedgwood's support. He presided at a meeting, at which I spoke; but I spoke in vain. The Sutherlands' offer was rejected, a shortsighted policy, it seemed to me, and Trentham was pulled down. When later I visited the Potteries, I could never forget what a chance was missed.

After my visit to Lilleshall, I heard from the Duchess:

June 25. 1910.

My dear Mr Rothenstein,

'Tis I that should thank you—for true unabashed words in public, & much kind merry give & take in moonlit hours—I am so glad one meets suddenly like that face to face—it lifts a veil of mal-knowledge that can never shroud again and you & I & a few of us have to *grope* rather, as others still greater have groped before in an odd world of soul blindness—but never mind, we can laugh & we have a secret liaison with the universe! Joy! Joy!

Ever truly
MILLICENT SUTHERLAND.
Hooking Hill, Woking.

A mate for Baudelaire

A drawing I made of Anatole France was bought by the Duchess of Sutherland. 'I hear Anatole France thinks you have failed to flatter him. Do you think he would suffer if he knew he was to be hung cheek by jowl with that old photo of Baudelaire?' she wrote. The Duchess's interest in the arts and in life too was unflagging. I thought one so radiant as she would be cherished and spoilt by the Fates. I saw her moving, as it were, swiftly, like a figure in the *Primavera*, on slim white feet along flowery meadows; but there was always a note of tragedy in her letters. She wrote to me from Lilleshall:

Dear Mr Rothenstein,

There are very few 'Futurists' in *this* Country—& the Pottery folk—even immortalized as they are—by A. Bennett's caustic pen—are not amongst them! I'm just now living in a state of bewilderment—between the awakening of democracy—in the shape of the Federated Borough of Stoke on Trent! & the suicidal despair of ruined aristocracy—in the shape of . . . !

An hour under your spreading tree & a talk on the East & its age-old peace—would be very relieving—For I too flew to Rio de Janeiro this winter—& that is *Beauty*: just so spelt—Unfortunately I cannot come to you yet because I am going to Scotland—away into the West about our Gaelic Societies —a feeble effort to renew the Spirit of the Land & to stem emigration.

In June I will come—& that most happily—Have much to show me & much to tell me—it will be a pleasure to see you again.

I am adventuring on 4 Fridays—bring with you any artists who are your friends—anyone amusing. It's delicious here—with all the new greens & white blossom—& the birds in unending song—but I've got to return to London in a mint. to present my girl at Court to-morrow night.

Such are the poignant contrasts of existence. They are very

tiring—I would rather spend all day painting sunshine on a wall!

Yours very sincerely,
MILLICENT SUTHERLAND.

And again:

'I was delighted to get your letter & thank you for all the kind things you said. Life is very difficult to face at transition periods—when one is young sorrow is rather like a nightmare—frightening—but interesting to remember. Now every tragedy that happens brands one with red hot letters that ever burn in hidden fire—& every time one figuratively sees the menacing hand of fate one winces & trembles at the apprehension of fresh pain.

'Presently one will get quite old & cold & calm—I do not think it's death itself that matters—but the things that bring death—the circumstances that surround it—but then so little matters to me after all; a handful—not that—of people we love—the birds, the Sunshine—& few wayside adventures make up the sum total of the thrills of life.'

I could not imagine the Duchess as either old or cold. She spoke of giving up Stafford House, in which, to us who were her guests there, she was ever the familiar goddess. But I was to see this, one of the last of the great London houses ('I have come from my house to your palace', Queen Victoria is reputed to have said to a former Duchess of Sutherland) turned into a museum, and was later to hear of the Duchess in Belgium, in the austere dress of a Sister, devoting herself to the care of the maimed and blinded, as though she had never known anything but suffering, and a passionate desire to alleviate and to comfort. She should have been painted thus; her portrait by Sargent, which hung at Stafford House, did her scant justice. But there were other portraits there, of men especially, which were dignified and, in their way, impressive.

I remember talking with Harold Nicolson about the impressiveness of the Victorians. He was inclined to think I was romancing. One day he came into the studio, when a pastel of Leslie Stephen, which I had made some years earlier, caught his eye; 'Who is that?' he asked, and when I told him he asked if Stephen had really so grand a head; had I not exaggerated? 'Well, if Victorians really looked like that' Nicolson added—'I can understand your attitude.' For I had told him how we, as youngsters, revered Browning, Tennyson, Swinburne, Matthew Arnold, Whistler, Watts, Burne-Jones, Holman Hunt and others who were still alive. 'Are there no elders about whom you to-day feel as we did?' I asked him. 'No,' said Nicolson, he didn't think so; and then he added—'Well, perhaps Max Beerbohm.'

It seems as though the men of to-day admit to having grand-fathers but not to having fathers. I imagine the great split between the older and younger painters in England came about through the Post-Impressionist Exhibition of 1910.

CHAPTER XXVI

A POST-IMPRESSIONIST EXHIBITION

I WOULD sometimes spend a week-end at Oxford, with the Fishers, the Raleighs or the Bridges, and later, with the Chaloner Dowdalls. Oxford friends, when Wooldridge resigned the Slade Chair, wanted me to be a candidate. I heard from Herbert Fisher:

> 37, *Norham Road*,
> *Oxford*,
> *March* 2. 1910.

Thy discerning eye, my dear Infant, will not have failed to appreciate a certain inane vacancy in the chair of Fine Arts in this great Academy of Knowledge. Hasten therefore to fill it with thine own appropriate and illustratious Person, lest the unworthy, coming like a thief in the night, forestall thine eminence and abuse our pride. Notify to me thine august pleasure and purpose and in the measure of his poor and humble powers your devoted slave will forward thy most honourable design.

> H. F.

Robert Bridges, who was always interested in the theory of the arts, and had persuaded Wooldridge to come as Slade Professor, wanted Fry at Oxford. In Bridges's study hung a portrait of his mother painted by Wooldridge, a scholarly work which reminded me of Alfred Stevens's portraits. I was devoted to Bridges; there was a grandeur about him—he looked like a great man—and sometimes a bearishness, which hid a warmth of friendship. So with his mind; he was avid of information, yet contemptuous of the gossip of art and literature, keen to hear of all that was new and vital in art, yet sharply critical of mental slackness and unworkmanlike ways. He had a rich and masculine intellect, ardent, searching and learned, yet again with something finally simple and childlike which was one of his endearing qualities. Essentially modest as are all artists, he was not without vanity. I remember writing to tell him that I was coming to Oxford and would bring my drawing things to Boars Hill; for I wished to draw him again. 'Come along by all means,' he wrote, 'but don't bother about the drawing. I am not worth it.' And when, on my arrival, he came to greet me at his door, the first thing he said was 'What about your paper and pencils?' I had taken him at his word and left them behind!

I was pressed by others, besides Fisher, to apply for the chair, by Lethaby especially; but I heard that Fry was a candidate, and knowing that, at this time, he needed a platform, I did not send in my name. Then I heard from Lethaby:

May 2, 1910.

Dear Rothenstein,

I hope you are applying for the Slade. My interest in the matter is this—a week or two ago I heard from an Oxford man that they had in view the possibility of appointing an architect, & from that point of view he suggested I should apply. I have consented, & if they do take the line of appointing an architect it would interest me very much to do it, especially as my work at the Central School has virtually terminated (I resigned some time ago, and they are going to make arrangements after the new Council is elected). I should doubt whether they do appoint an architect at Oxford, & if they do not I should like them to appoint you, & I should like to be in a position to tell them so. If the thing comes to me as an architect, well & good, but I don't want to be a place-seeker.

Very sincerely yours,

W. R. LETHABY.

But neither Lethaby nor Fry was chosen. As often happens, the 'safe' candidate was elected. Much as I respected Selwyn Image, I did not feel that what he had to offer equalled that which either Fry or Lethaby could have given. But Fry was soon to find an outlet for his restless and varied energies elsewhere.

When Fry had the offer of a Gallery, he wanted the older independent artists, who were outside the Royal Academy, to show their work, together with some of the more adventurous younger men. He approached Steer and Tonks, but they were disinclined to move. In spite of the somewhat strained relations consequent on the Sargent episode, I still felt the New English Art Club to be the body with which I had most sympathy. Further, remembering Carr's and Hallé's ways at the New Gallery, I did not feel inclined to work under Fry's dictatorship. As Fry had from the first been my warmest supporter he expected that I would now support him; but since I held aloof, the good Roger, who can always convince himself as magically as he convinces others, discovered that my work was no longer of any importance. Fry's first idea was to show a group of Russian paintings; finally he got together an exhibition of what was then, or just afterwards, called French Post-Impressionist painting, which provided a greater sensation than any collection of Russian paintings would have done. Fry thenceforth became the central figure round whom the more advanced young English painters grouped themselves. Some of them, however, broke away, and Wyndham Lewis issued a manifesto explaining why they dissociated themselves from Fry. Through his prestige as a critic, but chiefly through his enthusiasm for the new movement, Fry proved of great service to many of the younger painters. He became for the younger generation what D. S. MacColl had been for Steer and Conder and other members of the New English Art Club. Fry's great intellectual powers, his gift for clear exposition, his wit, and his delight in presenting the many facets of any attitude he took up—and he was thoroughly convinced of the rightness of each succeeding attitude—made him a brilliant advocate. Gifted with untiring energy, a copious writer and reviewer, an eloquent lecturer, he is an expert on every phase of art; indeed, Fry is the only English critic with a European reputation. In addition he is an industrious painter, who has made a place for himself in the movement for which he is the ardent propagandist. Fry is symbolic of his time, a time when opinions seem of supreme importance. A thirst to know what periods are the best periods, which individual works of art are the best works of art, and which should be treated with contempt, is a curious characteristic of our age. Men and women will hang on the lips of the connoisseur, the man who knows—the man who knows about art, about God, about the universe, about finance, about politics. Education has come to mean having the right opinions of things; *doing* rightly is a secondary consideration. Still if the people who do things gain the support of the people who know about things, the doers become quite important people. For my part I must confess to a sense of discomfort in the presence of most people who 'know about art'.

I was away in India when the Post-Impressionist show at the Grafton Gallery was held. Gill wrote to me:

'You are missing an awful excitement just now being provided for us in London; to wit, the exhibition of "post-impressionists" now on at the Grafton Gallery. All the critics are tearing one another's eyes out over it and the sheep and the goats are inextricably mixed up. John says "it's a bloody show" & Lady Ottoline says "oh, charming". As a matter of fact, those who like it show their pluck, and those who don't show either great intelligence or else great stupidity. The show quite obviously represents a reaction and transition and so if, like Fry, you are a factor in that reaction and transition then you like the show. If, like MacColl & Robert Ross, you are too inseparably connected with the things reacted against and the generation from which it is a transition, then you don't like it. If, on the other hand, you are like me and John, McEvoy & Epstein, then, feeling yourself beyond the reaction & beyond the transition, you have a right to feel superior to Mr Henri Matisse (who is typical of the show—though Gauguin makes the biggest splash and Van Gogh the maddest) & can say you don't like it. But have you seen Mr Matisse's sculpture?...'

Yes, I had seen Matisse's sculpture in his studio in Paris. I could not pretend to like it, notwithstanding that Matisse gave an elaborate explanation of his intentions. It was massiveness and significance of form he aimed at. 'But is form merely massive?' I asked; 'may it not be alert as an animal resting is alert, ready to spring?' I little thought when I saw this first example of the newest sculpture what was to follow. Indeed, it was puzzling, knowing the charm of Maillol's virginal figures, to meet with this sudden move away from the smooth radiance of form, so akin to that which Renoir had shown in his paintings of young girls, which had replaced Rodin's more restless modelling.

Why this dour heaviness, this solemnity which one was now to meet with? What total absence of movement, what megalomania; these cubistic sculptors seemed to be suffering from what might be called elephantiresomeness. There is a story of a saint, a lady whom a Roman general desired to share his bed. The lady thereupon sat on the ground, when first one and then several slaves were called upon to move her; finally a whole regiment was ordered up, but still the lady sat, immovable. I am reminded of this saint before the massive blocks that now are alone deemed suited to architecture; as though carving should not play, like a flame, about a building. Ornament is the flower of the human spirit; yet some frost has now nipped its bloom. Observe the flowering of the chestnut—as though ten thousand candles in praise of life were lighted on the tree. I believe the human spirit will flower again; when this tedious pedantry of inert mass will pass its dull and heavy record, and time and weather will refine with their merciful patina. Time is the master artist, who, with a touch or two, gives grace and style even to poor witless apprentice work.

I had also seen Matisse's paintings in Paris—chiefly studio-nudes. The nude was a Salon tradition; each annual Salon provided paintings of *Parisiennes* lying on divans in provocative poses, and each year reproductions of these brought a wide sale for the Salon catalogues. Matisse's early nudes were the honest studies of a serious student with a sense of good painting, who improvised well from the model, yet a student with no clear aim, with no imagination, and with little sense of composition. Pritchard, a friend from Lewes House, had taken me to Matisse's studio, and the Berensons introduced me to Leonard Stein and Gertrude his sister, whose flat was full of Matisse's paintings. Matisse had given up his rather dry studies and was now painting violent forms with violent colours. He was still an improviser from the model; an improviser of single figures, for his gift was too slender to master the more complex difficulties with which the older painters were able to cope.

Here were powerful studies, but how they smelled of paint! and the red hair he painted was too crude a red, the black eyes too large and black, and the drawing was over-deliberate. But Matisse was very intelligent, a man to be reckoned with. He knew his museums, had looked about him with a discerning eye, and was aware of the charm, not only of improvisation, but of direct statement of pattern. So he aimed at giving on canvas something of the quality of design which Persian potters and tile painters gave to their deft, fecund brush-work. A large clumsy design of women dancing, a prominent work at the Post-Impressionist Exhibition, which might have been suitable enough for tiles, seemed to me quite unfitted for oil-colours and canvas, materials adapted for representative painting. But Matisse happened to hit the taste of the time, when connoisseurs, scholars and dilettanti brought up on museums, were occupied with the comparison of styles and of schools, with attribution and denial of works to particular masters;

and naturally, such men are avid of theories which appeal to the mind. For the minds of experts are more sensitive and better trained than their eyes.

Henceforth criticism was to be occupied with a literary or philosophical interpretation of the arts, with elaborate theories about form, which soon became popular among those who wished to be in the fashion. The imaginative side of the painter's nature was now condemned as 'literary'; and literary faculties were concentrated on painting and drawing which could not be understood without verbal explanation. The height of absurdity was achieved when, at one and the same time, representative art was to give way before significant form, and highly complex theories concerning the third dimension, and of colour values, were evolved, which were now applied—to Giotto and the primitives! who, according to the theorists, could have been as photographically accurate as modern painters had they wished; it was their conscious aesthetic choice which dictated their naivety, not their place in time! Could anything be less 'unpsychological'—and at this time, when men pride themselves on their analytical insight?

But to-day the priest who knows all about God has been replaced by the expert, who knows all about art; and the orthodox throng to hear the latest word on creation from men who do not create. Even Matisse must have tired of the doctrine, for he has dropped 'significant form' and distortion, to return to direct drawing and painting. A charming colourist is Matisse, and a lively draughtsman. His aim is now a modest one; he remains true to simple studies, and has little ambition for any but a limited objective. He shoots his bolt; it may hit the target near the centre; but the target is very close to his bow. Yet for a man to impress his vision, as Matisse has done, on his own generation, is no mean thing. Always there are at the same time similar germs impregnating art, literature, science and philosophy. Indeed the fact that there is so general a response to Matisse's art is itself significant, though that response may be the result of confusion, or despair, or hesitation after a period of conviction, of sustained faith and hope. Perhaps, when our philosophers return to a belief in the relative truth of appearance, painters too will again concentrate on this shining symbol of reality. Meanwhile there is an intuition among artists, in sympathy with that of our psychologists, that dynamic shapes, swift angles and strong colours have a marked effect on our mood. The artists of the baroque period were well aware of this influence, and the early painters used horizontal and perpendicular forms to give dignity and repose to their panels and mural paintings. This sense of the emotional power of pure shapes and colours was lost by the academic artists of the nineteenth century, and it was against their irresponsible picture-making that the Pre-Raphaelites and Impressionists protested. To-day the younger men in their turn react against what they regard as the tyranny of appearance. It is not for our academics who try to be historians or retailers of anecdote to point the finger of scorn at our 'moderns' who put blinkers on their eyes to follow philosophers and mathematicians. Yet what irony in the fact that the very painters and sculptors we are asked to cherish (because, since disregarding romance and illustration, they alone give us pure art) turn their eyes away from appearance, to look, as it were, inwards, producing art so incomprehensible, that it must be expounded in books and articles by men of letters! The same fate has befallen Cézanne, whose good, solid, and powerful painting is enveloped in a fog of sentimental mysticism.

But a much stronger claim is made for Cézanne by his admirers; that he has revolutionised the painter's approach to form, as no one since El Greco has done, that he looked at nature more profoundly than a mere surface painter like Velasquez did, and, taking visible form as his raw material merely, passed the natural images made on his eye through the shuttles of his mind, whence it was transformed into a new material, an organised pattern, significant, illuminating, born of the marriage of sight and intellect.

He brought to painters a new sense of form, less obviously

representative, less like normal appearance, than was shown in the work of more skilful artists such as Manet and Degas. A solitary and impassioned worker, he was also a thinker, who saw that the value of a great work of art lies in its uniqueness, in the fact that what the painter did, that he experienced, that each touch of his brush was born of will and sensitiveness, and so through a series of single acts it became fused into a whole. In this spirit, as though no problem had yet been solved, he worked throughout his life. This exposition of Cézanne's aims was given me by a very intelligent young painter, who insisted on the doctrine of uniqueness, which was also, he declared, Marcel Proust's. Perhaps the best of those stirred by his influence will also feel their own uniqueness, and thus his example will lead to paintings, not like Cézanne's, but far otherwise.

My young artist stressed the rediscovery of volume; yet, to my mind, Cézanne never saw clearly, as did Millet and Daumier, that the sense of mass comes from our perception that parts of form are turned towards, and others away from the source of light. They learned this lesson, perhaps, from the old fashioned cube, though more likely from their firm grasp of this simple principle. Artists who have important truths to impart need a clear system of aesthetic. Daumier and Millet expressed the sense of volume more clearly and more completely perhaps than any artists before or since their time; yet because their aesthetic sensibility was used to present a more epic picture of the life of man than their followers conceived, the importance of their formal qualities goes unrecognised. A generation that sanctifies the austere devotion of a Cézanne and acclaims a Picasso is not easy to comprehend. But men travel by different roads, some toil up mountain paths, others speed along smooth broad ways through the valley. While one man looks out upon the landscape from a height, and sees a smooth sea, on whose bosom quiet islands rest, while around are hills, olive and vine clad and all seems eternal peace, the ears of another are split with the noise and confusion of a village which, to the first, appears but as a fleck of white on the crest of a hill or the sweep of a valley.

The impulse to replace vision by intellectual reason began in France, but the Frenchman has an innate classicism which gives distinction to his form and design, whatever his principles may be. It was not until some years later that the germ of this doctrine was carried to England. The urge to create pure form is, maybe, the first among many impulses; but an artist must relate his abstract conceptions to the evidence of his senses, for fallible though our senses may be, they are yet as it were a fixed point to which all experience may be related. Art and literature which do not combine form with human drama cannot satisfy mankind. The minds of artists are not so limited that they cannot both create form and associate it with those emotions which, attending on man's pilgrimage through life, bring the arts within the orbit of common experience. There are signs indeed that this is again being realised by some of our younger artists. Interest in form for its own sake has never distinguished English painters.

To-day, standing aloof from the 'abstract' painters, there are a number of young artists who give fresh and vigorous attention to the life about them. In English painting there is something akin to the provincial flavour of Mark Rutherford's and Thomas Hardy's writing, an imaginative quality set down with reticence, yet by no means wanting in passion.

It is not always the men who are most discussed during their lifetime who to succeeding generations stand as the interpreters of their generation. There is still surprising creative vitality in Europe; yet one asks one's self, seeing how naturally rich and fertile is the artistic field, whether the publicity given to artists in vogue does not corrupt many young, ingenuous natures, who, but for influences forced on their notice, would do more personal, more scrupulous work. Yet advertisement itself offers scope for much ingenuity, and the effect of contemporary painting on design, on the quality and pattern of our fabrics, pottery, book illustrations, posters, book-jackets, fashion plates, indeed, on everything connected with the making of books and magazines, has been highly stimulating. Elegance and finish, disdained by painters, are happily expressed in the minor arts; much that is inappropriate to canvas and paint is perfectly suited to the crafts, and herein Picasso's influence— I once called Picasso the gigolo of geometry—has been fruitful. We are singing, maybe, the swan-song of luxury before a new social order sweeps it away.

CHAPTER XXVII

OBJECTIVE AND SUBJECTIVE PAINTING

THE glory of Western painting has been the compassing of great achievement. So low a standard of skill as now permits men to practise painting has not been known since the dark ages. Invention, a fresh outlook on art and on nature, is rightly praised; some amateurishness, some technical incapacity may be condoned when true passion, or true innocence, is present. But the imitation of passion, the affectation of innocence, these have no worth, save in the eyes of critics and dilettanti, who assume that something, which looks like an acknowledged work of art, must share its qualities. The original Impressionists and Pre-Raphaelites, for instance, remain, while their imitators have disappeared. Up to the middle of the 19th century the followers of a sound master at least learned their trade as draughtsmen, painters or craftsmen, and could deal faithfully with the subject set them. Mulready, Landseer, Winterhalter and Frith, painters who are now held in contempt, could do whatever their fancy bade them with a virtuosity denied to the 'moderns'. I have often been asked to recommend painters for portraits of women and children; but the grace and charm the early Victorian painters commanded are no longer within our compass.

No doubt contempt for skill arises from impatience with the triviality or unreality of aim and vision, for which the academic Victorians were especially blamed. There was trivial painting done, too, in the 16th century and after; hence the growing tendency to look back to early periods of art.

Primitive paintings

Yet it is to my mind a fallacy based on comparison with later developments to insist on the more abstract quality of early painting and sculpture. For it is doubtful whether any art, even that which appears to us the most primitive, seemed simple when seen by contemporary eyes. Homer's description of the shield of Achilles denotes a highly realistic and complex art; yet could we now behold such a shield as Homer wrote of, we should deem it naïve and archaic. Stories of paintings which have come down to us—the birds pecking at the painted grapes, for example, point to an acceptance of painting as a completely representative art. Shakespeare's notion of a work of sculpture, in *The Winter's Tale*, suggests a like conception; and no doubt the Byzantine mosaics and illuminations appeared, to contemporary eyes, vivid and lifelike pictures.

We prefer the simple, direct and naïve qualities of early painting and carving to the false heroics of later artists; and need something of the austerity and conviction of the earlier masters in our work to-day. But we must look for a more profound explanation of a phase which is too characteristic of modern art to be overlooked. We are faced with a persistent effort, an attempt to replace the thing seen by the evidence of the intellect. Many of us differ profoundly from this attitude as applied to the arts. But it is in harmony with the challenge to our senses which is more and more occupying the attention of our all-powerful physicists.

Foreign critics first began to entice painters towards a new atheism: the denial of the material world. Painters and sculptors are no longer to trust their eyes, but must consciously use their intellects. They are unlikely to attend long to such unwise counsel. Indeed, if artists listened to this unseductive song of a blue-stockinged Circe, their art, like Humpty-Dumpty, not all the King's horses and all the King's men could set up again. Artists, always touched by genuine innocence, envy certain qualities which children—and sometimes amateurs—show in their work, a directness of vision and expression which seem beyond the compass of their own subtler eyes and more complex experience. The douanier Rousseau's painting is typical of this ingenuousness; so are the paintings of many working-men in England. But the pretence of artlessness is always ridiculous. Formerly there were harlots who walked in Regent Street, clad in the short skirts of school girls, with golden hair hanging down their backs, but which of these poor wantons showed the maiden's liquid eye, and sparkling innocence? Yet quite clever people are deceived by a similar pretence in literature and art. Picasso, that sad aesthetic rake, spends each weekend with a different style; and how many young foreigners, who envy him his gallantry, he has debauched by his example! I sometimes wish certain English painters would be a little naughtier, after his fashion—more true to Mary Anne and more faithless to Cézanne. Their bourgeois fidelity to this last becomes tedious. Our originals all paint alike.

Though a modern painter can, through his own inner passion, give significance to the everyday things of life, I was possessed by the idea that some subject of common interest to artist and public as well was needed if a healthy interest in the arts was to be born again. Aesthetic and technical problems, an essential part of their craft, are chiefly of moment to artists. Popular interest comes from subject and its presentation; the finer sensibilities grow therefrom. It is thus, too, with literature; interest of story precedes the attraction of style; moreover the recognition of familiar things in the form of art pleases everyone. Painters know the countryman's pleasure when he sees a familiar figure or landmark represented on canvas. In a village hall, the local hedger and thatcher, the carter and ploughman would be fitly portrayed against the familiar local landscape. In town or city the notables, the Lord Mayor, Vice-Chancellor of the University, Town Clerk, doctor, banker, warehouseman and others should serve as models for contemporary or past local history. For this local talent too would be well employed, and here and there a local school of painting might grow up. I pleaded with Sir Robert Morant to appoint in Yorkshire or Lancashire an inspiring artist to lead the way in some such direction, and when (in 1910) a committee sat to inquire into the scope of the Royal College of Art, I gave evidence towards this end. I still cling to this heresy; indeed the later developments of painting and sculpture, so little individual, so akin in their cosmopolitan sameness to the European tailoring, which is everywhere replacing dignified and beautiful local dress, have convinced me of the fruitlessness of mere aesthetic gesture.

Let an artist, by all means, work for *himself*: he has within him something which he, and no other, can say; but let him not confuse this honourable isolation with painting or carving or modelling to please the *cognoscenti*, or those who so eagerly follow the foreign artistic campaigns. To win the favours of these last is to risk an aesthetic disease, one from which many paintings and carvings suffer. Were I asked to name it, I would call it collector's pox, a mal de Venise, de Chine, or d'Afrique.

Style grows from within; it is intrinsic in all good work; it is the quiet good manners of art. You know a man by his speech, by his behaviour, by his dress; by the same tokens well-bred painting may be recognised. 'How like commonplace is a masterpiece,' said Gauguin.

The desire for perfection other than that dictated by the client, who wants 'finish', is innate in the artist. Perfection exists apart from accuracy; the Chinese or Japanese artist aims at precision of touch, at a suggestion of the grace he finds in every blade of grass, in the bend of a bough, in the petals of a blossom. He who desires to achieve this sweeping finish should not, to my thinking, use oil paint which entails a less immediate, a more complex process, fitted to render visual truth. In comparison with the graphic arts, too much prestige is given to oil painting. The essence of art is drawing, whereby body and spirit can be most perfectly united. Indeed, through drawing 'the modern movement' has perhaps been most legitimately expressed. Even in the pages of fashion magazines, in *Vogue* and *Harper's Bazaar*, the fine flower of modernity can be seen; some of the fashion plates have a quality akin to that of Greek vase painting. While painting sometimes seems to be a lost art, the numbers of men who do excellent drawings is surprising. Eric Gill, John Nash, Eric Ravilious, Gwen Ravarat, and Blair Hughes Stanton among others, have again raised English wood engraving to a high level. Some of their white-line designs are exquisite works of art. But the influence of Continental artists, of Matisse and Picasso especially, has seduced English painters from their old independence. Only a few among the younger painters have kept their birthright, notably Stanley and Gilbert Spencer. Ten years before this, John had written to me from Paris: 'I wish you could be in Paris these days. I don't want to work, that is, not on anything I'm doing. I want to start something fresh and raw. I feel inclined to paint a nude in cadmium & indigo & orange. The "Indépendants" is effroyable—and yet one feels sometimes these chaps have blundered on something alive, without being able to master it.' John too, for a time, looked on life with an 'early' eye. Like other virile men, his mind and heart were at the same time complex and simple. How often one hears the tedious cliché, 'though a great artist he is so simple'. The simplest persons are the egoists, who think overmuch of themselves; a superior spirit has more complex motives, which sensitive feelings allow him to educate. John's ardent soul dances before the ark of Leonardo and El Greco as it does before that of Giotto. He is a spiritual gypsy, and scorns the arm-chair thoughts of sluggish minds; he takes his subjects by assault, never by cunning. Epstein has similar courage, but he has not John's lyrical genius; it is in the external world that he finds his inspiration. That one should be head over ears in love with some aspect of life is what matters. An artist, who turns from his work to fulfil his duties as a citizen, may feel he is wasting precious life; for he is more ashamed of telling untruth with his pencil than of fibbing and prevaricating among his neighbours. Yet how tell the truth about the rainbow, about a blossoming almond tree, the lights and shadows that sweep over the mountains, changing their shapes from moment to moment, about the sun, about the night hung with a million million stars?

Behold a tree; it has grown, a miracle of strength and complex beauty, from a tiny seed; the sun has drawn it upwards, gravity has disciplined its growth, the winds have twined and twisted its branches against the sky—no painter can comprehend the complex laws which have woven its shape on their mysterious loom. But by subjecting himself intuitively to its appearance, by emptying himself and concentrating wholly on this shape and that, he may yet interpret the hidden forces of which the tree is the effective symbol.

How absurd to speak of realism as though objective painting were of necessity less interpretative of spirit than illustrative, romantic or abstract art. Creation is intuitive self-surrender, the entering into the thing loved. As the youth with the maid does not think of the miracle of childbirth that may ensue, nor even of the beauty of the maid he clasps to him, but surrenders himself that he may unite, body and spirit, with her body and spirit, so the artist is oblivious of the final picture, and loses himself in active union with the object of his desire. This is the value of the work of art—it is the supreme surrender of self and at the same time an act of masculine virility.

Herein lies the impossibility of any wide understanding of art—indeed, the relative unimportance of understanding. Appreciation is one of the social amenities of life; creation alone has positive value. Hence the ancient difference betwixt critic and artist, between artist and public. Criticism is refined gossip. The truth between man and woman is known only to the two concerned, but is yet the occasion of infinite surmise by outsiders; so only the artist knows what ecstasy, what agony, possessed him when he knew, simple and significant word! his subject. The truth between man and woman! If women told it, how many men would hide their heads. The true work of art wears on its surface, as it were, something akin to the radiance on the face of the fulfilled woman.

Yet how easily, with what cheap deception, can the appreciator be humbugged. An artificial accent, the frequent use of modish slang, *top hole, fed up with, I simply love it, too devastating*, offends a sensitive ear; but a similar accent and slang in the form of painting may seem the last word in refinement. Hence one prefers ignorant people to the initiated, who are too familiar with the shibboleths of Mayfair, Bloomsbury and Chelsea, to have preserved their ingenuousness. In the company of a few rare spirits we are possessed by our truest self; and we see the light, as through a prism, red, orange, yellow and violet. To speak of these colours to others were, for the most part, in vain. One can be truthful only with one's equals; with those who have not his whole respect the wise man is polite.

CHAPTER XXVIII

AN INDIAN PILGRIMAGE

DURING the summer of 1910 I returned to Vattetot, to paint cliffs and barns. While I was in France, Geoffrey Scott wrote enthusiastically about a Mohammedan Exhibition then being held at Munich:

Hotel Reichshof,
München.
Sonnenstrasse No. 15.
September 6th 1910.

My dear Will,

I am *perfectly* furious at missing you in England, & to hear that we really were there for a few days together & that I might have seen you. I saw Albert in London & inquired all about you & your doings, and he told me that you were all away in France & the villain never mentioned that you were just coming back although I was lamenting missing you. Heap a fat curse on his head from me when you see him. It is too tantalising when one is a lonely exile to lose any chance of seeing one's friends, especially yourself who have never written the said exile any letters since he went away—(or received any from him I am afraid, but then he is very busy & has never written any letters to anybody, but will to you if you promise to reply at great length in a merry vein)—& whom I want to see quite particularly.

My visit to England was an unforeseen one. Now I am on my way south again & stayed at Paris on Friday & at Nancy on Saturday. Nancy is the most perfect town archi-

228

tecturally that I have ever seen;—a consistently planned
Louis XV scheme which combines, as no other place does,
the strictest unity of design with the utmost life & variety—
perfect coherence without monotony—I daresay you know
it. Now we are for a few days at Munich to see the Mussulman
exhibition. You have heard all about it of course from
Mrs Chadbourne & Roger Fry; but if you haven't yet
seen it, you really *must*; cut the countesses who have
booked you to dinner, put away your own work, pawn
your possessions, and come. I kept thinking of you when I
was there to-day, for I know nobody who loves these things
as much as you do, & to me they were a revelation,—the
cumulative effect was so astonishing, & the pleasure of
seeing all the Persian things in succession without anything
to clash. In one way the effect is depressing, for it brings
home the sense of being, racially & by culture, hopelessly
out of it & separated from the finest art. There is some
splendid archaic sculpture—three or four things—in the
Glyptothek, but I was a little disappointed in the Aeginetan
work on a first impression. Beautiful as it is—an extraordinary touching moment in the Greek development—I
felt it to be plastically neither one thing nor the other—
missing the real archaic quality & yet not achieving the
mature grandeur of the next period. But that may be dispelled by another morning there. Of the pictures I have only
yet indulged in looking at one—the late Titian *Flagellation*:
so completely absorbing and mysterious in colour & imaginative conception that one cared nothing about the very
weak drawing in parts of it. All this is very dull for you to
read, but these are the things on the top of my mind & I
can't help writing about them. Munich, generally, I find
most appealing: in spite of all the classic snobbery of its
pseudo-Greek & pseudo-Italian architecture the people
themselves seem to be wholly indifferent to & apart from the
Graeco-Roman tradition, living without any noble dis-
contents & glorying in their paunches: a much more
beatific paganism than was ever realised further south,

causes them to beam at one in a way I find wholly irresistible. You will probably find me buried in a beer mug on your next visit.

No more now as it is late, but do write to me (I Tatti, or 3 Via delle Terne) like a good fellow.

Yours GEOFFREY SCOTT.

How intelligent Geoffrey was! Of all my lay friends he was to my mind the most sensitive to painting, not to painting alone, but to all the arts. Four years afterwards a book on baroque architecture was to appear, destined to have a decisive influence upon contemporary taste. Unfortunately the book appeared on the eve of the war, and received less notice than it would otherwise have done; but it has made its mark and become a work of authority.

I did not go to Munich to see the exhibition of which Geoffrey wrote. I was never a real student of the arts, and preferred pottering about the streets in my spare time looking for bargains, to studying seriously in overcrowded museums.

We were most of us collectors, but none of us were such fortunate hunters as Ricketts and Shannon. I say fortunate, but they were more than this; they had courage which equalled their knowledge, though their means were modest. By denying themselves many things, they were building up a magnificent collection of works of art. None of us could vie with them, but we all sallied out in the evenings to visit the antique shops. Steer had a keen eye for Chelsea figures, also a taste, which I shared, for Chinese porcelain and bronzes. But my special predilection was for Indian drawings. No one else, except Ricketts and Shannon, who had some superb examples, seemed to care for these. At Sotheby's they fetched insignificant prices; indeed, so little were they appreciated, that I find Campbell Dodgson writing to ask whether I cared to take some Indian drawings, offered to the Print Room for 3 shillings each, which they did not wish to acquire. These drawings are among the finest in my collection. I could never understand the lack of interest in Indian art. I had heard vaguely of a man called Havell, who in India was preaching its significance; but here in London Mrs Herringham alone supported me in my estimate of Indian painting and sculpture. She, indeed, who knew much more of the subject than I, spoke of going to India to make fresh copies of the paintings in the Ajanta caves, believing she could improve on those in the South Kensington Museum. Binyon encouraged her; he at least had an open mind, though he did not think Indian art compared with that of China and Japan. But I am forgetting Coomaraswamy, whom I met while staying with Ashbee at Campden. He had written a book on the art of Ceylon, and was now beginning to take an active interest in Indian art. He showed me drawings by Abanindranath Tagore and other artists of the Calcutta school, which he greatly admired. He then knew little of earlier Indian painting. I had noticed the difference between paintings which were named Indo-Persian and others I called folk-paintings. Coomaraswamy was to go more deeply into the matter, and to distinguish Rajput from Moghul art. But, as yet, only Indian craftsmanship was admired by the experts. Later, when Havell returned to England, he, Coomaraswamy and I went to hear a lecture by Sir George Birdwood, who while praising her crafts, denied fine art to India; the noble figure of Buddha he likened to a boiled suet pudding! This so disgusted me that, there and then, I proposed we should found an India Society. A meeting was held at Havell's house, and with the support of Dr and Mrs Herringham, Thomas Arnold, W. R. Lethaby, Roger Fry, Dr Thomas, T. W. Rolleston and others, the new society was formed. Mrs Herringham was now planning a second journey to India; copies she had commenced at Ajanta were unfinished and there were others she wished to make. She pressed me to go out with her. I had lately seen photographs, taken at Benares, the beauty of which had greatly excited me. There must be marvellous things to paint there; so I decided to accompany Mrs Herringham to

Ajanta to see the great wall paintings; then I would look for suitable subjects for work.

I spoke to the Ritchies about my intended visit. Sir Richmond asked me down to the India Office; he was not encouraging; he was afraid that my sympathy for Indians and for things Indian would encourage the Nationalists, now beginning to be heard through Gokhale and Tilak; I must promise to keep in touch with the officials, and to this end he provided me with letters to Provincial Governors. Thomas Arnold, then at the India Office, gave me different advice, and less official introductions.

I was to join the P & O boat at Marseilles. One could spend a pleasant day exploring Marseilles, but, as in most ports, there was something sinister about its streets at night. In the morning came a rumour that we were not to join the P & O boat; no one knew why. Then, while the steamer lay out in the bay, we were told there was illness on board; passengers would embark at their own risk. I did not hesitate; Mrs Herringham was expecting me.

I met her on deck, and found my cabin. We were soon in the Gulf, with a fine view of Marseilles and the surrounding hills, full of colour in the bright air. I thought of Puvis de Chavannes's picture of the Port of Marseilles, of the ship with Eastern travellers sitting on deck, so different from that on which I was travelling. It was not long before we heard what the illness was—a case of plague, perhaps more than one. The Anglo-Indians were indignant; such a thing had never yet happened on a P & O boat, and no one could find out precisely how matters stood. One of the lascars, it was said, was found to be suffering from the plague soon after the boat left London; now it was rumoured that one of the stewards had become infected.

At Port Said we found ourselves isolated. No one was allowed to land, or to come on board; but there was so much to interest me, so much to admire; the long files of Egyptians, austere and dignified figures, going to and fro between the ships and the shore carrying baskets of coal on their heads, reminded me of Egyptian wall paintings. To have seen this alone, I thought, had been worth the journey. And when, at nightfall, we passed through the Canal, with the desert stretching, silent and mysterious in the moonlight, on either side, I was deeply moved—such stillness, such solitude I had never known. A thousand ships, bearing countless people, pass through the Canal year after year, yet the desert appeared as remote and virgin as though the eyes of man had never beheld it, nor his feet yet trodden its wide spaces of sand. And such sunsets there were! the sunsets I had read of, which flamed up and died down so quickly; and the moonlight nights, as we steamed through the phosphorescent water, were indescribably beautiful. As we passed through the Red Sea the heat was intense. All who could slept on deck; I was the more glad to do so, since I was told that the plague was carried by fleas, and in my cabin I would wake up to imagine a flea was biting my ankles. I was soon to see enough of the plague. But there was something strange and menacing in this untoward preface to my journey, and I wondered whether I had been wise to go on what was perhaps a madcap adventure. Then we got to Aden, and seeing the great Dantesque, rocky mass towering sheer from the sea, I knew I had done well to come. At Aden again no one might land; our ship was outlawed, an object of fear and dislike. Then, after four broiling days, we reached Bombay. Here there were no difficulties about landing; no unfriendly feeling towards us. We were soon on shore, among a brilliant bustling crowd. Mrs Herringham and I were met by Colonel Fryer, with whom were two turbaned Indians, our servants to be, human treasures whose value I was now to discover. Miss Dorothy Larcher, who had previously assisted Mrs Herringham at Ajanta, and was again to work with her, had come by an earlier boat.

At the Taj Mahal Hotel I found my Russian friend, Goloubew, with his secretary Müller, a photographer, and a retinue of servants. The Pasteur Institute, he told us, had provided him with a large cabinet of antidotes against plague, typhoid, cholera and every kind of snake bite, and he was concerned, the good man, that we were not likewise supplied. He was keen to go at once to Elephanta to visit the cave-temples, so I went with him to Cook's to hire a launch for the next day. Cook's man told me confidentially that it was not worth while to hire a launch; there was nothing to see at Elephanta! When we landed on the island I felt, as I had felt some years earlier, at Torcello, that this was a wondrous and unique adventure. Though tourists visit both islands in their thousands, on this occasion no voice inspired by Murray or by Baedeker disturbed us: we were the only visitors. Silence suited the hour and the place. The rock-cut entrance to the cave-temple was simple and impressive; then deep within the shadow we came upon the great Trimurti, a brooding group of three heads of Brahma, carved with a breadth I had never seen surpassed. Then out of the gloom there emerged figures of Siva, of Siva and Parvati, and of attendant *apsaras*. I knew that Southern India had crystallised, in the *Nataraja*, in the dance of a single figure, man's profoundest intuition of the universe more simply, more perfectly perhaps, than in any philosophy. This figure, poised between one movement and another, symbolises the ordered movements of the planets through the contending forces of gravity and attraction; but here in Elephanta the powerful figures, menacing, or lost in meditation, suggest the terror and the peace, the destructive and the creative aspects of nature—the agony of birth, the peace of sleep, and of death. How much sculpture loses when detached from its original setting and placed in a museum, I felt here as never before. We were overwhelmed by the dynamic force of these great carvings, and returned to Bombay with a new conception of plastic art.

Though the main streets and buildings of Bombay look Western enough, in the native quarter swarm men from every part of India. Here I spent most of my time; but we did not tarry in Bombay; the nights were hot, and I wanted to get away from a semi-European city. Mrs Herringham, too, was eager to reach Ajanta. So we took the night train to Jalgaon, where we found bullock carts and a tonga awaiting us, the bullock carts for our luggage, the tonga for ourselves. I am told that there is now a new road, on which motor cars carry travellers up to the Ajanta caves. Twenty years ago it was less easy to reach them. Indeed the long drive, along an indifferent road in the hot sun, tried me; how disastrous were I unable to stand the Indian climate! It was embarrassing to feel ill when the two ladies were well. Fortunately the discomfort soon left me and never returned while I was in India. At Fardāpur we found tents, servants and provisions sent by the Nizam, a welcome attention, for there was only a primitive dak-bungalow at Fardāpur, and a few mud dwellings.

Up betimes, I borrowed a pony to get a first look at Ajanta, which was a couple of miles away, but found riding by no means easy; it took a while to get used to the stirrups, which were thrown over the pony's back, unattached to the saddle.

Before me rising from the jungle was a great escarpment of rock, crescent shaped, covered here and there with bushes, among which the entrances to the caves could be seen. It was as though nature had consciously provided a setting for a sacred site. A couple of hours later I was climbing up the steep path which led to the Chaityas and Viharas. Though I had seen a few photographs of the façades, I was unprepared for the magnificence of the temples. Still less than at Elephanta could I conceive these churches and monasteries to have been, with their porticoes and columns and courts, with their niches filled with sculpture, carved from the solid hillside. Once within the temples, the effect was bewildering—a forest of elaborately carved columns, rich ceilings, stupas, sculptured figures and walls covered with paintings—I wandered from cave to cave throughout the day. On the day following I was able to concentrate on the wall-paintings. At first I thought these paintings irreparably damaged; then I deciphered vast compositions wherein the whole life of India seemed to be displayed, with an observation and grasp of form, character and movement set down with swift precision and energy of line. Mrs Herringham's praise had not been extravagant. I understood better than hitherto her zeal and devotion in coming to India a second time to make copies of these astonishing paintings. She had wanted my advice in selecting the subjects for future copies—but how to find my way through this jungle of masterpieces! Yet one can see much in a couple of days' time; and reproductions seen since have kept my memory fresh. I could have spent many days studying these great Buddhist paintings. To look at things is inspiring, but there comes a nostalgia for work; looking and not doing becomes oppressive after a while, unnatural—a weariness to the spirit. So my servant packed my bed and my bags and I left the wild and beautiful scene at Ajanta and took my leave of Mrs Herringham. I was eager to begin my journey 'on my own'.

My first destination was Chitor, where I arrived at night, and walked gingerly in the darkness to the dak-bungalow, where my servant put up the bed, and prepared supper. It was my first experience of staying in one of these rest-houses. The Indian nights are marvellous; the moon seems to ride higher in the heavens than she does in Europe, and her light is far more brilliant; from outside came the cry of the jackals, and other strange sounds. It was long before I slept. In the morning I climbed up to Chitor.

I had read the tragic story of Chitor in Tod's book. From its now silent temples and palaces, trees and bushes grow; where men and women once lived, snakes and wild animals make their lair. As I wandered from ruin to ruin, and ascended the two remaining towers, I saw no human being; the desolation was complete.

Could there be anything more wonderful for me to see? I had asked the same thing at Ajanta; I was to ask it many times. Each time my servant laughed, and spoke of other places, much more beautiful; and when I reached Udaipur, I saw that he was right.

Udaipur is a dream city of shining marble palaces, mirrored in still lakes. Its streets, too, with little open shops, seemed streets from some Eastern story. There sat the merchants, cross-legged, dressed in green and scarlet against gaily painted and carved interiors, while up and down rode Rajput gentlemen girt with swords and bucklers, just as they appeared in the Indian paintings I was collecting. No one had told me of such unbelievable places. True, Bauer had made striking etchings of temples and palaces, and of Eastern crowds, but the English painters who had been in India were content, it seemed, to paint only Maharajas.

I had met the English Resident's wife on the boat, through whom I was invited to visit the Rana's Palace. The Rana, descended from the Moon through an unbroken line of ancestors, was the most honoured among the Rajput Princes. About the entrance to his Palace stood his retainers, beautifully clothed, while elephants, with their heads and trunks superbly painted, were led round the court-yard. I was taken through long passages to a room where the Maharaja, bearded, grave and dignified, received me. He spoke a few words of welcome in English; bowed in response to my expressions of admiration for his beautiful capital, hoped I was comfortable in his guest-house, bade me go where I pleased. I withdrew, touched by his noble aspect, and something sad in his bearing. Afterwards I met his son, whose delicate health, maybe, accounted in part for his father's melancholy.

Next day a state-barge was placed at my disposal, in which I was rowed to the lovely lake-palaces. I challenged my bearer to show me a fairer place than Udaipur. Yet though Jodhpur, whither I went next, was not so fair, I found there another, a graver beauty. Built on a steep mass of rock in the midst of a plain, Jodhpur, with its square houses of red sand-stone, and its tanks, put me in mind of a Greek city, though its medieval castle, having huge bare walls protecting and supporting its carved upper storeys, is unmistakably Indian. Thoroughly Indian too are the streets of the city, and the dress of its people, the women with swinging Rajput skirts, of red silk embroidered with gold, and bright shawls thrown across their shoulders.

I cared less for Jaipur, laid out as it is in imitation of a French or Italian city. The letters I carried gave me many advantages; for I had not long been at Jaipur before two elephants and a number of retainers stood at my door, ready to take me to Amber, the deserted city on the hill. I tried to behave as though I were used to having an elephant at my disposal; steps having been placed against the beast's side I climbed into the howdah. The intelligent animal, making a seat of his trunk, swung the mahout on to his neck, and lumbered up the hill towards Amber. Here again I seemed to be breathing oxygen instead of air, as I found myself wandering through a city of houses, temples, palaces and gardens, now entirely deserted. Only monkeys chattered from the roofs; and when the luncheon hour approached, at a sign from the mahout my elephant sank upon his knees and I descended, an insignificant figure among the Maharaja's tall but shabby retainers, who awaited me at a table set on a marble terrace, facing a great tank; here I ate a modest lunch of sandwiches. I had wished myself, and my meal, more worthy of the situation.

At Jaipur I saw the Maharaja's collections of paintings and manuscripts, jewels and works of art; and at Alwar, too, I visited the Prince's treasure-house. Most of the Princes were in Calcutta, to bid farewell to the retiring Viceroy, Lord Minto, and to welcome Lord Hardinge, the new Viceroy. A minister of the Alwar state, who showed me round the palace at Alwar, said, in response to my admiration for the collection of splendid jewels, 'These that remain were used as ornaments for the elephants. The jewels which belonged to their past Highnesses were of a different order'. He referred, of course, to the sacrifices made by the Rajput Princes during the long struggle against the Moghul power.

From Alwar I went on to Ajmir, where I came into touch for the first time with Moslem culture. I was taken over the great mosque and saw the *Imams* seated with their pupils round them, much as later I was to see the Hindu *Gurus* sitting with their *chelas* at Benares. I think my respect for the exterior beauty of the holy places and of the people therein was obvious, for wherever I went I met with marked consideration. To enjoy a foreign country, one should have love in one's heart, whereby many doors and many hearts will be opened. I left Ajmir with regret, as indeed I left every place, and went on to Agra.

Who is not moved by the beauty of the Taj? And again at Delhi by the beauty of the tombs scattered round old Delhi? From Delhi I turned southwards to pay a promised visit to the Maharaja of Chhatarpur, an old friend of Thomas Arnold and Theodore Morison.

Chhatarpur is a small state in Bhandalkund that contains one of the rare groups of Indian medieval temples which escaped destruction at the hands of the Muslim conquerors. Arriving at night-time I was met by a carriage which the Maharaja had sent to take me the 40 miles to his capital. As we drove, the carriage lamps lighted the fringes of the mysterious landscape. Now and then we passed buffalo carts by the road-side, beside which gray shrouded figures rose up out of the darkness. At Chhatarpur I found the usual guest-house and a message of welcome from the Maharaja, who seemed pleased at my coming—visitors at Chhatarpur were rare. He was a small man with restless eyes. Beside him sat his two *Gurus*; one, a beautiful old man with a long white beard, serene and kind looking, was dressed in the orange garb of the religious, with one hand in a small bag telling his beads; the other, in a blue coat trimmed with orange, was a stronger, more worldly looking man. Both sat gravely listening to our talk. Philosophy, His Highness told me, was his favourite subject, and he asked affectionately after his old friends and tutors, Arnold and Morison.

Chhatarpur, a purely Indian town, shabby and decrepit, was yet to my eyes full of interest. One day there arrived in the town a group of ascetics, with long beards and hair piled up on top of their heads, their faces and bodies gray with ashes, just as I had seen them in Indian drawings. All day men and women crowded round, bringing them food and presents, and asking their advice. While I was sitting with Chhatarpur in his palace, two of these men, stark naked, stalked into the room. They offered the Maharaja some small round pebbles, which had to do with good fortune, I gathered. Yes, he said, these holy men had free access to the palace; he had to treat them with respect, though many of them were doubtful characters. These were the first fakirs I had seen, and the first I drew. They were evil-looking men, I thought, certainly not holy, but what a picture they made sitting on their tiger skins, with the women covered in their red saris gathered round. I had not been long enough in India to know the difference between these fakirs who played on the superstitious natures of the Indian peasantry, and the true Sanyasis, men of a very different character. The group of temples at Khajurahu I had come to see were some miles from the capital. Thither the Maharaja took me in his car. Motor cars were then new to India, and the Maharaja had built some miles of road especially for driving. How I disliked to see the poor frightened peasantry get out of our way, dragging their buffalo carts into the ditches to let us pass. The temples, reflected in the water of some neighbouring tanks, shone white in the distance. Remarkable though the temples were, I was more interested in the carvings with which they were covered. In the medieval sculpture there is little of the static quality associated with Indian Buddhist art, though I was put in mind of the Amarāvati carvings on the staircase of the British Museum. Here all was motion; the buildings appeared at one and the same time to rest solid and square upon the ground and, through the tiers of ardent figures carved upon them, to quiver with life. The mastery shown in these carvings, the plastic beauty of the forms, the energetic and subtle postures of the figures playing in and out of the light and shadows of the mouldings, the design and rhythm concentrated in each panel, delighted me.

Not only the buildings, but the ground was covered with figures, many of which were half buried in the soil.

My enthusiasm for the beauty I saw everywhere touched the Maharaja's heart, and he confided to me many of his troubles. He was eager too to hear anything I could tell him of philosophy, literature and science. In his State there was no one, he said, with whom he could talk. Finding that I wished to see one of the traditional Indian dramas, he arranged a special performance for my benefit. It was strange to find myself sitting on a divan alone at the end of the Durbar Hall, the sole audience of a marvellous performance. Here were living figures who took the same hieratic poses I had just been seeing in the temple carvings. I was reminded of the Javanese dancers I had seen twenty years earlier at the Paris Exhibition. And how beautiful were the women. When I praised them to the Maharaja he laughed—they were not women, they were boys! No women ever figure in these religious plays.

One day I found His Highness poring over catalogues. He was choosing Christmas presents and would be glad of my help; and he handed me an illustrated price-list of cheap German jewelry from a Calcutta firm. Now I daily admired the gold ornaments, made by local goldsmiths, which the townspeople and villagers wear at Chhatarpur, indeed throughout India. But the Maharaja preferred the commercial products of Europe to native workmanship. He could not possibly offer the work of humble Chhatarpur goldsmiths to his friends. I have heard the decay of Indian crafts laid to the charge of British rule. This is unjust; I met with few Indians who valued their own art.

I liked being in Chhatarpur, but I was eager to get to Benares. It was a photograph of Benares shown me by my American friend, Mrs Chadbourne, which had first made me want to visit India.

In Benares I put up at Clark's Hotel, in the cantonment, a couple of miles away from the city itself.

Here the landscape was flat and dull, and I was impatient

to see the sacred city. Early next morning I hired a *ghari* and drove into the town. Each place in India had seemed to me more wonderful than the last, but Benares was overwhelming. Havell had told me that the architecture there was not remarkable, but as I was rowed along the ghats and saw the great massive buildings of apricot-coloured stone which towered above the long flights of steps leading up from the river, I could imagine no lovelier or more radiant scene—the crowds bathing in the river, women in their *saris* with joined palms, men, stripped of their clothing, standing like bronze statues, others splashing themselves with the sacred water—above them, all down the river, under vast umbrellas made of wood-fibre, sat cross-legged figures in every attitude of prayer and contemplation, while women in bright *saris*, looking like Tanagra figures, walked, on bare, delicate feet, up and down the steep steps leading to the town, their silver anklets tinkling as they went. Indeed, the crowded, coloured, agitated scene put me in mind of a classical city; of Corinth or of Carthage; and again, in the densely packed streets, of medieval Rome. The beauty and variety of the colour was overwhelming. How was I to choose among the thousands of subjects I saw during a single journey down the river?

Day after day I drove into Benares, in the mornings to study the ecstatic scene of the bathing, in the afternoons and evenings to watch the quieter life of the ghats.

After seeing all this marvellous life along the Ganges, I explored the streets of the town, looking for subjects to paint. But so bewildering, so crowded and varied was the Indian scene, it seemed impossible to decide. How to find a quiet spot was another difficulty. Finally I settled down on the Dhasaswamed Ghat, under the shadow of a huge umbrella. My servant tried to keep back the people who crowded round me; until the bathers who frequented the ghat got used to my presence, and protected me from the curious. But, 'Why was I painting here? What made me come so far? Did people buy my pictures? How much

money did they pay for them? Wouldn't I do better to paint
Maharajas?'—To these questions I replied: 'Anyone can
dress up to look like a Maharaja; but no one can look like a
Sanyasi unless he has found peace.' A remark which won
their sympathy. In Benares I found that which I had come to
India to discover; but each evening, to return to the hotel,
with its self-satisfied tourists, became more distasteful. A
majestic bearded Bengali, in the dress of a Sanyasi, often
stopped to watch me as he passed by. He was friendly and
took me up to his cell, high above the ghat. It had been
Kabir's dwelling, he said. He was pleased at my interest in
the *Sadhus*, and I went with him to places where they
assembled, and into the *Matts*, where the pilgrims and
ascetics, come from afar, could stay. These hostels were
noble buildings from without, but within, were close and
dark. I was happier in the court-yards, or, sheltered from the
sunlight, in a small building on one of the ghats, where a much
venerated *Guru* sat stark naked with his disciples; this was
illegal: a loin cloth at least must be worn, but no one molested
the holy man. The *Guru*, who spoke no English, nevertheless
befriended me, and induced many of his visitors to stand
or sit to be drawn. My new Bengali friend, whose name was
Narasingh Sharma, pointed out that no one would come to
sit to me at the hotel; why not come and stay in the city?
He introduced me to a Mr Biswas, who offered me quarters
at the Maharaja of Vizianagram's house. When I told the
Commissioner and the Collector that I thought of moving
into Benares, I met with immediate opposition: I should be
running great risks of plague, typhoid and cholera. They
meant well. But they could not follow my liking for
'fakirs' of whose loyalty they were, moreover, doubtful.
But I had not come so far to live in an English cantonment;
I must be in touch with the people whom I wanted to draw,
near the scenes I wished to paint. So I went.

What had before been difficult was now easy; all sorts of
people came to sit for me. In the evenings I painted on the
ghats, which were now less frequented. Here and there a few

elderly men sat together, or walked quietly along the terraces watching the sun set. I would sometimes join some group and listen to the talk. Each evening I was exalted by the peace and beauty of the scene. Over the water came the sound of women's voices, chanting hymns, as the boats glided down the swift-flowing river. One day I was greeted by a grave looking figure, in *chadur* and *dhoti,* who spoke my name. He was Sir Pannambalam Arunachalam, a cousin of Coomaraswamy—he had been told I was painting at Benares, whither he had come as a pilgrim. A Tamil, and a practising Hindu, he was an old Cambridge graduate, a friend of Edward Carpenter and of Lowes Dickinson. I found him to be a man of wide culture and of quiet charm; and though he was at first surprised at meeting some of my Sanyasi friends, he quickly approved of my choice of acquaintances. He joined me in my visits to Narasingh Sharma and together we learnt something of the tenets and practices of the Hâtha Joga. To attain *Samadhi* would take long; therefore it behoves a Jogi to acquire perfect bodily health. Incidentally he must learn to control the organs of his body. Of his own powers of control Sharma told us some astonishing things. Whether I was moved by the religions and philosophy I heard discussed or more by the beauty and dignity of the men with whom I sat, I know not. Certainly the combination of personal dignity with a subtle insight into the springs of mental life gave me a profound happiness I have never experienced before, or since. I remember one evening especially when I encountered, sitting on one of the ghats, a venerable figure, whose aspect so moved me, I asked if I might sit with him. A retired Civil Servant, he had come to spend his last years at Benares, he said: and he had indeed found peace. But he had not yet been able to sever his last ties with this world. He still loved his wife; though he hoped, before he died, to overcome even this frailty. I was rash enough to tell this to some English friends, who thought it extremely funny. How different were these quiet afternoons and evenings on the ghats, from the crowded, noisy, passionate mornings! And again,

how different from the life of street and temple, the life the
tourist is shown.

Enchanted as I was by the beauty I found at Benares,
there were many things that shocked and repelled me.
Everywhere along the ghats sat men, and women too, in
contemplation, reciting prayers and doing breathing exer-
cises, while poor country folk, who had come into Benares
from long distances to visit the temples, to bathe and to
drink from the sacred river, were being cruelly exploited by
the Pandas, who, spider-like, waited for their prey. No
doubt pilgrims in Europe were once similarly exploited; yet
the indifference shown by the more educated religious
surprised me. One day a youth from Allahabad, named
Makandi Lal, sought me out. He was a student from the
University there who had been sent to look after me. He
meant, he said, to devote his life to serving his country.
Yet while he was speaking there arose a clamour—a *tonga
wallah* was trying to brow-beat some villagers he had brought
into the town. 'But can one devote oneself to a whole
country?' I asked. 'Why not begin by helping these poor
people who are being exploited?' Help them he did, and
was the happier for his action. In Benares I was meeting men
with remarkable religious insight; but in Europe the religious
spirit is best seen in our social civilisation. It would be long,
I felt, before India developed a similar social sense; though
the Indian teaching, that men must first do their duty in
the everyday world, marry and bring up a family, before
attending to their spiritual duties, is a sane doctrine. But
nothing is gained by untruth or exaggeration. It is not true
that the Indians are treated as equals by my countrymen;
it is equally untrue that they are being exploited and im-
poverished under British rule. I saw for myself that Indians
are often more harshly oppressed by each other than ever by
us. The real grievance against England is a social one; and
I feared, were it to continue, it would change to political
discontent.

Sir Montagu Butler had sent me a letter to the Maharaja

of Benares; his *Dewan* called on me. After many compliments and some desultory talk—I felt that he had something on his mind—the *Dewan* came to the point. A painter visiting India could not be disinterested. What Maharajas had I already painted? He feared that the fee of so eminent an artist would be too high for His Highness. He was surprised as he was relieved to hear of my strange taste for the life of the ghats. His Highness would at once place a state-barge at my service. A state-barge manned by some 20 retainers awaited me next morning. Sir Harry Stephen and his wife, and Sir John Woodroffe had come to spend Christmas at Benares, and together we saw the entire length of the city from the river. We enjoyed the experience, but I preferred to go on the river in a more modest equipage—and in a more thrifty one, too, for retainers and rupees are synonymous. Among others who visited me was Mirza Kamrān Bux the lineal descendant of the Moghul Emperors. He invited me to his Palace; it was so named, but I found it to be a large, neglected looking house, poorly furnished within. It was pathetic to know this subdued and kindly gentleman, in whose veins flowed the blood of Bābur and of Akbar, an obscure pensioner of the British Government. All that remained to him of past splendour were a few fine Moghul paintings which hung on his walls. He was now a respected member of the Benares Municipal Council.

On another occasion I was bidden to a temple (it was, I think, a private temple of an orthodox branch of the Tagore family) where a musician, reputed to be the most famous in India, was to be present. He was an elderly Hindu, who chanted to the accompaniment of a *Vīnā*; then first one and then another, becoming excited, would take up the singing, which lasted, without a pause, late into the night. The songs were religious songs; their melodies seemed to wander through the air like disembodied souls, never touching earth. It was by no means the most beautiful voice which aroused the greatest enthusiasm; perfection of voice is but a small thing, I was told, compared with the inner sense of music.

I, who am set on edge by the notes of a piano, delighted in the frail, silver chords of the *Vīnā*; and there was a simple fervour in the singing musician which touched my heart. I was also to see a famous nautch-dancer, who was visiting Benares. For long we sat and waited; time means little to Indians. At last the lady, muffled in a great cloak, arrived and was assiduously greeted. Expecting to see a houri, slender waisted and high breasted, I was somewhat embarrassed at the sight of a lady of such ample proportions. True, I had admired certain massive heads and torsos in one of the museums; but scarcely connected such a figure with a nautch-girl. Now the musicians began beating with their hands on their long drums, and the lady advanced an arm, loaded with bracelets, and then a foot, whose toes, beringed and bejewelled, were as sensitive as her supple fingers. At first her hands, arms and feet moved slowly and rhythmically, and as the music quickened her body swayed and turned in unison. As the superb creature danced, I forgot her stature; still I was content, later, with a lesser celebrity and a more youthful figure. But Coomaraswamy and an Indian lady who together had brought me, were loud in their praises.

Life at Benares had seemed like a dream, whose beauty was beyond compare, that would never return. But I had dreamed it, and I was the richer for this vision of the antique world, for so I held it to be. Why, I wondered, should such beauty live with poverty, disease, superstition and injustice? Someday the dark interiors of Benares will be swept and garnished, marigolds will no longer be left to decay in the temples, and the bright *saris* of the women, the *chadurs* and the *dhotis* of the men, and the apricot garments of the Sanyasis will be exchanged for dingy clothes of western cut, and with sanitation and universal suffrage, beauty will leave India, as she has left Europe.

To-day there is still such beauty, it seems too much for one pair of eyes to look on. The magnificent buildings, the ever-changing crowd, coloured like a great border of flowers, the processions carrying litters and banners; and then the

247

austere figures sitting like bronze images of Buddha and Bhoddisatvas—was I in truth awake, or living in a dream? What were English painters doing, to miss such subjects as these I was seeing, which no one but the Dutchman Bauer had attempted? And think of what Zoffany saw a century and more ago, and that a succession of painters have since come to India, and painted only Maharajas! I saw clearly, too, that the images by Indian, Chinese, Tibetan and Japanese sculptors and painters which I had previously believed to have been the result of a fine style, were in fact based upon accurate observation. Here were men sitting in contemplation, draped in garments whose folds the greatest stylist could not surpass. It was all too bewildering; and though I made more than 150 drawings of ascetics, I felt as I drew each one, how much time was needed to do him justice. I must return some day, not to Benares, perhaps, but elsewhere, and concentrate on a modest subject, in a less exciting, a quieter spot.

Before I left Benares, Coomaraswamy, who was directing an arts and crafts exhibition, asked me to join him at Allahabad. I found him living in a tent; and, provided with a similar one, I stayed to see the famous *mela*, the annual religious fair, and the fakirs and mendicants who came there from all parts of India. Some of these had young boys with them, whose faces were gilded, and who wore on their heads tinselled crowns, familiar in the paintings of Krishna. I was fascinated by these living images; a pity, I thought, that by ridding religion of its superstitious elements we end by banishing wellnigh all its beauty. Artists, who care little for creeds and dogmas, love their accompaniments. Idols, idol worship, priests with their distinctive dress, processions and fairs, all the outer forms of India's many religions, attracted me strongly.

Meanwhile I could not help noticing a steady increase in the number of bodies brought to the burning-ghat. The plague was claiming its victims.

My time was coming to an end; before leaving Benares,

I paid a last visit to Narasingh; as I bade him adieu, I urged him to look after himself. 'Nothing can touch me,' he said, proudly; 'neither plague nor other bodily illness.' There comes, with departure, a weight over the heart. Is it a foreboding of final departure? And as the train crossed the bridge, and I saw for the last time that great sweep of the river, with its rich border of temples and palaces, I was miserable. Should I not have stayed awhile longer to continue my painting, and given up my plan of going to Calcutta, Darjeeling, and Puri? Had I done so, I should never have met Tagore.

Sir Harry and Lady Stephen had asked me to stay with them in Calcutta; and wonderful as Benares was, I confess to a grateful feeling at finding again the ample comfort of a well ordered English household. I met Goloubew once more in Calcutta, who opened his arms and embraced me as though he had scarcely expected to find me alive! He had been, among other places, to Kashmir, where he had shot a bear, beside which he and his friend Müller were photographed in turn. There was only one bear.

Then Abanindranath Tagore and his brother Gaganendranath came to take me to their home at Jorasanko; a delightful house, full of lovely things, of paintings, bronzes, stuffs, and musical instruments. Their collection of Indian paintings was the best I had seen, made, as it was, by artists. Gaganendranath, a man of singular charm and culture, was a kind of Indian Ricketts, who seemed to have seen and read about everything. I was attracted, each time I went to Jorasanko, by their uncle, a strikingly handsome figure, dressed in a white *dhoti* and *chadur*, who sat silently listening as we talked. I felt an immediate attraction, and asked whether I might draw him, for I discerned an inner charm as well as great physical beauty, which I tried to set down with my pencil. That this uncle was one of the remarkable men of his time no one gave me a hint.

Sir John Woodroffe, who, with Sir Harry Stephen, had visited me at Benares, knew the Tagores well; it puzzles me that he told me nothing about Rabindranath, for we discussed both Abanindranath and Gaganendranath. Sir John Woodroffe, of all the Englishmen I met in India, showed most desire to plumb the depths of the Indian spirit. With a Pundit he was studying the Tantric writings, on which he became a learned authority.

I was eager to see the medieval temples at Puri and Bhuvaneshwar; so was Coomaraswamy, who had come on to Calcutta from Allahabad, and thither we went together. The Tagores put their Puri house at our disposal; and although half a dozen domestics met us at the station, yet the house was bare, so simply do Indians live, but for two Spartan beds made of plain wooden boards. Puri was crowded with pilgrims come to worship at the famous Jaganath Temple. The Uriya *pandas* wore violet *chadurs*, the folds arranged as in early Greek sculpture, beautiful to see.

I saw a procession of temple priests, naked to the waist, their brown, round bodies shining in the sun, carrying on their shoulders naked children covered with golden ornaments. Here was the world of Dionysus living before one's eyes!

Scenes like these, of which no one had given me a hint, make India seem a classical land. The processions which poured in daily put me in mind, too, of medieval Europe, and I wondered whether pilgrims had formerly visited Christian shrines in such numbers. Herein lay the secret, I thought, of India's religious greatness. Whereas Europe adopted an alien religion, whose ancient sages and prophets, and, finally, the noblest of all teachers, belonged to an alien race, whose language, customs and environment, were foreign to Europe, India's gods and prophets were born of her own seed, with intimate racial and local roots. Where Krishna sported with the milkmaids, where Buddha preached, where the Heroes fought, was sacred and native soil; and while our crowds flock to Brighton and Blackpool, the Indian villagers make pilgrimages in their thousands to Benares, Hardwar and Puri.

Indian genius

Everywhere the women, russet browed and with grave faces, placed their offerings of flowers before the lingams in the shrines by the roadside, or before the images under the great peepal trees, and to watch one of them doing puja, with her flowers and conch shell, was an exquisite sight.

At Bhuvaneshwar, close to Puri, is a remarkable group of medieval temples. The buildings themselves are simple, not unlike the structure of a corn cob with beautifully articulated stone work, and the walls are enriched with carvings similar to those I saw at Khajurahu. What I had surmised in the *apsara* cast twenty years earlier at Degas' flat I again realised in overwhelming fashion, and I wondered, in front of these superb creations, that the Gandharan heresy still survives, a crude injustice to the Indian genius. The medieval craftsman showed that combination of disciplined power and intuitive impulse which only the greatest modern artists have achieved. That India evolved on the one hand, in the figure of the seated Buddha, a perfect expression of static repose, and on the other, in the invention of the dance of Shiva, a superb expression of the creative and destructive elements of nature, is a great achievement. That the earlier archaeologists, when Far-Eastern art was imperfectly understood, should not have recognised this is scarcely a matter for blame; but that students of the art of Persia, of China and Japan should still undervalue the unique plastic qualities of the best Indian sculpture is less excusable. There is, too, a tendency to pass too lightly over the creation of form, of gesture, of poise, invented and perfected by Indian artists before Buddhism reached the Farther East. The creation of a great mythology, the peopling of a vast heaven with credible gods, is an extraordinary achievement. The carvings at Bhuvaneshwar play about the walls and roof of which they form a part like flames, making the temples seem to quiver like trees and rocks in mid-day sunlight.

Wherever I went, my English friends spoke of the Taj Mahal as though this were the one work of art in India, adding that this was in part due to Italian influence. It was as though Indian visitors to France should praise Versailles only, ignoring Rheims, Amiens and Vézelay. Archaeologists have shown a like lack of sensibility when they have praised the debased Eurasian Gandhara sculpture to the disadvantage of the superb, dynamic carving of pure Hindu artists.

But I found cultivated Indians surprisingly ignorant of their own art, and embarrassed by my enthusiasm for the carvings on the Bhuvaneshwar and Khajurahu temples. For they deemed these ugly; while for my part the furniture and pictures in the palaces of the Maharajas and in the houses where I was so hospitably entertained, set my teeth on edge. Perhaps the effect on a Japanese artist of the bamboo tables and Eastern knick-knacks of the average English home, even of the overcrowded rooms of men who pride themselves on their good taste, is similar to that which the upholstered interiors in India made on me.

While there are signs everywhere of the past genius of the Indian people, there is little evidence, save in their dress and in the jewelry of the peasantry, of its endurance to-day. But an Indian visiting Europe might well say the same, though at least Western art still retains something of its old vitality. It seemed strange to me, witnessing the fervour and devotion among the crowds at Benares and Puri, that the creative energy of a people so passionate should have spent itself.

At Calcutta, at the Tagore house and at the Government school of art I met a group of charming young artists, who gave me a touching welcome. Had I but come to India earlier, I would gladly have stayed among these students, so perplexed betwixt two traditions. Nanda Lal Bose, Asit Kumar Haldar and other gifted young painters, under the guidance of Abanindranath Tagore, were reviving a purely Indian tradition of painting. But no artist of marked creative impulse had yet been sent to India, to teach, by example, how much good Eastern and Western art have in common. In the active departments of life, in government,

in law, in engineering, no finer or more devoted set of men
has ever worked for the good of others than is to be found in
the Indian Civil Service. But we have been less sensitive to
the intellectual and creative needs of India; men like Lock-
wood Kipling and Havell, who have appreciated the genius
of the Indian people, have been all too rare. And the archaeologists have been busy looking for what is hidden under the
ground. Had India's rulers a sense of beauty, their understanding of India and of Indians would be profounder,
I thought, and there would be less friction between rulers
and ruled.

When I saw two Pathans meeting, each placing his
hand above the heart of the other, my heart went out
to the Muslims; when two young Hindus walked hand-in-
hand, I was touched by the beauty of Hindu ways. Everywhere in India I saw this beauty, so that each day seemed
fuller and richer than the last, and each hour of life a
privilege.

At Darjeeling, whither I went from Calcutta, I saw many
Tibetans, the followers of the Dalai Lama. Some of their
faces showed a simple goodness which touched my heart.
I have met with this same goodness in priests of every
creed, Christian, Mohammedan, Hindu, Buddhist and Jewish,
and always, on meeting it, I lay down my arms. These
Tibetans were strikingly like the figures in their bronzes
and paintings. Why does the recognition of pure racial
qualities give one so much pleasure? Psychologists may
know the reason; for my part, I know only the peculiar
response which purity of race excites in me. I saw again that
the style which we believe primitive artists give to their
paintings and carvings is inherent in their models. And how
unconsciously and subtly the racial character is rendered in
the art of every country, but how clumsy the attempts to
give a Chinese or a negro character to European painting
and sculpture! The Greek type, at least, was European, and
not one alien to our sculptors.

Besides Tibetans, there were men and women from

Bhutan and Sikkim, some of whom I was able to draw. Again I was sad at turning my back on all these wonders. Before leaving Darjeeling a telegram came from Rabindranath Tagore, asking me to join him at Bolpur; but my passage was booked, and I must reluctantly refuse.

At Bombay I was joined by Mrs Herringham; the state of her health alarmed me. She had overworked, as women will, and the long hours in the close bat-haunted Ajanta courts had done her grave harm.

Before I left India Gokhale came to see me. I was disturbed by what he told me of the growing unrest, the more so since he appeared to be both moderate and wise, and without personal bitterness. Moreover, he was not a Bengali. I mention this since, when on my return I spoke of my fear lest social grievances might turn into general political discontent, I was told I had been listening to a few disgruntled Bengalis —that the heart of India was sound. I found the German Crown Prince was returning on the boat on which I had booked my passage. He had been recalled by his father; rumour had it that his conduct had been somewhat unconventional for the son of the All Highest during an official visit. He made himself agreeable enough during the passage, joining in the games and amusements, and inviting the more eminent passengers to join him at his table. I became acquainted with a journalist in his suite. His views on Anglo-German relations were disquieting. 'You see', he said, 'you are sometimes an Empire and sometimes a European power. Leave us free to deal with Eastern European problems and we will fall in with your extra-European policy; as things are you insist on interfering in matters that we feel to be our special concern.' Had he never heard, I wondered, of the balance of power in Europe, which, for a century at least, had been the mainspring of British foreign policy?

I was no card player and took walking exercise on deck, towards evening especially, when the sunsets were marvellously beautiful. The Crown Prince very likely thought me a nuisance, for I would come upon him with some young lady. When he left the boat at Port Said, there was at least one young woman in tears.

I brought from India three paintings and some hundred and fifty drawings, chiefly of ascetics, which I exhibited at the Chenil Gallery. H. G. Wells wrote a few words on these for the catalogue. Though the drawings were but slight, they gave at least a hint of what might be done by an artist willing to spend some time in India. It is surprising, seeing our close connection with India, that no English painter has been so tempted as Bauer and Besnard were, as Gauguin was by Tahiti. I would return, I decided, whenever a chance offered itself; but when this came, ill-health prevented my going.

CHAPTER XXIX

AMERICAN PORTRAITS

Now I was asked to paint a portrait, and at the same time to hold an exhibition of drawings and paintings, in New York. Of the four months I spent in the States I need say little. The real America I scarcely saw, staying as I did with people comfortably circumstanced and cosmopolitan in outlook. But for a short visit to Boston and Chicago, I spent all my time in New York. Like everyone else I admired the skyline of New York. The Woolworth Building then seemed a magnificent peak; but I am told that the other skyscrapers would now appear insignificant by the side of those recently built. Stanford White's Pennsylvania Railway Station and the Municipal Library were then regarded as typical of the best American architecture. Ralph Adams Cram was occupied with the new Cathedral, only a part of which was built. He complained of the dearth of good craftsmen; he was envious of the many in England. I saw something of the American landscape, being taken by motor into the Adirondack mountains; it was late autumn, yet the leaves on the trees, gloriously painted bright red and yellow, seemed neither to shrivel, nor to fall. When staying near Boston, too, to make drawings of Mr and Mrs Storrow and of their son, I had a glimpse of Thoreau's country, beautiful under the snow. It was pleasant to meet old friends again, Kenneth Frazier, Philip Hale, Howard Cushing, Howard Hart, and the Herters. My painter-friends complained of their neglect by American collectors, while foreign artists found their country a gold-mine—I understood their feelings and felt a little ashamed of being among these last. My success, however, could arouse little jealousy. One small landscape only, and a few prints and drawings, were sold after exhibitions of my work in New York, Boston and Chicago. I saw little of American painting in the houses I visited. Indeed, I used to say that I recognised Anglo-American interiors by the Buddhist paintings on the walls; while when I saw Byzantine reliquaries and crucifixes and chalices, I knew I was the guest of Jewish-Americans. I admired the museums; but I wondered whether the acquisitive passion was not detrimental to the rise of a vigorous school of American art. The painter whose work I thought most typically American was Winslow Homer. I remember especially two of his paintings, one of a river scene with a canoe, the other of figures dancing by the seashore by moonlight. Berenson and Ellen Terry had given me letters to friends in New York and Boston, and I tasted the fruits of American hospitality. I made new friendships—with the Simon Flexners, the Carroll Dunhams, the gifted Miss Belle da Costa Green, who showed me the treasures of Pierpont Morgan's house; the Robinsons of the Metropolitan Museum, the Spingarns, Kenyon Cox and Arthur B. Davies.

While in New York, I saw much of Davies, who had something in common with Ricketts, and with Shannon also. Shy and sensitive, he led the life of a recluse; and he at least was fortunate in that a few amateurs bought wellnigh all he did. I respected Kenyon Cox's conservative views, though I cared little for his mural decorations.

Indeed, I spent my spare time with my artist friends; but staying as a guest in various houses, my time was not my own. Of the then young writers and poets—Theodore Dreiser, Edwin Arlington Robinson, Willa Cather, Edgar Lee Masters—I heard only vaguely. I did fall in with George Santayana; it was a privilege to talk with a man of his delicate understanding. For to converse with the many attractive people I met at dinner parties was often to find no experience taken for granted; it was as though, when playing tennis, the court had to be marked out afresh for each game. I remember an evening spent with George E. Woodberry, a man of great charm who must have had a great vogue at this time, as there was a Woodberry Club in New York. One day, while I was sitting in the Century Club, of which I was made a temporary member, there came in a striking looking man, dark-bearded, with a head like a wild boar. I asked Frazier who he was: he was John Jay Chapman, a letter to whom, from Berenson, I had with me. There was a power in him, an authority and conviction, which set him apart from other men. He asked me to paint his youngest son, and I stayed with him and his wife at Barrytown-on-Hudson; their house was a notable example of early Colonial building. I read his books and was struck by his plays, some of which I sent to friends in England, who shared my estimate of Chapman's gifts, which were too little appreciated, it seemed to me, in America.

From New York my paintings were sent on to Boston. There I renewed old relations with Philip Hale; also with Mrs Jack Gardiner, this time in her own home. Her house was in fact a museum—is now, I believe, a public museum. At the great Boston Museum I saw the splendid Chinese paintings which Denman Ross had collected. But I was chiefly impressed by the pastels of Jean François Millet, from which Van Gogh got his technical, as well as his imaginative inspiration. It was Millet, and not Van Gogh, who conceived those passionate, rhythmical strokes by which he built up his designs; Van Gogh exaggerated what Millet invented.

I was invited to show my paintings at the Chicago Institute. In Chicago I stayed with a sister of Charles Crane, whose house looked over Lake Michigan. With its border of sparkling snow the lake was beautiful. But Chicago had not then the character it has since attained. There were no lofty skyscrapers. I saw something of the great steel works, wherein the directions were written in half-a-dozen foreign languages; and, by way of contrast, I stayed for a while at Hull House—an American Toynbee Hall, doing admirable work—with Miss Jane Addams. Returning to New York

I made drawings and lithographs, and besides the portrait of Chapman's son, I painted one of a beautiful young girl, and a third of Samuel Untermyer, to whom Berenson had recommended me. This last portrait was a failure; I was ashamed to accept payment for it, but was weak enough to do so. Perhaps because of the effect of the heated rooms, or the strain of constant sittings, I fell ill, and my visit was cut short. I was asked to return to America to do other portraits, but one experience of the life of a professional portraitist was enough. If I went back to America it would be as a free man, to travel whither I wished—to Arizona and to New Mexico, and to mix with men of all kinds.

It was pleasant to be again with my wife and children and to start fresh work. I had a charming letter of welcome from Francis Darwin, showing his love for birds, which endeared him to Hudson.

> 10 *Madingley Road,*
> *Cambridge.*
> *Sunday May* 19—12.

Dear Rothenstein

I am so glad to hear that you are safe at home. I want to come & see you very much. I have just been having a week in Holland during which I only had ½ hr in a picture gallery, isn't that barbarous? But we went to see wild birds and travelled almost straight to the Isle of Texel where we stayed in a funny little town which is so innocent it has no name but Den Burg. On our way there we stayed at Alkmaar for an hour between trains to see the weekly cheese market which appears to be a regular sight. The whole place was strewn with orange coloured cannon balls which were brought up to the public weigh-house (made of a disused brick church); they were carried in a sort of litter by ridiculously clean men in spotless white, & with orange coloured ribbons round their hats. The litters were like the rocker of a rocking horse and were hung to the men's shoulders by big loops of leather; they held out their hands in a queer stiff balancing way & walked with a funny shuffle. They were shuffling in all directions & finally rolling the cheeses in streams down wooden gutters into barges. It was a strange mixture of orange colour & rather ridiculous movement. We saw all manner of rare & beautiful birds and heard the booming of great invisible bitterns hidden in the reeds of a marsh. One of the most beautiful sights is a godwit showing off, coming down to earth in a series of zig zags or rather like a skater changing edge; they showed confused changes of colour, grey white chestnut, and cried all the time *roo-to roo-to* in a wild sort of tune, quicker and quicker, till they came to earth. The birds don't seem to be shot at & are tamer than I expected. We sat by an old thatched pumping wind-mill for a long time watching the birds sleeping on one leg or quietly feeding. The avocets are the most elegant birds I ever saw, white with long black wading legs and delicate black lines marking the outline of their wings. Their beaks turn up instead of down and we could see them delicately stroking the surface of the water as if they were mowing, I believe they gather little beasts from the surface. However it is impossible to describe the effect of these nice creatures.

I do hope you are getting on & will soon be up to work.[1] I hear from F. that you have read Francis's book,[2] I haven't yet but I can see that I shall like it. The dedication to me pleased me extremely, it was of course a great surprise.

Yours ever F. D.

During 1912 I was invited to give the Hermione Lectures on art at Queen's College, Dublin. I found myself in Dublin, for the first time, at an exciting moment, when the great strike, led by Larkin and Connolly, was still unsettled. I was taken to Liberty Hall, where the Countess Markowitz was cooking food for the strikers, and Connolly and others

[1] I had fallen ill in America, and on my return underwent an operation, from which I was now recovering.

[2] *From Religion to Philosophy, a Study in the Origins of Western Speculation*, by Francis Cornford.

were encouraging the men to hold out. Connolly reminded
me of Steinlen and of Gissing; by nature he was gentle and
tender-hearted, but the poverty and ignorance of the people
had stirred him and made him bitter. I was impressed by
Connolly's faith and fairness, though in public he said things
that were not fair, being carried away, he admitted, by his
audience. In this he differed little from most politicians.

Connolly asked me what I thought about the strike.
I knew too little, I told him, of labour conditions. But
I couldn't bear to see all those strong, capable-looking men
lounging about, with their hands in their pockets, day after
day. Were there not things they could do at home, and for
one another? Must they perforce remain idle? Connolly, too,
deplored the waste, but Trade Union rules hinder manual
work during a strike—or perhaps my memory is at fault and
some other reason was given.

I heard from Orpen: '8 South Bolton Gardens. My dear
Rothenstein, Thanks for your kind letter—hope the lectures
went off well—as I'm sure they did. Are you with Larkin?
He's the greatest man in some ways I ever met. I had a grand
fortnight with him at Liberty Hall before he was booked up.
Give my love to Bailey.... Yours, William Orpen.' But
Larkin was not in Dublin; neither was Yeats nor James
Stephens, but A. E. and Lennox Robinson were there and took
charge of me while Bailey, the Land Commissioner with
whom I stayed, was at his office. With Lennox Robinson
I went more than once to the Abbey Theatre and I was
surprised to find how small it was and how small, too, the
audience. After the play I would go round to drink the 'good
red tea' with Miss Sara Allgood and the other players; it was
a pleasure to be with such good, simple, intelligent men and
women. I was happy in Dublin; I liked the small company
of enthusiasts living unpretentiously and vividly, as poets
and artists lived in the eighteenth century, in a small and
homely capital. A. E. was the sage, from whom everyone
sought counsel, and who gave all the wealth of his mind,
making others seem misers beside him.

CHAPTER XXX

RABINDRANATH TAGORE IN LONDON

I HAPPENED, in *The Modern Review*, upon a translation of a story signed Rabindranath Tagore, which charmed me; I wrote to Jorasanko—were other such stories to be had? Some time afterwards came an exercise book containing translations of poems by Rabindranath, made by Ajit Chakravarty, a schoolmaster on the staff at Bolpur. The poems, of a highly mystical character, struck me as being still more remarkable than the story, though but rough translations. Meanwhile I met one of the Kooch Behar family, Promotto Loll Sen, a saintly man, and a Brahmo of course. He brought to our house Dr Brajendranath Seal, then on a visit to London, a philosopher with a brilliant mind and a child-like character. They both wrote to Tagore, urging him to come to London; he would meet, they said, at our house and elsewhere, men after his heart. Then news came that Rabindranath was on his way. I eagerly awaited his visit. At last he arrived, accompanied by two friends, and by his son. As he entered the room he handed me a note-book in which, since I wished to know more of his poetry, he had made some translations during his passage from India. He begged that I would accept them.

That evening I read the poems. Here was poetry of a new order which seemed to me on a level with that of the great mystics. Andrew Bradley, to whom I showed them, agreed: 'It looks as though we have at last a great poet among us again,' he wrote.

I sent word to Yeats, who failed to reply; but when I wrote again he asked me to send him the poems, and when he had read them his enthusiasm equalled mine. He came to London and went carefully through the poems, making here and there a suggestion, but leaving the original little changed.

For a long time Yeats was occupied with Tagore: 'I have been writing lyric poetry in Normandy. I wish I could have got down to you for I find Tagore and you are a great inspiration in my own art. Thank you for asking me,' he said in a letter.

Tagore's dignity and handsome presence, the ease of his manners and his quiet wisdom made a marked impression on all who met him. One of the first persons whom Tagore wanted to know was Stopford Brooke; for Tagore, being a prominent member of the Brahmo Somaj, which was closely allied to Unitarianism, had heard much of him and of Estlin Carpenter. Stopford Brooke asked me to bring Tagore to Manchester Square; 'but tell him', he said, 'that I am not a spiritual man'. I think the dear old man, with his love of beautiful surroundings and of the good things of life, was a little nervous of Tagore's purity and asceticism, as it appeared to him; and when we sat down at the Brookes' generous table, though the talk might be of angels, Stopford must be true to himself. 'You and I', he said to my wife, 'are going to drink champagne.' But how could anyone not love Stopford Brooke, with his delight in nature's sumptuousness? Roses and peonies are hers, and the ripe beauty of women, as well as violets and daisies. It was in the high summer of the year that he gloried, above all in the rich landscape of Italy, among the olives and vines seen against the clear blue of the Carraras or Apennines. 'This world is so beautiful', he said to Tagore, 'and I have seen so little of it; when I go I feel that my spirit will haunt it. No, I do not want to be absorbed into the All before I have had much more of this tiny world.' And Tagore told him how he, too, cared for beauty; how he had written: 'When I go from hence let this be my parting word, that what I have seen is unsurpassable.'

Of course, the two men became great friends. Now

Tagore wanted to meet Hudson, for he had read *Green Mansions*; it was his favourite modern book, he said; and then to the Temple, to a party at the Woods's—for Woods was now Master of the Temple, where Margaret Woods, with her gracious presence and lovely mind, was a centre of attraction.

The young poets came to sit at Tagore's feet; Ezra Pound the most assiduously. Among others whom Tagore met were Shaw, Wells, Galsworthy, Andrew Bradley, Masefield, J. L. Hammond, Ernest Rhys, Fox-Strangways, Sturge Moore, and Robert Bridges. Tagore, for his part, was struck by the breadth of view and the rapidity of thought that he found among his new friends. 'Those who know the English only in India, do not know Englishmen,' he said. 'All you people live, think and talk while a strong, critical light is constantly focussed on you. This creates a high social civilisation. We in India, on the contrary, live secluded among a crowd of relations. Things are done and said within the family circle which would not be tolerated outside; and this keeps our social standard low.'

George Calderon dramatised one of his stories, *The Maharani of Arakan*; the play was acted at the Albert Hall Theatre when it fell to me to introduce Tagore to his first English audience. Meanwhile Tagore was translating some of his own plays, one of which, *The Post Office*, was acted later in Dublin; a beautiful edition of this play was printed by Miss Yeats at the Cuala Press. I most admired *Chitra*, and next to this *The King of the Dark Chamber*, which he read one evening to a number of friends at our Hampstead house. We asked George Moore, among others, to hear Tagore. Moore was curious, but, except for A. E., suspicious of idealists.

My dear Alice Rothenstein,

I owe you many apologies for not having answered your kind letter inviting me to Hampstead to hear some poems by the Indian poet. Yeats tells me they are very wonderful and that he is going to write a preface. I am sure I should enjoy the poems if '*Salve*' were off my mind. But I am writing the last chapters, and there are bits that I find very difficult to arrange, and until all the ...has gone to the printer I am not my own master. I should like to come to see you very much for you are one of the pleasantest talkers I know of, and I'll try to get up to Hampstead Sunday week. Do not forget however that if you happen to be in town you will always be welcome either for lunch or for tea.

Always sincerely yours,
GEORGE MOORE.

I do not think Moore and Tagore ever met; I could not readily imagine them together; nor could Shaw come to hear the play read; he wrote:

10 Adelphi Terrace,
W. C.
18th September, 1912.

My dear Rothenstein,

My own mother (82) has just had a stroke; Charlotte is blue and gasping for life in paroxysms of asthma and bronchitis; and I am rehearsing no less than three plays: therefore my reply to your letter is a hollow laugh. It will be a good solid month before I can fix an hour for lunch again, and I will come with the greatest pleasure.

The Rodin bust is getting devilishly young.

Yours ever,
G. BERNARD SHAW.

But they did meet, though I was away when the Shaws came to dinner. My wife told me that Shaw was rather outrageous, while his wife was all admiration—'Old bluebeard,' said Shaw to mine while he was leaving, 'how many wives has he got, I wonder!' Nearly 20 years later, at a reception given to Tagore by Evelyn Wrench and Yeats-Brown, the two met again, now white headed and white bearded, and sat and talked together, two noble looking elders.

It was pleasant to see homage paid so readily to an Indian;

nothing of the kind had happened before. I was concerned only lest Tagore's saintly looks, and the mystical element in his poetry, should attract the *Schwärmerei* of the sentimentalists who abound in England and America, and who pursue idealists even more hungrily than ideals. Tagore had, indeed, all the qualities to attract such. It was easy to protect him at first, for he enjoyed the society of men whose books he had read but whom he never expected to meet. Then, when the summer came, we escaped to Gloucestershire, where Tagore joined us. It happened that the summer (1912) was one of the rainiest on record. 'A traveller always meets with exceptional conditions,' said Tagore, when I apologised for the cold and rain, and the absence of sun. When kept indoors, he busied himself with translations of more poems and plays.

Fox-Strangways wanted Oxford or Cambridge to give Tagore an honorary degree. Lord Curzon, when consulted, said that there were more distinguished men in India than Tagore. I wondered who they were; and I regretted that England had left it to a foreign country to make the first emphatic acknowledgment of his contribution to literature.

I now proposed to the India Society that they should print, for its members, a selection of Tagore's translations of his own poems. Yeats, when the Committee agreed, generously offered to write an introduction; he had previously gone carefully through the translations, respecting Tagore's expressive English too much to do more than make slight changes here and there. Indeed, Yeats was as keen over the issue of the book of poems as he would have been over a selection of his own lovely verses. He wrote to me:

Sept 7.

Coole Park,
Gort,
Co. Galway.

My dear Rothenstein,

Your letter of August 24 only reached me to-day—sent on from London. I sent the text and book to Tagore yesterday, and I expect my essay back from my typist on Monday. I think I had better send it to you. You will, I think, find it emphatic enough. If you like it you can say so when you send it on to Tagore. In the first little chapter I have given what Indians have said to me about Tagore—their praise of him and their description of his life. That I am anxious about—some fact may be given wrongly, and yet I don't want anything crossed out by Tagore's modesty. I think it might be well if somebody compiled a sort of 'Who's Who' paragraph on Tagore, and put after the Introduction a string of dates, saying when he was born, when his chief works were published. My essay is an impression, I give no facts except those in the quoted conversation.

Yours w. b. yeats.

I will talk over the question you raise when we meet. I am here, have been pike fishing and am tired.

The poems were published by the India Society with the title of *Gitanjali*. They were well received and were favourably reviewed in *The Times Literary Supplement*. Tagore was in America at the time:

508 W. High Street,
Urbana,
Illinois,
U.S.A.
19 Nov. 1912.

My dear Mr Rothenstein,

Your two letters of the same date amply made up for the long delay and eager waiting. They are delightful. I thought I had come to that age when doors to my inner theatre must be closed and no more new admission could be possible. But the impossible has happened and you have made my life larger by your friendship. I feel its truth and its preciousness all the more because it came to me so unexpectedly in a surrounding not familiar to me at all. That I should, while travelling in a foreign land, meet with some experience of life which is not temporary and superficial fills me with wonder and gratitude. It is to me a gift from the divine source and I shall know how to value it.

I am so glad to learn from your letter that my book has been favourably criticised in *The Times Literary Supplement.* I hope the paper has been forwarded to me and I shall see it in a day or two. My happiness is all the more great because I know such appreciations will bring joy to your heart. In fact, I feel that the success of my book is your own success. But for your assurance I never could have dreamt that my translations were worth anything, and up to the last moment I was fearful lest you should be mistaken in your estimation of them and all the pains you have taken over them should be thrown away. I am extremely glad that your choice has been vindicated and you will have the right to take pride in your friend, supported by the best judges in your literature. Remember me kindly to Mrs Rothenstein and give our love to the children.

Ever your affectionate friend,
RABINDRANATH TAGORE.

Since only a limited edition of *Gitanjali* had been printed I wrote to George Macmillan, with a view to his publishing a popular edition of *Gitanjali*, as well as other translations which Tagore had made; Macmillans, after some hesitation, finally published all Tagore's books, to his profit, and their own.

The India Society deemed it fitting to touch on the much debated problem of the New Delhi, for which Lutyens and Herbert Baker were to be the architects. Was it to be European or Indian in character? Together with Rolleston, now secretary of the India Society, I drafted a letter to *The Times*. There was no reason why buildings which were to be occupied—so we then thought—by Englishmen should not be frankly European in plan, and in elevation too; while Indian Princes should employ Indian builders, masons and carvers for their Delhi residences.

Neither Lutyens nor Baker cared, I think, for Hindu art; their sympathies were with the later Moghul builders. Indeed they had visited none of the great Hindu centres, neither Bhuvaneshwar nor Khajurahu. Yet Lutyens's genius for striking effects combined with charm of detail was to serve him well. I asked Lutyens to meet Tagore, when he cracked jokes all the time. It was not easy to convince Tagore that Lutyens was the right man for Delhi.

Before Tagore left for India, Yeats and I arranged a small dinner in his honour. After dinner we asked Tagore to sing *Bande Mataram*, the nationalist song. He hummed the tune but after the first words broke down; he could not remember the rest. Then Yeats began the Irish anthem—and his memory, again, was at fault; and Ernest Rhys could not for the life of him recollect the words of the Welsh national anthem. 'What a crew!' I said, when I too stumbled over *God save the King*. Re-reading some of Hudson's letters I am reminded that previously a public dinner had been given to Tagore, to which many distinguished men and women came. Hudson had written:

40 *St Luke's Road,*
W.
July 13, 1912.

Forgive me my dear Rothenstein for not replying to the card about a dinner to Mr Tagore, for days past I have been so much troubled with palpitations I left letters unanswered. But you know I never dine out now—I can't go to a dinner at the conventional hour and eat & come home at some late time without paying for it heavily. If I could stand being chloroformed I would go to some surgeon & ask him to cut me up in pieces & take out as much as he thought proper, then sew up the remnants, in order to see if that would give me a little more life. But these be idle thoughts. I should have liked to hear Yeats read the Tagore poems; I hope he has got a poet to translate them. Not many of our poets know Hindustani; but these things can be managed another way. For example, Blunt's splendid translations of the Seven Golden Odes of Arabia were not done direct from the originals—he doesn't know Arabic; but he took them from Lady Blunt's literal translations into English and turned them into poetry.

> With love to you all
> Yours ever,
> W. H. HUDSON.

Poor Hudson! he was continually worrying about his health, about his heart especially; but this did not prevent his bicycling up hills as well as down, for he wrote to my wife:

> *Goits Moss Farm,*
> *Nr. Buxton,*
> *Derbyshire.*
> *May 19th.*

Dear Mrs Rothenstein,

Your letter has come on to me in this remote place when a postman with letters arrives on *Thursdays*—that is to-day, but I don't know how long ago you wrote it as it is undated. I've been staying some days at Buxton, then found this desolate spot in a hollow or *cleaugh* as they call it, in the Axe Edge Mountain and I think you would consider it a wretched place to be in—treeless, dark, stony, bitterly cold, always foggy or raining, or both; no cultivation, so that you can't have a vegetable to eat, and of course the house is very very small. I am afraid of hurting my head when I stand up in my bedroom. There is no road leading to the place, only an ancient stony track, and the country is awful to cycle on, as we are about 1500 feet high at this point, though in other parts of the hill it rises to over 1800. Well, much as I like nature and solitude I don't find it very satisfactory and don't think I shall remain very long. The fact is I am here to watch a certain species of bird common in some parts of England, and nowhere nearer to London than the Peak district, so I've come 130 miles just to look at one little bird!

> Yours affectionately,
> W. H. HUDSON.

A helping hand

A man who could cycle 1500 feet up had a heart that would last him for many years, as indeed Hudson's did.

Hudson's books brought him but little. Even as late as 1916, the Ranee of Sarawak told us that, Hudson's wife being seriously ill, he was hard put to it to send her away to the sea-side. A sum of money—£200—was collected among his friends, and, through Edward Garnett, was discreetly placed to Hudson's account, without his ever discovering the secret. Sir Edward Grey was then Foreign Minister; when I wrote to him of Hudson's difficulties, he replied in his own handwriting; a delicate precaution, I thought, on the part of a man so beset as he was.

CHAPTER XXXI

MIGRATION TO GLOUCESTERSHIRE

DURING the summer we spent in Gloucestershire my wife and I, walking one afternoon with Tagore, came upon an old farmhouse overlooking the Golden Valley. The house was in a state of decay; there was no gutter to gather the rain and the walls were soaked with damp. But we saw its great possibilities. My wife, impetuous as usual, said we must rescue the place. We made inquiries; the property belonged to a Miss Driver whose family owned most of the land thereabouts. She was willing to sell the house, with 55 acres, part of which was woodland, for £1300. I borrowed £1000 from my father, wrote out a cheque for £300 (my savings from my American journey) and became the possessor of a tiny estate. Oh the pride with which I first explored each field, and the lovely beech wood, and the house and barn! I was too ignorant to notice the lamentable state of the walls and fences.

Built on the edge of the hill, the house, with its plain stone front and irregular mullioned windows, faced due south, opposite Sapperton and Frampton Mansell. An orchard fell away from it steeply, and below were fields and a fringe of beech wood running down to a canal, a proud engineering feat of the 18th century, and nearby was a tunnel which ran for four miles under Sapperton, hereabouts out of repair, through which barges could no longer pass. Nature had now taken possession, and everywhere weeds and rushes grew, and there were wild water-lilies, and kingfishers nested along the banks. Here and there a lock still held enough water, in which the children could bathe and fish.

There were too many locks to be tended. Thus far and no further; man can say nay to nature, but he must not let go of that which he makes; so long as he watches over his handiwork nature respects it. At Chalford, two miles away, the canal was in use again, and boats were built between Chalford and Stroud. The old mills thereabouts with the millers' houses attached put me in mind of those near Bradford. There were many such at Chalford; and between Stroud and Painswick, and at Longdon, where the Playnes lived, was an 18th-century mansion, with a mill in the park, telling of past prosperity.

First our house must be made habitable, so I consulted my friend Alfred Powell. No one knew better than he how to repair an old building; hence my disappointment when he refused his help—I had told him that the local builder advised me that £50 would make the place decent. During the next two years I spent sixty times that sum! It was the middle of the winter when the house was ready for occupation. But outbuildings and walls had still to be put in repair: there was enough work to occupy a waller for a year.[1] Since Giverny I had painted no winter landscape, and I now found myself so happy I could not think of returning to London. Village life was new to me. The old Tolstoian mood returned, with more cogency. Country life, too, would be good for the children. My wife required some persuasion at first, but she retained some of the rooms of our London house and felt we were not altogether cut off from Town. From Ernest Gimson and the Barnsleys, now our neighbours, we got clean new furniture, a delight to the eye, and from Gimson beautiful fire-irons and sconces. I was in a new world and each day seemed happier and fuller than the last. The tawny winter landscape, the bare trees, suit the English scene better than her too lush, too green summer dress. Then came the early spring, covering the woods with a rosy blush, interspersed with the bright tender green, as the buds unfold themselves. But how fleeting were these effects, fleeting too

[1] The rate of pay for a waller was then only 4*d.* an hour.

the blossom of the cherry, the plum, the pear and the apple, as they burst into lyrical life; each season I was too overwhelmed by their beauty to collect myself, as I should have done. It was during, as it were, the masculine seasons of winter and high summer that I could best use my resources. In the changing drama of the year I found constant inspiration. In London, when no model came, I would feel at a loss; not so in the country, and the Cotswold buildings are especially paintable. Stone buildings always move me—austere in gray weather, pale, livid even, against a stormy sky, they are warm and sparkling in the sunlight. In our house and outbuildings and in a great wych-elm in a field below, I found subjects to my hand. Just before the war we threw a wing betwixt the house and a barn adjoining. I would have no builder, but entrusted the work to the village stone-masons: my friend Norman Jewson acted as architect. The Oakridge masons were noted throughout the countryside, but naturally this job at home was too good a thing to be quickly finished. Idealism has to be paid for. I certainly paid for mine, but I gained an experience in building I had otherwise missed. A ruined cottage on our land and some stones we quarried gave us superb coigns. The new floors must, of course, be of English oak, while to replace rotten beams in the barn roof we cut down oaks in our own little wood, our horse and pony dragging them out with chains. I found it exciting and fruitful work to extend the life of a fine building. For this I wanted to use local labour only. We had an excellent cabinet-maker, carpenters and a blacksmith in the parish, but they were all employed by Gimson, and Gimson, I discovered, was averse to their doing private work. Now I admired Gimson; no one designed or produced better furniture. Profit was of little consequence to him; his integrity was indisputable. No matter at what cost of time, everything that came from his workshops must be of the finest possible workmanship. But the world is suspicious of men whose motives are higher than those of their neighbours. Gimson, a disciple of Morris, had chosen this corner of England in which to revive the traditional crafts which still linger there; yet in effect, I said to myself, he withdraws the capable village blacksmiths and carpenters from local occupations to make furniture and iron work for wealthy men living in distant towns. Either I must get the things I needed made at his workshops, or I must go farther afield for men to make cupboards, oak doors, casements and hinges. This made me feel a little sore, for being a convert I was eager to be orthodox; and who, I asked, better fitted to provide what was needed, than our own villagers? Nevertheless we got many pieces from Gimson, among others a cupboard, painted by Alfred Powell, with pictures of our house and the local landscape and flora and fauna, a delight to our children; I found now how much more amusing it is to have things made for one's immediate needs than to buy things in antique shops. I owe a debt to Gimson, and to the Barnsleys, inasmuch as I learnt from them of the partnership that should exist between patron and craftsman. Yet there were many who found them somewhat too doctrinaire. I had urged Arthur Benson to use Gimson for work he needed at Magdalene College.

In a letter from Benson I heard that nothing came of the proposal:

'I have had to part company with Gimson, he wouldn't design me what I wanted, only what he thought it right of me to want.

'Yet I recognise exactly what you say about Gimson. If I did not feel so unsatisfactory already, I should have been feeling wicked ever since my correspondence with Gimson— and he has gone on cracking the whip till the last, though he has really treated me *abominably*, and I shall never advise anyone to apply to him for any design or advice, or consult him in any way. He wouldn't do what I asked him to do, and he had every right to refuse; but he didn't tell me he wouldn't till we had wasted precious months and infinite correspondence!'

I know that Gimson lived according to his conscience,

that he was a man of vision and high achievement. The usurpation by the machine of that which he deemed was man's province distressed him, as it had angered Ruskin and Morris, and he wished to preserve in one corner of England at least, the old handicrafts. He was planning to get others of his way of thinking to join him and the Barnsleys in Gloucestershire, when he was struck down by untimely illness which ended his life. Afraid lest his scrupulous standards should be commercialised after his death, he left directions that his workshops should be disbanded. His foreman, Peter Waales, set up a workshop at Chalford where he continued Gimson's tradition of design and fine workmanship. Daneway House, a noble Tudor manor, leased to Gimson by Lord Bathurst, in which he exhibited his furniture, was later occupied by Sir Emery Walker. Gimson would have desired no more fitting tenant.

Our house, being a farmhouse, differed in no wise from other farmhouses, suggesting nothing of the class separateness that shrubbery and drive, high garden walls and greenhouses, give to a house. Since I carried easel and canvas about the fields, and painted in all weathers, I felt near to others who worked in the fields. There were now some seventy acres attached to the farm—we had horses, cows and a pig. I would fetch a horse from the field, bridle and saddle him, and ride, my painting things on my back, to the more distant places where I worked. But most of my subjects I found nearby, and was thus able to use fresh canvases according to the time of day, and I could paint on the same canvas year after year, to its advantage, I found. During the war, pressure was put upon farmers to plough up pasture and to sow corn; I was no farmer, and the breaking up of permanent pasture, and the work attendant on drilling, hoeing and harvesting needed more hands and more attention than I could provide when all who were fit were in France. I joined in weeding and hoeing, in haymaking, in picking up stones, in planting potatoes, and, later in the year, in binding and propping up sheaves to dry, in carting them to the rickyard, and in threshing operations. It was a good life, and the physical work was exhilarating and satisfying, and I gained knowledge thereby that I value. I have already mentioned my friendship with Sidney and Ernest Barnsley. Sidney made his beautiful furniture with his own hands; he employed no assistants. Ernest Barnsley was the least doctrinaire among the craftsmen-architects. In appearance and manner he was like a bluff farmer. For this reason, maybe, he appealed to a country neighbour, Claud Biddulph, who had lately received from his father his Rodmarton estate, and he asked Barnsley to build him a small residence there. During the eight years we lived at Oakridge, we watched this house growing until it finally stood, stately, strong and bold, a worthy descendent of the noble family of Gloucestershire manors.

Now Claud Biddulph and his wife did what I would that others tried to do. From the beginning they employed the village blacksmith, carpenters and masons for all the work in hand. Stone was quarried and dressed, trees felled and adzed, while iron work, window frames, door-hinges, garden gates, fire-irons—all these were given over to the Rodmarton smithy. So for years an English village carried out all that was needed for building a great country-house, and what so many of us preached was here quietly and efficiently done. The result is a triumph of modern craftsmanship. Furniture came from the carpenter's shop, and 'appliqué' tapestries, depicting the village with its church and barns and cottages, the villagers at their tasks, the local hunt—were made by the women of the village. A chapel was added, wherein the hangings and embroideries, designed by Mrs Biddulph, were likewise carried out by the village dames. I have seen nothing so heartening done in England, for here is proof positive that given the opportunity, the old skill and poetry still live under the crust of neglect which covers them. It is true that, but for the pioneer work of Ernest Gimson, of Ernest and Sidney Barnsley and of Alfred Powell, the Biddulphs would not have carried their ideas through so perfectly. But patient encouragement, and the training which one task after another gave to the village craftsmen proved their worth. It is not museums and picture galleries, but this practical encouragement, and the training that active work gives, that could bring back prosperity and skill to our villages.

Some of my friends believed I would soon tire of the country; others knew better, among them Conrad and the Michael Fields. Conrad wrote, August 2nd, 1913:

Dearest Will.

I was glad to see your handwriting—that next best thing to your bodily presence. It found me in bed—the wearisome gout again, but I am out of bed now, a little shaken but not much worse for this bout—which was mild. I understand you perfectly; and I am glad to hear you have found peace and inspiration; I am much happier thinking of you *there* than thinking of you in London; and as I think of you daily (without exaggeration) you understand it makes a considerable difference to me to know that you are away from too many people, too many voices—too many interests, which great as they may be are foreign to the inherent greatness of your art which lives in you.

Yes my dear fellow—we ought to see each other more often; yet, as you know, I have such long periods of sterility (from one reason or another) that I can never spare any time for the needs of my heart. There are moments when I positively miss you—who understand me so well. But I haven't even the time to indulge in regrets. Everything seems to grow so difficult! Every moment is given to the task. I am tired my dear Will—and I daren't own it to myself or I would stop, which I mustn't do. It is as if the game wasn't worth the candle, already more than half burnt down, while necessity drives one to save every gleam of the flickering light. But enough of this.

Send me the address of Mr Tagore. Directly I've finished this novel I am fighting with now I shall drop him a line—if

I may proceed so unceremoniously. There are 30,000 words at least to write and I can't come to grips with the thing. No combination of words seems worth putting down on paper. I assure you that just now I am not fit to see anybody but the veriest intimates—such as you for instance—if you were near.

Yours with unalterable affection,

J. CONRAD.

How little men realise, when they read work printed, or see it framed, its cost to the author!

Then Michael Field—Henry, Field called herself, wrote to my wife of our days at Far Oakridge:

1, *The Paragon,*
Richmond,
Surrey.
May 16*th,* 1913

We have heard from Far Oak Ridge—*an address of pure Fairy-land,* ridiculously impossible in a country of the ordinary world!—That 'Far'! We are beyond the end of the World! 'Oak'—we are with the Dryads—'Ridge' with the Oreads of the mountains—'Far Oak Ridge' we are, as I say, deep in Fairyland. H. D. will try to see us for some moments of his little run to town next week. So we shall look to seeing our cornfield Noli—no longer little golden nurse to her babes—the week after. We will spend days and hours. How we envy you that farmhouse beyond the setting sun, where you can all live out the simple impulse of life! Your letters are so like you, Goldilocks Noli, that no pen has ever better imitated red lips, nor tart laughing voice better.

Alas, my trouble is returning and now I have to learn to bear it better than I did—with sweet resignation—not the sour kind. But dropsy is a loathed foe, and the spirit flares against it, till gentleness is given by grace and the opportunity of grace, which perhaps for me is just now. Love to that circle of bright coloured happiness and health (I hope) at *Oak Hill* this time.

> Your friend,
> HENRY.

But alas! 'Henry' was now mortally ill, and before the year ended her bright flame was extinguished. Before this Michael begged for a drawing of her beloved fellow. Henry wrote from her bed.

> 1, *The Paragon*,
> *Richmond*,
> *Surrey*.
> *June 8th*, 1913.

Dear Heavenly Dog,

I trust you got your palette, 'dipped in heavenly hues' and your most precious sheets of paper quite safely; they were sent off promptly. More and more we love your lyric of my suffering self. Ricketts found it a 'lovely drawing' and was struck by the general likeness to me, and by the particular truth of mouth, nose and spring of the brow. The frame is being made for it. Though it is the linear music of my trial, I still look now and then with fascination at my face as it will appeal at the last judgment—at those eyes of mine you have filled with the extensiveness of pain.

Dear H. Dog—I am ashamed we have not, till now, sent you the inscribed copy of *Mystic Trees*. It comes to you with this; and our united gratitude is the perfume in which it is packed.

I have had a letter from Eric Gill,[1] wondering that we all find his work has an Eastern element in it—a nice letter— an artist's letter.

May the coming June week bring you inspired and glorified hours!

> Your Friend,
> HENRY.

---

[1] I showed Michael Field a little coloured cast of a Madonna and Child and they wrote to Gill for a similar one.

Prayers for Michael Field

I had sent a Gimson table for our friends; in acknowledging it Michael sent us the sad tidings:

1, *The Paragon,*
Richmond,
December, 1913

Beloved Heavenly Dog and Noli.

Speed the little table on its way—it will be welcomed.—Only perhaps you have heard, ere this, it will not pause at the sun room for the welcome of her eyes. My beloved and I parted on Saturday morning—So still she lay beside me and the mirror yielded no breath. For nearly an hour I kept her hand in mine—incredulous—till a doctor came and said in truth that a very gentle spirit had passed away. But in unclouded consciousness she had received the Last Sacraments, and been anointed—with clear ringing voice she said the last words the priest asked of her—among the last things she said were '*Better*' and 'Not just yet, Master', with so sweet a smile, when I said for her one of the commendatory prayers. Requiem Mass at our Catholic Church, Richmond, Thursday 11. Interment at Mortlake 12. You will be praying for us. Ask Billy to pray! 80 school children at Nazareth House have been praying for her.

Our love,
MICHAEL.

Michael without Field seemed unnatural; but they were not long to be parted. Michael confided to me a secret she had kept until now—that she was stricken with the same malady. Before another year passed her spirit rejoined that of her beloved partner. I have never known pain borne so blithely as by these bright-souled poets. But it is their lives I remember, a duo of ecstasy over the beauty of the world, which later became one of adoration.

CHAPTER XXXII

TAGORE AND THE NOBEL PRIZE

DURING the summer of 1913 came the news of the award of the Nobel Prize to Rabindranath on account of *Gitanjali*. The poet wrote from Shantiniketan: 18 Nov. 1913.

'The very first moment I received the message of the great honour conferred on me by the award of the Nobel prize my heart turned towards you with love and gratitude. I felt certain that of all my friends none would be more glad at this news than you. Honour's crown of honour is to know that it will rejoice the hearts of those whom we hold the most dear. But, all the same, it is a very great trial for me. The perfect whirlwind of public excitement it has given rise to is frightful. It is almost as bad as tying a tin can at a dog's tail making it impossible for him to move without creating noise and collecting crowds all along. I am being smothered with telegrams and letters for the last few days and the people who never had any friendly feelings towards me nor ever read a line of my works are loudest in their protestations of joy. I cannot tell you how tired I am of all this shouting, the stupendous amount of its unreality being something appalling. Really these people honour the honour in me and not myself.'

Tagore had the courage, at a ceremony given in his honour, to comment on the adulation which followed, not on his work, but on his success in Europe.

He was not often to escape the tumult and peace was to

be his but at rare moments. Henceforward Tagore was to become a world-figure.

But great fame is a perilous thing, because it affects not indeed the whole man, but a part of him, and is apt to prove a tyrannous waster of time. Tagore, who had hitherto lived quietly in Bengal, devoting himself to poetry and to his school, would now grow restless. As a man longs for wine or tobacco, so Tagore could not resist the sympathy shown to a great idealist. He wanted to heal the wounds of the world. But a poet, shutting himself away from men to concentrate on his art, most helps his fellows; to leave his study is to run great risks. No man respected truth, strength of character, single-mindedness and selflessness more than Tagore; of these qualities he had his full share. But he got involved in contradictions. Too much flattery is as bad for a Commoner as for a King. Firm and frank advice was taken in good part by Tagore, but he could not always resist the sweet syrup offered him by injudicious worshippers.

Lowes Dickinson, who had lately been elected to the first Kahn Fellowship, visited India on his way to China and Japan. He had, in fact, felt depressed in India; he was happier in China and Japan. After reading Dickinson's report of his travels, Tagore wrote:

'Lowes Dickinson's Essay on The Civilisations of India, China and Japan has made me feel sad. Not only he is entirely out of sympathy with India, but has tried to make out that there is something inherent in an Englishman which makes him incapable of appreciating India—and to him India by her very nature will be a source of eternal irritation. Of all countries in the world India is the East for him—that is to say an abstraction. Possibly he is right in his observations—but then it is a hopeless misery for India till the end of this chapter of her history and it is utterly bad for those who have come merely to govern her from across the sea. I only hope Dickinson is not right and that it was heat and hurry and dyspepsia that blotted out the human India from his sight leading him into the blank of a monotonous mist of classification.'

I agreed with Rabindranath; Dickinson was hardly fair to India, not on account of any prejudice, but because he was not at his ease there.

Just before the war I heard again from Rabindranath, who was now where he always wished to be—away from the crowd, sitting quietly, as he writes, under Father Himalaya. He was always at his happiest thus, and his letters show it.

> *Ramgarh,*
> *Kumaon Hills,*
> *June 2. 1914.*

My dear Friend,

Your letter gave me great joy, because it is your letter and because I got it when I had regained my peace of mind under the kindly care of the Father Himalaya. I have been wishing every day since I came here that you were here. This is just the place in the world for you. My house here will wait for you even if it is in vain. I cannot imagine that you will never visit Shantiniketan and this little nest of ours among the hills. It seems perfectly absurd to think that you have never seen Shilida and never lived in boats with us in the lonely sandbanks of the Padma. But, my friend, if you fail to come to share with us this feast of colour and light and love you will have to pay for it in your next birth. I do not know what your punishment will be—possibly you will have the heart of a Yogi and yet be born again and again in London. I know you and your own atmosphere—I have seen you alone and in crowds, I have sat with you at your dinner table and sat to you in your studio, I have walked with you in the unimaginable shady lanes of Hampstead and in the solitude of your Gloucestershire forest, I have drunk your words sparkling with wit and wisdom and I have shared with you the silence of the sunset sky in that beautiful terrace at Oakhill Park, but I came to you like an apparition blurred and out of focus—at best like a statue, somewhat unreal, because bereft of all atmosphere. Do you not think it is unfair to me and that you should bring me out of the casket where my fate carefully placed me while sending me oversea—that you should hold me in the light turning me round to have a fair valuation of my personality?

Very affectionately yours,

RABINDRANATH TAGORE.

I too was living far from the crowd, finding constant inspiration in the changing scene under the open sky.

There was a jest in Paris in my student days—he gave up art and took to landscape painting. Yet for pure pleasure, there is nothing to equal painting out of doors. There is the excitement which the changes from sunlight to shadow give to the scene; or maybe the strange elation that comes when one is fused, as it were, with the object of one's desire, and a tree, a barn, a hillside, seems to be possessed with a shining life whose rays penetrate the soul, stirring one's bowels in an ecstatic love—is it the love of God? Sometimes, while painting a tree, I would feel its youth or its age—the firm round bole and slim branches of a young tree, or the thick trunk, creased and lined and twisted with the years, while the worn attachments of its heavy limbs were like the pitiful armpits of an aged man. And a tree seemed like a sentient being, wise, strong and resolute. Strong, too, are the stone barns, standing square to the world, roofed with stone, with their noble coigns and jambs, and the great timbers across the lintel. I would imagine, while painting them, the old-time villagers placing stone upon stone with careful skill; so every stone had its own shape and character, and to paint carelessly seemed a sin. Moreover, there is magic in correctness; for on each foot of surface there lies a lovely pattern; each tile on a roof, each stone in a wall has a beautiful and vigorous life, which conscience urges one to treat with respect. Too often, through weakening concentration, I have failed to listen to the still, small voice, and have cheated my work of its due. To achieve something between dry copying of detail, and the excitement of the glowing breadth of the whole, patience combined with swift daring is needed; as when on horseback, one gives free rein while retaining control. This disciplined swiftness has nothing in common with a lazy timidity which wears the look of 'finish'. I believe all painters instinctively desire finish; but beginning with care, they have to give life, and an ardent life, to the work of their hands, and so must often undo what was carefully begun. To the minutest conceivable matter the gods have given colour and form, radiance, detail, pattern, energy, swiftness, poise, rhythm, strength and delicacy; the artist strives and fails, but his aim at least is godlike, and while at his task there pass through him sparks and currents of the Divine; and when, turning his eyes away, he puts down his brushes, he becomes even less than a man; a sorry amateur, whose virtue has gone from him, until he takes up his palette, to become an instrument through which the spirit again, for a spell, possesses him.

CHAPTER XXXIII
EARLY DAYS OF THE WAR

I LEARNED through being with my village neighbours how little they know of the obstacles our fallibility sets in our paths. Some one would tell a story and say, 'Now, is that just?' they believed in the possibility of perfect justice; that there is only rough justice in the world they could not understand, though towards one another they were far from just, and altruism was not common among them. The school had no water supply and eleven houses in the village were without water. When a ram and a cistern were to be provided for the village—'Why should us as has water pay for them as hasn't?' was the usual reply to an appeal for a small subscription towards the cost. Alas, centuries of hardship have made it necessary for the peasant and the small farmer to be calculating, shrewd, suspicious and economical to the point of meanness. This meanness laid a load on my spirits; it was this alone that made me regret the town. Yet I knew that only through sustained shrewdness could a farmer live; that the labourer's hire was unworthy of his labour. Why, our tenant-farmer's man with a wife and child to keep was getting no more than 11s. weekly. When he came to us, I gave him 18s., under promise he should tell no one. I could do nothing right, my man could do nothing wrong, about the farm; and the freaks of the weather, the habits of beasts and birds—the ways of hedger, thatcher, mason, rickbuilder were all known to Parker; yet as a farm labourer, he stood lowest in the social scale. The skill and knowledge shown by my village neighbours, the wallers, the tilers, the masons, the carpenters were a source of endless wonder and interest. And what things the old men could still do! Phelps, over 80, when the wood, long neglected, needed thinning out, himself felled the trees. Henry Bishop, another octogenarian, succeeded him; Sam Gardiner, one of the best of the masons, was well over 70, Eli the thatcher, George Hunt the tiler, George Halliday the waller, were close on the seventies. I made drawings of these veterans, and was looking forward to painting them. Then came the shock of the war. What its effect would be, no one in the village knew; men still went on working. But at Stroud and Cirencester officers in khaki bustled about, examining horses, buying provender, recruiting men. Across the valley we heard trains passing all night; it was said that the bridges and tunnels were all guarded, and rumours of German spies, of station-masters being shot, of German defeat at the hands of the Belgians were brought us by the vicar. We knew from the papers that the expeditionary force had been safely landed in France, but for many days we heard nothing more. We could not yet grasp the power of the German armies which the French and our small expeditionary force had to face. I recollect reading French's first long dispatch aloud to the men busy about the building. Recruiting became urgent, some of our young men left and were lost to us. But others came along, pleading for work. Was work to go on, or should it stop? No one knew; then came the word 'business as usual'. It was hard to deny men who wanted work, but was I likely to earn? Painters would not be wanted. What was to be done? I bethought me of my Rembrandt and my Daumier drawings. I consulted Holmes—my Rembrandts were worth £200 each. It was hard to part with these. But human life is more important than property; and it seemed wonderful to me that a few lucky purchases could now enable me to keep 20 men in active work. Soon pressure was put on the young, and one by one men left the village for the training camps. Then rumours began to reach us—our house dominated the valley: we had laid down concrete floors, to be used for gun emplacements.

I joined others in drilling at Bisley, a village near by; a lady with whom we had been friendly spread fantastic stories. Lord Beauchamp, the Lord Lieutenant, sent a curt message, threatening to disband the volunteers unless the charges against us were withdrawn. Oakridge stood gallantly by us, and the rumours died down. Month by month came news of losses of friends and of the sons of friends, of victories and defeats. Those who could not enlist, who were over military age, or else were unfit, now offered their services. I was called up to London, to the Ministry of Information, to join with others in making lithographs, to show what England was doing in the war.

I need not dwell upon the emotions and anxieties, common to us all, of those first weeks of the war. No one has set these down better than Wells in *Mr Britling Sees It Through*.

I had written to Raleigh, among others, of my grief at the loss of so many brilliant young men. He replied:

> *The Hangings,*
> *Ferry Hinksey,*
> *Near Oxford.*
> *14th Nov.* 1914.

My dear Rothenstein,

We shall be delighted if you will come along, as you say. Meantime, cheer up and don't read horrors. What people forget is that with death all round you all the values change —not wholly for the worse. Hilary's post-cards which had a certain sense of strain in them while the Leicesters were being held back, are now wholly gay—from the trenches, in water, with 'coffee pots' dropping all around.

The papers live in an atmosphere of pathos and horrors— indeed pay heavily to thicken it. It's a miasma exactly like an elderly celibate's dreams of adultery. Hilary says that the only thing that he's sorry for is that he hasn't yet killed a German. He saw an old woman shot by them (by brutal carelessness, I presume) behind his trench. Since when he's been all right. He's clear sighted and high-hearted—he may be broken, but he can't be twisted.

Damn the Germans, anyhow. It's funny that their slight overvaluing of their own importance to the world should cost all these millions of lives to correct. I am waiting for the German papers to begin to say that, after all, there's something in the English, and perhaps they had better be spoken of respectfully. Yes, I think they will.

Yours ever,

W. A. RALEIGH.

Raleigh's courage was striking, for both his sons were away fighting—one in the Navy, the other in the Army, and both returned.

During 1915 I went to Dorset to paint a portrait of Ernest Debenham, a gift from the staff of Debenham and Freebody on his fiftieth birthday. He had recently bought a large estate, and was full of projects for the improvement of his villages, and of new methods of farming which startled the conservative natives. A young architect, Macdonald Gill, Eric Gill's brother, was transforming old and building new cottages. I began my portrait in a room on the ground floor of Morton House, where I found that the sunlight, reflected into the room and on to the face of my sitter, created difficulties which, with more forethought, I should have avoided.

I went more than once to visit Thomas Hardy and his wife, and made several drawings of Hardy, slight ones merely, for, alas, he was getting on in years and might be tired with long sitting. Hardy, modest and self-effacing as usual, commanded all one's affection. He was pleased at my praise of his drawings in the *Wessex Poems*, and went upstairs and brought down the originals, together with some of his old sketch books, full of touching little drawings of buildings and architectural details. There were big trees round his house, and I remembered he had told me that he had planted these himself, and how they began to sigh directly the roots touched the soil. I drew too some of the noble Dorset barns, with their roofs closely thatched as though with mole-skin.

During the early years of the war I made drawings of

Colonel Repington, Sir Ian Hamilton and Lord Haldane. One morning, at Queen Anne's Gate, I found Lord Haldane somewhat depressed. He was used to abusive letters, he said, but to-day had come a letter threatening his life. How shameful, I thought; but while discussing the dress in which he should be drawn, by the time we had settled on a Scottish Chancellor's robes and cap, and the Order of the Thistle, his usual genial mood had returned. Although, when politicians sit I am careful not to refer to politics, I usually find they will speak on various matters. On this occasion Lord Haldane gave a dramatic account of his visit to Germany and of his interviews with the Kaiser and with Von Tirpitz. Like Mr Balfour, Lord Haldane was interested in the theory of aesthetics. He was surprised at my ignorance and at a painter's indifference to the subject. Lord Balfour, when later I made his acquaintance, was curious about the philosophical basis of taste; he doubted whether there was any fixed standard by which a work of art could be judged. I fell, as did most people, completely under Lord Balfour's charm. He was said to be selfish; I thought him singularly gracious, attentive to the opinion of others, a man who gave himself unreservedly in discussion.

Besides Lord Haldane, I drew Lord Bryce and the Duke of Devonshire. During the war Devonshire House was given over to the Red Cross while the Duke lived in a corner of the building. He took me all over the great house, so simple outside, so splendid within. I was to see it again but once, before it was destroyed for ever. How we all regretted the disappearance of that long wall, with its great gates through which the court-yard and plain front of the house could be seen. The destruction of this historic house portended a change, which made one uneasy; and there was the actual architectural loss. The modesty of the Georgian houses was everywhere being replaced by pretentious façades. Ever since the once-homely Bird-Cage Walk was 'Potsdamised', one felt that something alien to the English spirit was being forced upon London. Would that

Kipling had protested against its vainglory, so alien to the Queen's character! The rebuilding of Regent Street was not yet thought of; the view looking up Lower Regent Street from the steps below the Duke of York's Column, the United Services Club and the Athenaeum buildings on either hand, always appeared to me one of the finest sights in London. Now Regent Street, and most of Lower Regent Street, have gone. Lincoln's Inn and the Temple remain. James Bone lived in the Temple, so did Arthur Fox-Strangways, and Sir James Frazer, whose portrait I drew in his pleasant rooms there. Modest as he is learned, Sir James Frazer would none the less open out; he was now engaged on the Old Testament, an even richer book from his humanistic point of view, he said, than the New Testament, fuller of folklore, of history, of wisdom, than any other work that has come down to us. Shy and silent as Sir James could be in society, I was to find Lord Rayleigh a still more silent man. Perhaps he thought a mere artist could understand nothing of the things that matter; perhaps, like Lord Kelvin, he was little interested in intellectual matters outside the scientific field.

CHAPTER XXXIV

LETTERS FROM THE FRONT

ALL the time one tried to figure to oneself what life was like at the mysterious front. Letters told little, of course, for the censorship was strict. But of all my friends, it was Frederic Manning who gave me the most poignant account of his life in France. Manning was offered a commission, but he insisted that he had none of the qualities required by an officer, and he enlisted as a private. It was difficult to realise Manning, with his fastidious tastes and habits, living with Tommies in the trenches. Fifteen years later his experiences were to be crystallised in a great book, *Her Privates We*; its character was now foreshadowed in his letters, four of which I here reproduce. The first came from Bush Camp, Pembroke Dock, and deals with his first experiences as a private in training:

> 19022 Pte. Manning. E. Coy.
> 3rd K.S.L.I.
> *Bush Camp,*
> *Pembroke Dock.*
> 26. XII. 1915.

My dear Rothenstein,

The greater part of the camp are now recovering from a three days' saturnalia, which culminated last night in something like a gladiatorial show. When I first came here I told everyone that I was a teetotaller, simply as a measure of self-protection, because this life is so rough and hard, that it is easy to find an excuse for drinking, simply as a way of escape from the pressing and imperious necessities of it. I am heartily glad I did. No one bothers me to drink with them, and both the N.C.O's. and men seem to like me, because I can go out with them and let them go as they please, without either joining in their orgiastic rites, or seeming an outsider to them. That is only one of the things which makes me glad I came. These men are like children. When drunk their acquired character is all dissolved away, and they are simply traversed by their emotion. A mixture of discipline and drunkenness is funny enough: it exemplifies Bergson's theory of the comic, the disparity between the ideal and the reality: but perhaps the addition of piety to the other two brings it too close to tears. The orderly sergeants were both drunk, one of them put his fist thro' a pane of glass, cut an artery, and came in covered with bright blood. We stopped the bleeding, and in return for this kindness he threatened to lock up our corporal who came in two minutes late, excusable enough on Xmas Day. Then the corporal went mad and wanted to fight him. I was the first person to interfere, and then with some more stalwart men held our corporal until the 'orderly sergeant' got away. There were other minor fights and squabbles, but the sober section of us didn't care so long as our corporal, who is really a splendid fellow, didn't get into trouble and lose his stripes. Mid-night brought quietness. Well, this training develops the brute in us, but at the same time there is a curious inward reaction from the brute: just as the middle ages brought forth the ideal of Galahad as a reaction from the reality of this life. These people have the primitive passions, and broad simplicity of an earlier age: 'we be sinful men' they say, and don't know how close that spirit is to the true heart of religion. I suppose the type is only another instance of my 'double-minded man'.

Then came two letters from France.

19022 Pte. Manning. Hdqrs.
7th K.S.L.I.
B.E.F.

In one of your letters to me you said how strongly you wished to paint these young men in khaki. I wish you were here to paint them as they come in from the trenches, weary, splashed with grey clay, in their steel helmets that are like Chinese hats and the colour of verdegris. These Shropshire lads, too, have bright blue eyes, and a high, clear colour in their cheeks, relieving the grey and green and tawny of their uniform, telling clearly against these neutral or degraded tints, and yet without violence. The weariness of those faces, and the almost animal patience expressed on them, would fascinate you as it has fascinated me. After a night's rest, it goes; and an animal gaiety replaces it. When we are not grey with mud, we are as white as millers with dust. Or you could paint a platoon or company of us in one of these huge French barns, which are so Gothic and episcopal in their architecture. I wonder if Gothic architecture began with a barn. It is just one of those features which succeeding ages do not elaborate: those curved beams for instance.

I have been out a month now, and came straight to the hottest part of the line; now we are quieter. We had a bit of a 'strafe' last night but I slept right through it. Debussy or Walter Rummel might compose music from the guns, full of overtones blending into each other. One hears a big gun; it is not simply an explosion in a single note, it comes shattering through the air with a roll of notes, and then there is the 'wind music' of a shell ending miles away in a dull and muffled thud; the only drum note in the whole. I forgot Archibald. Every bomb has its own note, and there's something curiously shrill about a Mills's hand grenade.

Does all this bore you? But, as a matter of fact, I can't sort out and analyse my experiences yet—they're too immediate—tedium, and terror, then a kind of intoxication—one can only put the bare heads—we really deal not with the experience itself but with the traces of the experience.

Four men and a dog

And again, later:

> 19022 Pte. Manning. H.Q. Coy.
> *Signals Section.*
> *7th K.S.L.I.*
> 31. X. 1916.

My dear Will,

You will make me bankrupt of thanks. At present we are four men and a dog in a dug-out—the dug-out being the reconstructed cellar of a shattered house: the dog is suffering from a slight shrapnel wound and shell-shock, and the men are very grateful for a cigarette—yours, in this case. The weather is horribly wet, and there is a great deal of shelling. I am acting as a relay runner between the trenches and Brigade. At first I took up my quarters in a comfortable dry barn, until Fritz began dropping shrapnel and high explosive round it. I stood it all night, some very close, and then migrated to this damp but healthier refuge, during the first lull. It is not pleasant to hear a whole iron foundry being hurled thro' the air. I stand it better when I have something to do.

I can't tell you how much I look forward to seeing you at Stroud, when the tempest and the whirlwind have passed, and there is time for the still small voice to make itself heard; and yet, curiously enough, even here the mind is free. We become more or less indifferent to what is going on about us, and to consider it all as tho' we were, in a sense, only spectators of an incredible madness: this, even while the same madness infects one's own blood. I am horribly dirty, and there is a smear of wet clay on the top of the page, but these are merely the inherent incidents of our life, and you will forgive them. Dirt, misery, and madness are the realities of war. We are cooking our dinner now over an improvised brazier, and the damp wood has filled the dug-out with smoke that stings the eyes. There's one thing that matters in war time, I am generally on duty from 12 midnight until six a.m. and it means a couple of long walks, on a road which is continually shelled. We are supposed to go in pairs but so far I have always gone alone, and it is a curious sensation. I am not ashamed to say that I have felt fear walking beside me like a live thing: the torn and flooded road, the wreckage, mere bones of what were living houses, and I have always felt the character or personality of a house; absolute peace of the landscape and indifferent stars, then the ear catches the purr of a big shell, it changes from a purr to a whine and then detonates on concussion. Another comes, then a third. After that a short space of quiet. Sometimes, as I have said, I feel fear, but usually with the fear is mingled indifference which is not pious enough to be termed resignation.

1. XI. 1916.

We have been relieved, but we don't get much rest from the noises of the guns. I must try to sleep through it. Good night, my dear Will: thank you for your kindness, and my love to you all.

Yours always affectly

FRED.

19022 Pte. Manning. H.Q. Coy.
Signals Section.
7th K.S.L.I.
10. XI. 1916.

My very dear Will,

I have to thank you for cigarettes, a most interesting letter and the delightful tracing of Max's caricature. Yes, as you say, in their heart of hearts the majority of people seem to regard God as one of the brute forces of nature. Similarly they attribute to him the ultimate responsibility for war, with all its inexcusable brutalities; forgetting that it arises from their own brutal instincts. War is in the nature of things; and, for my part I must separate the notion of deity from the nature of things. God to me is an adventure which perhaps ends in a discovery, but I am not going to calculate the chances of the hazard as Pascal did. I prefer Spinoza. When I attempt to form any notion of God the whole of life becomes quite irrelevant to the matter. If I were an orthodox Christian this war would have shattered my belief in Christianity; but being a Christian to whom 'Christianity' is a merely formal symbol, the war does not affect the question for me. The spirit of Christ was one which considered every particular case entirely upon its own merits: he did not set out to measure life by means of any principle or set of principles. That is why his words on one occasion will often seem to contradict his words on another. The attraction of Christ's personality consists precisely in this, that he formulated no system.

We have had a week's rest now, so I expect we shall soon be put through it again. Even when out of the line our life is miserable, and one to which no man should be condemned. We sleep on the floors of barns, we are tormented by lice, and we haven't had a bath for weeks. I think the heroism of these men is in proportion to their humiliations; the severest form of monastic discipline is a less surrender. For myself I can, with an effort, I admit, escape from my immediate surroundings into mine own mind. But they are almost entirely physical creatures, to whom actuality is everything: that they can suffer as they do and yet respond to every call made upon them is to me, in some measure, a vindication of humanity.

Well, my dear Will, I can write no more; and you, I should imagine are heartily glad of it, for I have given you a dull screed. Isn't it amazing that for about fifteen years we should have been silent to each other. I am more than grateful to you for having broken the silence; and to see you and talk to you again after this weary nightmare is over is one of the anticipations which help me to bear the present.

Yours always affectionately,

F. M.

I happened to be at Oxford where I witnessed the conferring of degrees when the last of those letters reached me. The sight of a number of youths, booted and spurred, with their gowns over their khaki, kneeling before the Chancellor to receive their degrees, put me in mind of the age of chivalry, so touching and beautiful were these young figures; and I thought what a fine subject for a memorial painting this would make. When Henry Wilson was planning an exhibition at Burlington House to illustrate future memorials of the war, he asked me to paint a large decoration, and I bethought me of what I had seen at Oxford. I therefore painted a group of representative figures, Vice-Chancellors, scholars and men of science surrounding a Chancellor conferring a degree upon a young soldier, with a group of undergraduates, Rupert Brooke, Julian Grenfell, Raymond Asquith, John Manners and others, walking up, hand in hand, to receive symbolically what could never now be given them. Unfortunately this exhibition was premature. When the time came for the planning and executing of war memorials, the projects shown at Burlington House were forgotten.

While I was at Oxford Robert Bridges spoke of his plans for his *Spirit of Man*; he was asking his friends to suggest poems worthy of inclusion. He thought of including some poems by Kabir, and one or two by Tagore, but these last he believed he could improve. The changes he made seemed to me so suggestive that Tagore, I felt, would approve; but all didn't run smoothly.

My dear Rothenstein, (Bridges wrote)

I feel sorry now that I indulged a notion of dealing with Tagore's poems; but when you were here, your liking for the version that I had sent him of the one that I had ventured to alter must have overset my judgment. I see now that I would do nothing with them without his consent and approval, and I had sent him the one that I worked on, in order that he might tell me what he would wish. I certainly could not bring myself to altering anything that he had written, and then allowing it to be published without his approval.

Tagore wrote to me after hearing from Robert Bridges and explained his hesitation:

> *Shantiniketan.*
> *Bolpur,*
> *Bengal.*
> *April 4. 1915.*

My dear Friend,

I give up Japan, at least for the present. Not for any sudden failure in courage or enthusiasm but for the same blessed reason that brings a modern war to its halt. My finance is hopeless, mainly owing to the European complications.

I got a letter from Dr Bridges with his own version of a *Gitanjali* poem. I cannot judge it. But since I have got my fame as an English writer I feel extreme reluctance in accepting alterations in my English poems by any of your writers. I must not give men any reasonable ground for accusing me—which they do—of reaping advantage of other men's genius and skill. There are people who suspect that I owe in a large measure to Andrews's help for my literary success, which is so false that I can afford to laugh at it. But it is different about Yeats. I think Yeats was sparing in his suggestions—moreover, I was with him during the revisions. But one is apt to delude himself, and it is very easy for me to gradually forget the share Yeats had in making my things possible. Though you have the first draft of my translations with you I have unfortunately allowed the revised typed pages to get lost in which Yeats pencilled his corrections. Of course, at that time I never could imagine that anything that I could write would find its place in your literature. But the situation is changed now. And if it be true that Yeats's touches have made it possible for *Gitanjali* to occupy the place it does then that must be confessed. At least by my subsequent unadulterated writings my true level should be found out and the faintest speck of lie should be wiped out from the fame I enjoy now. It does not matter what the people think of me but it does matter all the world to me to be true to myself. This is the reason why I cannot accept any help from Bridges excepting where the grammar is wrong or wrong words have been used. My translations are frankly prose—my aim is to make them simple with just a suggestion of rhythm to give them a touch of the lyric, avoiding all archaisms and poetical conventions.

I am sending you some more of my translations—keep them with you till we meet, if you have any doubts about their fitness. I still cherish the hope of seeing you and the dear children in your green solitude and bury there under the fallen leaves all the artificial laurels lurking in my wreath.

With love,
yours affectionately,
RABINDRANATH TAGORE.

Andrews does not admire the alterations made by Bridges, but that does not affect me. In fact I am not so much anxious about mutilations as about added beauties which I cannot claim as mine.

R. T.

I knew that it was said in India that the success of *Gitanjali* was largely owing to Yeats's re-writing of Tagore's English. That this is false can easily be proved. The original MS. of *Gitanjali* in English and in Bengali is in my possession. Yeats did here and there suggest slight changes, but the main text was printed as it came from Tagore's hands. I could readily understand Rabindranath's hesitation, but he respected Bridges's judgment, and the poem was included in the *Spirit of Man*.

Tagore was modest about his English, about his prose especially. In a letter in which he charmingly acknowledged a book of six drawings which Macmillan published, he refers to his difficulties in this direction; also to his love for England. Tagore was not without his grievances, but he was emphatic in his acknowledgment of India's debt to Englishmen.

No man's company gives me more pleasure than Tagore's;

but among his disciples I am uncomfortable; easy idealism is like Cézannism, or Whistlerism—no, away with the smooth talkers, with those who wear bland spiritual phylacteries upon their foreheads! These men who specialise, as it were, in idealism give me the sense of discomfort that I feel among other men who do not practise but preach. I marvel always at Tagore's patience with such, who weaken his artistic integrity by flattery, as they weakened Rodin's. Degas, Fantin, Monet and Renoir closed their doors against such half-men, parasites and prigs. I imagine Tolstoy's house to have been infested by these, to his wife's despair.

CHAPTER XXXV

A VISIT TO THE BELGIAN TRENCHES

BELGIAN refugees were still coming out to England; all who could took them into their homes. We had a family of Belgians at Oakridge; and Émile Vandervelde, whom I met in London at the Binyons, came to stay with us. He wanted to take me with him to the Belgian front, there to make a drawing of the King. For like everyone else, I wished to do something to help the Belgians, and reproductions of such a drawing, Vandervelde believed, would have a wide sale. He was to start in a week's time, and undertook to get me a passport. Here was an unlooked for chance of seeing something of the war. A telegram came to say that all was arranged, and a day later I stood, the only civilian besides Vandervelde, on a ship crowded with soldiers bound for Calais. I was in a new world of men and of action at Calais, but there was little time in which to explore it; a car was awaiting us, and we were soon on the road, challenged every few miles by French sentries, who examined our papers. The road took us through dullish country past red-roofed cottages and farmhouses, to the frontier. Then we reached Belgian Headquarters. La Panne was a sea-side pleasure-resort in the sand dunes, full of tawdry little villas, built for prosperous bourgeois families, and, save for the presence of thousands of soldiers, there was little here to suggest that we were near the seat of the war, though I was told that the German lines were but four miles away. We lodged in the house of two officers, Captains Thys and Ullmann, both of whom had helped, working night after night, to open the sluices which flooded the Yser, and thus checked the German advance.

I visited various parts of the Belgian trenches with Vandervelde, who, as a Minister who had resisted the German demand to pass through Belgium, was popular with the army. Though now and then there was a short bombardment, the front was quieter than I expected. A farmhouse, just after we left it, was shelled; so were some empty trenches, but each day the firing ceased at about 5 o'clock, as though the gunners were called off for afternoon tea. Now and then an enemy aeroplane would fly over La Panne, but dropped no bombs. I commented on this during a visit to the British Military Mission, where I found Major Baird[1] and two other officers, one a tall figure with big black moustaches, the other a stocky fellow, who remarked, 'Of course they don't bomb us. Why, we are all Bosches in La Panne—there's the King and Queen, and Prince Alexander here, and Rothenstein; we're alright'. It is true that outside La Panne, towards Dixmude, things were more uncomfortable.

We were all right; but a little dull, and I wanted to get a sight of Ypres; so did Vandervelde; but Ypres being in British occupation, Vandervelde said I must get a special permit. The Military Mission were a little suspicious of Vandervelde; wasn't he a bit of a socialist? I reassured them, and when they met Vandervelde, they were charmed by his eloquence. We motored through Cassel, the first place in British occupation, to Bailleul, which as yet showed no signs of war, but was three years later to be completely destroyed. As we approached the war area, though the day was still, and there was no sound of firing, something heavy, sinister and menacing hung in the air. Near to Ypres this sinister silence grew yet more threatening. Outside the town a sergeant with two or three of his men barred the way. Orders were that no one was allowed into Ypres. We showed our papers, but the sergeant was obdurate. Happily ignorant of military discipline, I said a word to the chauffeur, who started his engine, and we left the sergeant behind. The ominous silence continued; not a soul was in the

[1] Now Lord Stonehaven.

streets, and as we drove on we saw that the houses were mere empty shells. It was like a city of the dead. Soon we entered the square, and suddenly came on the great Cloth-Hall and the adjoining Cathedral, livid and scarred with white wounds against a lowering sky, a magnificent and unforgettable sight. It came as a sudden shock, awful and distressing, as though the great buildings felt the agony of approaching death. It was like witnessing the anguish of a stricken lion, and I vowed that I would return to make some record of what I had seen. But something warned us it would be dangerous to linger; the silence was like that which heralds a storm; and we passed through Ypres to Poperinghe. There we were told this had been one of the rare intervals when Ypres had not been heavily shelled. Three years were to pass before I found myself in Ypres again.

I visited other places with Vandervelde, but none so dramatic as Ypres. When we motored through Furnes to Nieuport, which was held by French troops, we were warned not to walk up the main street; but Vandervelde, to show his courage, which was never in doubt, took no notice, though I felt uncomfortable, hearing the zip of the bullets past our ears, and was relieved when the French sentries stopped us and made us proceed by the communication trenches. At night the front was lit up by Verey lights and rockets. I was so impressed by the dramatic character of the scene, both by night and by day, that I determined when I got home, to petition that artists be attached to the British forces, to make records of the scene of war. Meanwhile my return to England was nearly prevented by an absurd misadventure.

I was visiting part of the line with Vandervelde, when we were entertained at lunch by Belgian staff officers. I was astonished at the profusion of the food and wine. But never a good trencherman, I wandered away to make drawings. Presently a French officer strolled up, of whom I inquired whether these trenches were held by French troops. If so might I continue my drawing? I had a written authority from Belgian Headquarters. He must first ask his superior officer, he replied, and returning shortly, invited me to follow him. A motor car was standing close by, which he asked me to enter. Within sat another officer; we were soon travelling at a great pace along the high road. I inquired where we were going. 'To Dunkirk', was the grim reply. At Dunkirk I was taken to the French H. Q. where, after long waiting, I was closely questioned. What was I doing, drawing French *fortifications*? It was an awkward situation, for my explanations were brushed aside. My sketch book in which were drawings of Belgian soldiers, notes of landscapes, and of trenches too, was sent up-stairs to be examined. A Colonel descended, who took a grave view of the matter. I was a civilian, what business had I in the French lines? my passport meant nothing; anyone could have a forged passport. The position was getting serious. War is war. The French were intensely suspicious and one heard tales of suspected spies being summarily executed. Suddenly an idea struck me; would the Colonel telephone to Belgian H. Q. where my identity could be explained. Fortunately this was done, and I found myself at liberty and provided with a military pass to take me back to La Panne.

An incident remains in my mind, concerned with the first visit of a theatrical company to the Belgian war zone. A performance was given in a great hangar, followed by the singing of the Marseillaise, Rule Britannia and the Belgian National Anthem, in which the Belgian and French troops joined. Afterwards Vandervelde was asked (and I was included in the invitation) to join the company of players at supper. We sat among gay young actresses; it was a joyous party, healths were drunk and Vandervelde was called on to speak, when he launched out into a grandiloquent oration, such as Mr Lloyd George or Mr Winston Churchill might have made at a great political gathering. On this occasion it was slightly embarrassing.

It was from this hangar I went up in a 'sausage' balloon

with a Belgian officer sent to make observations, whence a wide prospect of the Yser front was revealed. I returned full of enthusiasm for the scene of war. I implored my friend Colonel Repington to plead at the War Office that artists should be allowed out in France. Repington spoke to Northcliffe, who wrote to me:

'*11th April* 1916.

'I heartily agree with you, and have long ago suggested that we should copy the Germans (whom we always have to copy much as we dislike them) and send distinguished artists to the front.

'As for the British authorities, they are absolutely impossible people, but in regard to the French army I think I might be able to do something.'

The French army be damned, I replied; it was the British front of which records should be made. Two days later Northcliffe wrote again, 'Why does not the Royal Academy or somebody approach the War Office on the subject? If they will do so I will support them. If I were to approach the War Office they would kill the scheme at once. They have had more than enough of me—although they are still going to get more!'

I appealed to Repington again, who interested Lady Cunard, while MacColl and others began to move in the matter. As a result Muirhead Bone was sent out to France, with a Lieutenant's commission. No better choice had been possible; and no finer records have been made than those due to Bone's skilful pencil. Then Orpen, too, was sent with a Major's commission. Finally the project received full official support. I wrote to thank Northcliffe for his help. He answered: 'The carrying out of your scheme as to artists was very little helped by me. I spoke of it at G. H. Q. several times, and urged it, but it was carried through by young Sir Philip Sassoon.' The Ministry of Information, advised by Arnold Bennett and Campbell Dodgson, sent

Kennington, Nevinson, Paul Nash and finally myself to France with the rank of 'Official Artist at the Front'.

I knew nothing of Kennington until, going by chance into the Goupil Galleries I saw a large painting on glass of a war scene in the snow, *The Kensingtons at Lavantie*[1], and was at once struck by its power. Some forceful studies were also shown, one of which I bought. And I wrote to the artist. He turned out to be a son of T. B. Kennington, a sound but unadventurous painter, whom I had known for many years. I went to see young Kennington at his father's house, and there saw more of his work. He had volunteered at the beginning of the war, and was now back, after a trying time in France. He showed me some remarkable studies of soldiers. Here was the man, I thought, to draw types of the fighting men. I wrote to Sir Ian Hamilton, now back from Gallipoli. After seeing Kennington's picture he replied:

'I have seen and have enthusiastically admired the wonderful imaginative picture by Kennington of *the Kensingtons*. Being out of power it is difficult for me to do the sort of thing you wish me to do. Especially as only few of our soldiers would be in sympathy with the artistic side of such an appeal. Still, Macready, the Adjutant General, is not only a friend of mine, but has eyes to see ahead into the future and a mind to appreciate the value to posterity of having the work of British soldiers during the Great War imperishably chronicled. So I will ask him to see whether anything can be done.'

But in vain he approached the military authorities. This is what he sent on to me:

25th July, 1916.

My dear Sir Ian,

I find that Kennington is No. 1799 Private E. H. Kennington, 13th County of London Regiment, somewhere in France, and I have been unable to trace that anybody in the

---

[1] This fine work was at once acquired by Annie, Viscountess Cowdray.

Sixty feet of canvas

War Office is willing to consider the claims mentioned by
Mr Rothenstein. If anything comes through about him I
have kept your letter and his and will go into the matter.

Yours sincerely,

x.

But finally, through Masterman, now head of the Ministry
of Information, and Campbell Dodgson, Kennington was
sent out to France, but under unsatisfactory conditions, I
gathered. He had no car, and he found great difficulty in
getting about and was, he wrote, being often arrested. But
before this happened, he stayed with us at Oakridge, where
I was busy on the large decoration for Henry Wilson of which
I spoke before. Kennington helped me to square out and
transfer my drawings on to the canvas, and he painted in the
architectural details of the background, and the ornaments on
the robe which the Chancellor wears in the painting. I was
glad of his help, for there were sixty feet of canvas to be
covered with life-size figures. These were representative
university types whom I drew at Oxford and Cambridge,
or else when they came to stay at Oakridge. Among these
last were William Bateson, Michael Sadler, A. E. Housman,
Henry Hadow, Sir Oliver Lodge, Sir Isambard Owen,
Sir Alfred Dale, and Sir Henry Miers; while Rupert Brooke
and other heroic young men who had lost their lives in the
war, I painted from photographs with which Eddie Marsh,
ever helpful, had provided me. After seeing the decoration
at Burlington House, where it was shown in the autumn of
1916, Marsh sent me a heartening letter:

5, *Raymond Buildings.*
Oct. 16. 16.

My dear Rothenstein,

I went to the Academy on Saturday, and was deeply
moved by the group. I think it very beautiful. You have
given a lovely vision of Billy Grenfell, and in essence it's very
like what he was when I first knew him—about the time the
photograph you had must have been taken—Julian is like

309

too, but more superficially—the photograph gave no clue to his strength or his depth. I hear Lady Manners is delighted with the portrait of John, I expect she's written you about it. I think you've given a very beautiful version of Rupert. Will you forgive me if I express a feeling which I know always annoys the artist intensely, but which the beholder of a sketch can hardly help feeling—the fear that to go on with it will spoil it? In this case there's a practical reason for saying it—because I want you to leave this particular version as it is. The white is such a great beauty, it gives the spiritual look that the thing has now, and I think much will be lost when the gowns are what a herald would call 'proper'—(also the white goes so beautifully with the pale green of the background). I suppose it wouldn't be possible to treat the gowns, even in a final version, as a kind of surplices, and have them white for good? It would be such a fine 'romantic' contrast with the blacks and reds of the dons' gowns.

Yrs ever,

E. MARSH.

There was no final version. After the Exhibition my 60 feet of canvas were rolled up and forgotten.

Kennington's first visit to France was a short one. Meanwhile, plans were made at the Ministry of Information for other artists to go out. Paul Nash, who was on active service in Flanders, was anxious to be used as an artist. It was Campbell Dodgson again who arranged that he be set free—a wise action on Dodgson's part, for Nash did remarkable work at the front. So, too, did Nevinson, but all grumbled that the time allowed was too short. Muirhead Bone and Orpen were the two fortunate ones, for no limits were set to their service.

John, too, wanted to go out to France; he wrote of his chances:

28, *Mallard St.*
Chelsea.
Ap. 26. 1916.

Dear Will,

I went to the country after I got your letter and was much annoyed to find on getting there that I had left your letter behind, as I intended answering it from the country and I couldn't bring your address to mind. I have had the idea of going to France to sketch for a long while and I have hopes now of being able to do so. But I am still in suspense. I have applied for a temporary commission which I think indispensable to move with any freedom in the British lines where the discipline is exceedingly severe. A friend of mine who went sketching in France avoided the British Army as one avoids death but got on very well with the French. I fully sympathise with your proposal and am convinced there's enough material to occupy a dozen artists. Of course the proper time for war is the winter and I very much regret not having managed to go out last winter. I cannot say I have any personal influence with the powers that be. Blow however has done his best for me and I await the verdict. I have been advised at the same time to keep my business quite dark. You might suppose I could do something with Lloyd George but I fear that gentleman will never forgive me for painting a somewhat unconventional portrait of him. Northcliffe's popularity is a very variable quantity I should think and he and the Military are probably very much in agreement, so that he might do more than another to effect your purpose.

When you are in town do come my way. I wish I had the power you credit me with to be of service. I have spoken to Blow but he's afraid of bothering K[1] too much at present.

I hope Alice is as well and beautiful as ever and your children flourishing.

---

[1] Lord Kitchener, for whom Detmar Blow was acting as Private Secretary.

Max again

My own lot are all right barring a few ailments common to infancy.

Yrs

AUGUSTUS JOHN.

Later, John was attached to the Canadians, with the rank of Major.

I referred earlier to the propagandist drawings to illustrate what England was doing in war time. Max, who had come over from Italy, hoped he too might do something useful.

'I am intrigued to know what kind of "lithographic" work you are doing for the safety of England. I received an invitation to Queen Anne's Chambers the other day, and went there on Tuesday; saw two amiable men who seemed to like me; one of them made notes about me and gave me a card from which I learn that my Enrolment Number is 131,853—so that I gather I am up against a formidable amount of competition. Nevertheless I live in hope that I may save England yet by "some kind of clerical work".'

Masterman suggested that Max might try his hand at propagandist cartoons; but with his usual modesty, Max said he would be no good at anything so ambitious. Raemakers was their man; he had the right outlook and the powerful style needed for propaganda. Later, Max and his wife joined us at Far Oakridge.

For a time they consented to be our guests; but finding Oakridge to their taste, they moved into a furnished cottage nearby.

It was here that Max wrote *Savonarola Brown*, and produced his masterpieces of caricature *Rossetti and his Circle*. While they slept at the cottage, which was but a stone's throw from our house, Max and his wife had their meals with us, when every day Max, carefully dressed, would take stick and gloves to walk the few yards, bringing his drawings, carefully wrapped in a folio, in the same manner taking them back each evening: he couldn't bear to leave them behind! During frost or snow, Max would appear with socks over his boots, (still begloved and carrying his cane) lest he should slip, and the precious drawings be scattered in the lane.

What fun we had while Max and his wife were with us! Such words Max invented to be sung to current tunes! And in the evenings he would read to us what he had been writing during the day, and we would play the sonnet game, whereby few of our neighbours escaped being libelled. Or Max would see people whom we knew well and produce caricatures, showing such observation, such convincing likeness, that it was difficult to believe he had seen his subjects for a few minutes only.

We had a dog called Rover, about whom Max wrote a poem called:

Brave Rover

Rover killed the goat,
He bit him through the throat,
And when it all was over
The goat's ghost haunted Rover.

And yet (the plot here thickens)
Rover killed the chickens.
They thought he was a fox—
And then he killed the cocks.

And now events moved faster:
Rover killed his master,
And then he took the life
Of his late master's wife.

And we must not forget he
Killed Rachel and killed Bettie,
Then Billie and then John.
How dogs do carry on!

To Bradford he repaired.
His great white teeth he bared
And then, with awful snarls,
Polished off Uncle Charles.

Albert in London trembled,
An aspen he resembled.
His life he held not cheap
And wept (I heard him weep).

Brave Rover heard him too.
He knew full well who's who,
And entered with a grin
The Fields of Lincoln's Inn.

The Elysian Fields begin
Near those of Lincoln's Inn.
'Tis there that Albert's gone.
How dogs do carry on!

No wonder Max was nervous of leaving his Rossetti caricatures in an empty cottage; for they are now regarded as classics. What a remarkable reconstruction of a period! So intuitively truthful, that one of William Michael's daughters wrote that no person living within their circle had given so accurate a picture of its physical and spiritual composition. Max, with his air of delicate sprightliness, is the profoundest critic of men I have known. When Lytton Strachey made his bow to the world, and shy, retiring, slightly flushed and confused, sent from his youthful catapult a shower of sharp pebbles against the foreheads of the great, Max was generous in his admiration. My only quarrel with Max, I told Strachey later, was when Max insisted that he, Strachey, was as good a writer and critic as himself. Some day a complete collection of Max's caricatures will appear, when the full weight and range of his genius will be realised. There exists no other such discerning comment on men and movements of our age.

While Max seems to take life lightly, to be charming and patient with everyone he meets, his will, when he wishes to exert it, is as strong as Lord Snowden's. His no is No, though he would rather approve than disapprove. To maps and itineraries of future life, to Russian literature, the works of Proust, cruelty to animals, D. H. Lawrence's novels, Mr Lansbury's improvements of London, the Sankara system of Indian philosophy, the Proletarian State, he says emphatically no; in most other things he sees a kernel of virtue. Indeed Max, of later years especially, shrinks from offending people; the once pitiless satirist has become the most human and understanding of men. I know so many with wandering eyes, who feel their time wasted with any but important persons. Max, who charms everyone, finds most people charming. And how quickly he discovers the essence of each personality. What pleases me, too, is his loyalty to his own age. The young come to pay him homage, and he readily recognises new talent; but his comments on pretentious modernity are withering.

On one occasion an unsuspected side of Max's character appeared. A rick at a neighbour's farm caught fire; we all hastened out to help extinguish the flames lest the fire spread to the other ricks. All the neighbours turned out. Buckets were filled at a well, carried across the yard and thrown over the burning straw, where Max, gloved as usual, worked as strenuously as any. It was a dramatic scene, such as Legros or Millet would have painted—the excited figures of men and women, hastening to and fro, while flames and heavy smoke issued from the burning stack. For all the villagers knew what was at stake, what the loss of the year's straw and hay would mean. Happily, the fire was put out before it spread farther.

Max took a fiercer view of the Germans than I did. I had qualms about the war and sometimes leaned towards views of which Max would hear nothing. Like others, at the commencement I believed the cause for which we were fighting to be a just one. But doubts about the righteousness of war as a means of settling disputes between nations, as the carnage continued, troubled me.

There were rumours of a German move towards peace and of its rejection. Surely, in the face of so terrible an event as war, and one so long drawn out, it was legitimate to question the infallibility of statesmen. John Burns, Lord Morley, Ramsay MacDonald, Bernard Shaw and Bertrand Russell had the courage to express their doubts. The feeling against the last three was ferocious. I wrote to Russell after reading something he had written, and he answered:

315

Two letters

1 *January*, 1916.

Dear Rothenstein,

As we enter upon another year of war and hatred and blood, I must tell you how very glad I was to get your letter about my little book. I wonder whether this year will see the end of the madness, and what will be left of Europe when peace returns. We who knew life before the war will come to seem odd survivals of a softer age, like the Romans who lingered on after the barbarian invasion.

Yours ever sincerely,

BERTRAND RUSSELL.

Another letter, from Arthur Fox-Strangways, put, from a different angle, a wise and sane construction on the tragedy of war.

12. 6. 16.

My dear W.

Your short note supplies texts for three or four treatises on war and peace—'destruction of youth'—'outlasting a good deal of the passion of the first year'—'what modern war leads to'—'most statesmen in France and Germany would like to find a basis for settlement'. I wish you would consider this seriously; this war originates in (1) England's indolence, ignorance, selfishness, supineness, (2) Germany's mistake in handing over all responsibility for thought, (*a*) the women to their husbands, (*b*) the men to the police and the rulers behind it. (Grey and B. Hollweg plan about with Agadir, Casablanca, Sarajevo etc., but those are summer lightnings.) Some of us say, and I have to look for *some* sort of interpretation of it, this is a war to end wars. I can only explain this apparently absurd statement in the sense that the only thinkable abolition of war would be, first Europe, and then the World, under the assured domination of some one power, and that the Anglo-Saxon and Teutonic races are trying conclusions on this point. That makes sense, though it is again ridiculous, as peace would then last exactly as long as the predominance of the conqueror, which would not be long. All this weeping and wailing over war, or 'modern war', is beside the mark; we can weep over the individual victims, and I'm sorry to hear that you have cause, or fresh cause, to do so. War is terribly beneficent exactly as tempest, earthquake, and fire is; and we don't spend time wailing over them, we only try to alleviate the suffering. War cannot be laid to the charge of man, in the sense that he makes or declines to make it. No man in Europe made or could have prevented this war. Nature is punishing mankind not for their motives, but, as she always does, for their mistakes; in this case the mistakes on the one side of being indolent and on the other of shelving responsibility. In this punishment the innocent have to suffer, because we live in communities, and in every community all reward and punishment is vicarious, as Christ, among others, preached in life and death. War terrifies us by its size and suddenness; but we turn our eyes away from the far vaster mass of misery which steadily dripped and dripped through the 100 years of peace which preceded it. It seems to us waste; but we do not see yet the way in which it strips off all unrealities and brings us face to face with truth; we shall. But if war is beneficent, as I believe, what are we doing when we try by words and persuasions to interfere with its course? There is only one end, the defeat of one side or the other or the exhaustion of both. If we try to stave this off in any way we are blasphemously thwarting a divine purpose, exactly as much as if we called in war to hasten ends which should have ripened by the slower methods of peace. The millions of lives, bitter as it is to think, will have been well spent if the belligerent countries learn their lesson; they have not learned it yet, and we have no business to put obstacles in their way. But if your Lord Courtneys and Ramsay Macdonalds and B. Shaws would turn the *constructive* side of their minds to thinking out some plan by which the ultimate decision between two paramount and slashing ideals could be cast more mercifully than by war, they would be doing some good; personally I don't think such a plan will ever be found. Till that plan is found we had better accept this cataclysm of nature with the philosophy which we find it easy to exercise upon the many such cataclysms which are recorded in History, and give up talking of 'modern' war as if it was some sort of exception. Now we gas our enemies; then we tortured, burned, starved, poisoned them. Then twice as many died of disease as of lethal weapons; now the great majority of those who have to die meet death in the field. That is all. There are worse things than dying. War kills bodies; that 'dreadful peace' which went before was killing souls. And there are worse deaths than sudden death—but I said this before. Well—I expect we agree about a good deal of this at bottom, but have learnt a different set of shibboleths. One does fatally become the victim of a phrase.

Yours always,

A. H. F. S.

CHAPTER XXXVI

THE FOUR WINDS

I ADMIRED Stopford Brooke's courage when, nearing 80, he built himself a large new house, making therewith a rose garden. He would press me often to join him there; to bring my paints with me, for he wanted to see me at work. For his own paintings were done from memory, and he wished to see how one worked directly from nature.

'You will not be dull if, outside, you love woods and flowers and clouds....There are many walks and you can sketch to your heart's content. I sit in the garden & bid good-bye to doing anything at all. The only thing which bores me is that I cannot look forward to seeing grown up the trees I plant or the ideas I have for the garden all fulfilled. *That* is my shadow, but there is plenty of sunshine in the present, & it is perhaps enough.'

Brooke liked·to hear what I was doing at Oakridge.

'Your search for a subject and the happy chance of the sudden discovery of one, which sent its own emotion into your heart and desire, was happy reading. There is a sonnet of Wordsworth's which describes a little farmstead, whole in itself and owed to none, which has the same note of feeling in it as you felt. I've painted a bit, things I have seen within, but I have read nothing worth reading. Why should I read when I am so soon going to change the air? When my dust has added an element or two to the roses at The Four Winds what shall I care about the Insurance Act, or Social Progress, or the follies of Kings or the loathsomeness of Russian villanies; or of Philosophy always skipping the truth

319

under its eyes, or Science wading through its own hypotheses, or Theology hiding God by the clouds it engenders?'

Brooke had four years to watch his garden grow under the loving care of his daughter Evelyn, and to look on his roses. But he now walked with difficulty, and though his last years were saddened by the war, he enjoyed, up to the end, the beauty of the face of the world, and while, as he writes, he could no longer work, his interest in others' work was unfailing. I spent some days at The Four Winds and did some painting and was shown the glories of the garden. I drove out with the old man and enjoyed long talks with him in the evenings—about books, pictures and men and women—he avoided the subject of the war.

Stopford Brooke, knowing my love for Rossetti's drawings, gave me a delicate pencil study of a child (the son of his landlady at Blackfriars). But the good Brooke—who but a Victorian could have done such a thing?—deeming that one of the feet was awkwardly drawn, had rubbed it out!

Stopford Brooke was an admirer of A. E. and read me some poems he had lately written. I wrote to A. E. to tell him of Brooke's admiration and of my own, and A. E. at once replied:

Many thanks for your kind letter. The little book of poems you refer to I printed privately to give away to my friends. I was moved to write them but did not think they were good enough to publish otherwise, with the exception of two or three, and they were so different from my other work that I was dubious about them. I send you a copy with pleasure and am glad you find something to like in them. I wonder where Stopford Brooke got a copy. I did not send him one. I only gave away about three dozen copies altogether to personal friends but I am pleased one found its way to him. Dear man, I give the book such as it is to you willingly and with no thought of return. If you have a print of Yeats I would value it, or of Tagore if you have not Yeats.

The Irish rebellion

We are outside the world in Ireland and only receive such news as is carefully cooked for our consumption by the censor and refashioned again and diluted and distorted by the commentaries of our illiterate journalists. So we vary from general neutrality to an enthusiasm for battle on one side to a pro-Germanism on the other side, and all are equally ignorant of what they are talking about I imagine. I try to continue civilization, paint and write in the hope the world will come round to the worth of art and literature again. I think art and literature will both be freer in the future and that many old modes of thought will get broken up and we may begin unhampered by prejudice to build nearer the heart's desire. That is the young may. I am nearing the old fossil period of life. I will be fifty in a few weeks.

Good bye and best wishes,

Yours ever, A. E.

A. E.'s letter was written before the armed rising in Ireland which few foresaw.

Yeats was staying with us when the news came, and was much upset. These men, poets and schoolmasters, he explained, are idealists, unfit for practical affairs; they are seers, pointing to what should be, who had been goaded into action against their better judgment.

I hoped that James Stephens was not among them; no, he was too wise, said Yeats; Pearce and his friends were good men, selfless but rash, throwing their lives away in a forlorn hope.

The future Senator foresaw neither the dark days ahead nor the brighter to come. The rebellion, and the later troubles, would have horrified Stopford Brooke. But he was spared the knowledge. When the rising happened he was no longer alive. I had a last wistful letter from this grand old man, showing his unfailing interest in life.

The Four Winds,
Ewhurst,
Surrey.

13 *March,* 1916.

Dear Rothenstein, you wrote to me on Feb 17 and I have
never answered your goodness. This is not that I have anything to do—I have not—but because I have felt so in-
competent. The doctors in London discovered far too much
sugar in my system and have dieted me furiously &c. &c.
There is a kind of malaise everywhere in me, but I am getting
better to their surprise, and I hope to be able to join the birds
in singing in the Spring. Spring is all very well, but an aged
gentleman loves the Summer best. I like fulness of life
better than the beginnings of life. When I was young glad
beginnings, which God so often gives us, were my greatest
pleasure. I felt sure to be able to cross the hills into the new
country, and I lived half in the unknown. Now I know and
I love fulness and satisfaction, even though I am certain of
the passing of fulness into decay. Perhaps I think I shall
never live to see decay. I am glad you are so full up with
work, for the world will be the better for that and it pleases
one who can do no work that others can. To sit on the cliffs
and see the ships tossing in the gale, all attempting to conquer
their haven, is not disagreeable. We have had a wonderful
snow-time, more than a foot deep for three weeks on end,
and at first full of extraordinary beauty. With what amazing
delicacy Nature works when she is not out of temper; every
twig, every spine, every shoot was encased in the lacing of
the frost, and radiant with righteousness and happiness, and
no wicked thaw disturbed them. Pitch Hill looked as big as
Monte Rosa. It is all gone now, and it was time, for its
whiteness was being darkened over. The thaw began yesterday. I enjoyed the keenness of it all. So, you have been
drawing Thomas Hardy. How did he impress you? He is
one of the few men who cut into the quick of humanity.
The last Vol. of Poems was not as good as its predecessor.
That was a book of poems, from many of which I used to see

living blood pouring over the page. I never read *The Dynasts*, except one page at my booksellers. I don't think I could tackle it. Still, it is a big thing to have done, if all I hear be true. The daffodils promise well, so do the tulips. When they are all out, perhaps you can find time to come down. And with my love to your wife I am

Ever yours,
STOPFORD A. BROOKE.

This was the last letter Stopford Brooke wrote to a friend. Five days later he died, and I lost a friendship which counted as one of the assets of my life.

A slight acquaintance with another senior, T. J. Cobden-Sanderson, also ripened into a close friendship. With his finely cut features and pointed beard, wearing a sky-blue embroidered blouse, he looked the aristocrat-craftsman he was. But his outlook was more cosmopolitan than was that of William Morris and others of the craftsman-socialist circle. On his walls hung, side by side with drawings by Burne-Jones, a painting by Degas. Like William Rossetti he was charming to his juniors, and I loved to visit him at The Doves, a house scarcely bigger than a doll's-house. For he was one of the profoundest and wittiest talkers of his time, with a note of persiflage worthy of Anatole France. Of an affectionate nature he was inclined to be suspicious, and would close his door against doubtful friends. He had quarrelled with Emery Walker, his old friend and partner in the Doves Press, and one night, from Hammersmith Bridge, he dropped the Doves Press type into the Thames. Legally, this was a crime; but I can respect a man who, once or twice in his life, will boldly do a wrong thing.

Now a new friendship was to come into my life. One day Joseph Southall, with Arthur Gaskin and a young poet, John Drinkwater, arrived at Oakridge. They had walked over from Minchinhampton, and were tired, so we pressed them to stay the night; Drinkwater was persuaded, but Southall must return; they had promised to be back for supper, and being a Quaker, Southall would not break his word; Drink-water fell in love with Oakridge, and inquired whether there was a cottage nearby to be had; and soon after, the cottage where the Beerbohms had stayed being empty, it was taken by Drinkwater, who henceforward spent a part of the year at Oakridge. He and his wife were perfect neighbours; they loved country life as we did, and John found the Cotswold scene as good a subject for his poems as I did for my painting.

Besides poetry, he was now writing plays; the latest of these, *Abraham Lincoln*, he read aloud at our house. This was in 1918. The play so impressed my brother Charles that he offered to help finance it. *Lincoln* was happily accepted on its merits, and when it was performed, took the town by storm and made John Drinkwater's fame and fortune. He had, up to this time, lived modestly, like Southall, at Birming-ham, devoting himself to the Repertory Theatre there; for which loyalty to local life I admired him and Southall. Later the Drinkwaters took a house in London; left Birmingham and the Oakridge cottage, where they had lived so simply and joyously. Now John Drinkwater had written a charming poem on his life there, which Max, after the rigours and discomforts of a winter in the country during the war, thus parodied:

Cottage Song	*Same Cottage—but Another Song, of Another Season.*
Morning and night I bring	Morning and night I found
Clear water from the spring,	White snow upon the ground,
And through the lyric noon	And on the tragic well
I hear the larks in tune,	Grey ice had cast her spell.
And when the shadows fall	A dearth of wood and coal
There's providence for all.	Lay heavy on my soul.
My garden is alight	My garden was a scene
With currants red and white,	Of weeds and nettles green,
And my blue curtains peep	My window-panes had holes
On starry courses deep,	Through which, all night, lost souls
While down her silver tides	Peered from the desert road,
The moon on Cotswold rides.	And starved cocks faintly crowed.

Cottage songs

My path of paven grey
Is thoroughfare all day
For fellowship, till time
Bids us with candles climb
The little whitewashed stair
Above my lavender.

John Drinkwater.
Far Oakridge
Summer 1917.

My path of cinders black
Had an abundant lack
Of visitors, till time
Bade us with boxes climb
The train that hurries on
To old warm Paddington.

For J. D. from M. B. August
4. 1917 with 1,000,000 apologies
for this wicked echo of so lovely
a poem.

CHAPTER XXXVII

AN ARTIST AT THE FRONT

ALTHOUGH I had something to do with the initial idea of war records, I scarcely expected, in view of my name, to be among those to be sent to France. But there came a letter from Campbell Dodgson, from the Ministry of Information, asking whether I would be prepared to go out to France during the winter as one of the Official Artists. I jumped at the chance, and in November 1917 I crossed the Channel. I was met at Boulogne by a Major, who first drove me to G. H. Q., where I was introduced to Major Lee, who was in charge of the Official Artists. He asked to which front he should send me. Knowing nothing of any of the fronts, I proposed joining Kennington, and was soon speeding through the fertile Picardy country, when suddenly all signs of fertility ceased—we were in the area of the Somme. How different the war-scene to that I had witnessed two years earlier in Belgium. Then, when I looked over the country about Messines from a hill on which a windmill still stood, there was little sign of the thousands of men facing one another in a death struggle. The landscape was still green; there were trees in leaf—even men and women working in the fields. Now all was mud coloured, and of trees one saw only splintered boles. But soon we entered a lovely, rose-grey, ruined town—Péronne. The unwonted shapes of the ruined buildings, the pink flush of the red bricks, deepening to blood colour where the impact of a shell had made a wound in the walls, made a scene more dramatic than any stage setting. I wanted to linger; but we had time only for a hasty meal at the Officers' Club, when we rejoined the car.

Montigny Farm

Leaving Péronne, I noticed, written on wooden boards, 'Gas masks to be worn'; now we must be nearing the present war zone; and soon we drew up at a desolate spot, where a few tin-huts were grouped together in a flat, muddy landscape. Here Kennington greeted me. This was, he said, Montigny Farm. My luggage was deposited in a rough shack, wherein my bed was a wooden frame with wire netting stretched across it. I was welcomed by the Camp Commandant, Major Irvine and by Lieut. Piesse, a New Zealander. There was little that attracted me at Montigny: a ruined sugar factory, with its rusty girders and machinery twisted into fantastic shapes, was my first subject. Fortunately a car, for my use, arrived from G. H. Q.—to Kennington's relief, for he told me of the difficulties he had found in getting about— and I lost no time in exploring the neighbourhood. We were close to Hervilly, a small village of which a few walls remained, now occupied by a trench-mortar company; a place livelier than Montigny Farm, and more picturesque. It was now snowing and the windows and doors of the white shrouded ruins looked like blinded eyes. Deep down in cellars and dug-outs lived the trench-mortar men, a noisy, hospitable company. Some miles beyond was Hargicourt, a still more exciting place whereat to draw. Here I began a study; but on a journey thither some mounted men, and a couple of lorries, had been caught on the road just before I passed, and the sight was a sickening one. This particular stretch, being on rising ground, was under enemy observation. Hargicourt, now occupied by the Munsters, my friends at Montigny warned me, was a most unhealthy spot, and I was persuaded to work elsewhere. With my later experience, I should have known better, but the care these men, who were themselves constantly facing danger, took over non-combatant visitors was embarrassing.

Instead of returning to Hargicourt I went to Jeancourt, a mile or two distant, where a friend, Captain Lissant, was in charge of a battery. While I was drawing, an aeroplane came over, hovered and then turned back to the German lines.

Lissant cursed; some heavy guns, it appeared, had lately been parked in the open a hundred yards away: the Taube had spotted them, and now Lissant feared for his battery, hitherto unobserved. Sure enough while we were lunching a shell came over and burst close to the mess-room, which, roofed only by tin sheeting covered with earth, was not a comfortable place to stay in. My gunner friends were concerned for my safety, but not for their own, though my nerves were not frayed as were theirs by months of exposure to shell and rifle fire, to bombs and high explosives. We took refuge in a dug-out below the battery, but it soon appeared that the parked guns were the objective, and coming up, I watched the shells as they burst throwing up clouds of brown earth, and later was able to finish my drawing. Whenever I visited the advanced trenches I felt a childish elation at sharing for a short space and in small measure—how small it was I knew well—the danger and discomforts in which these men lived hourly. What I had heard, and was later to read, of the marvellous spirit evoked by war, I now knew to be true; and my admiration was the more profound since the habit of untruth, which distressed me so much at home, was here less noticeable; where life under conditions of incredible risk and hardship was patriotism itself, there was no need of heroics. Moreover men were ready to hear something other than newspaper clichés.

Kennington was content to draw tents and shacks and camp rubbish at Montigny. I was more attracted by places like Péronne, and thither I motored to make studies, discovering other places on the way. To make records of the movements of the troops I felt was beyond me. There were men who could do such things better than I; but the physical beauty of the scene of war affected me deeply. Northern France was now a country of ruins which to me seemed as beautiful, as consecrated, as the sites of famous abbeys. Was not each corner, where so many had suffered agony, so many souls had been so swiftly freed, in fact a hallowed spot? To make records of such places seemed a sacred task. Some day these ruins of humble homes, farms and châteaux and churches, so pathetic in their common misery, would be swept away and forgotten, I thought, as the suffering of those who lay beneath them would be forgotten. Others, more gifted than I, would show the more heroic side of war.

Though the winter of 1917 was one of the coldest on record, absorption in my task allowed me to work under conditions which otherwise I had believed impossible. It was often so cold that my brush froze between water flask and paper. These were physical discomforts not worth mentioning, but for the fact that never once did I know such things as a common cold or indigestion.

All day long guns, transport and mounted troops looking magnificent in their cloaks and helmets, passed along the roads. At night officers and men went up to the front to lay barbed wire and dig and repair trenches. For the Fifth Army Front, but recently taken over, was being feverishly prepared. The comparative quiet which prevailed was felt to be ominous, implying German preparations for attack. Kennington and I, ignorant of military matters, yet commented on the poor defences on this part of the front. A company of American Engineers under Colonel Thompson was stationed at Montigny, laying railway-lines, and others were building a bridge at Doignt. On Christmas Day Kennington and I were invited, with Captain Irvine and Lieutenant Piesse, to a party at the American quarters—to begin at 8 o'clock. We arrived to find a huge Christmas tree, and a roomful of men, and heard speeches and then Christmas gifts were offered all round. The names called out, as each man walked up to receive his present from the tree, amused us, Private Schwartz, Private Schmidt, Corporal Prellwitz, Sergeant Bergmann, and so forth; but we were getting hungrier and hungrier, since we believed we had been bidden to dinner! Fortunately a muslin stocking full of nuts, sweets and biscuits was presented to each of us, which we ate in secret.

With Kennington I stayed for a while with the Jodhpur Lancers at Devise. The troopers were Indians, mostly

Rajputs, under their own Indian officers; three or four British officers were also attached to the regiment—Colonel Hyla Holden, Majors Wheatley and Gell. With their ready help I made many drawings of Indians belonging to other units, among them one of Gobind Singh, of the 2nd Lancers, the first Indian to win the V.C. I was sorry for the men, living in rough shacks in the snow, snow that was churned into mud round the camps. From the Jodhpuris I got a mount whenever I wanted one, and with an Indian orderly, rode out to various villages, to Frêsnes and Misery, Athies and Monchy Lagache, where I could work quietly. Attached to the Jodhpuris was a French interpreter (a nephew of Puvis de Chavannes), and the Mayor of Devise and the châtelaine of Athies were both courageously roughing it in what remained of their houses, so we tasted of French hospitality. Then the Indian troops were ordered out to Palestine. I went to join Colonel Holden—I think our friends liked us to visit them when they took their turn in the front lines—when he went up for the last time. He was restless, for he hated the inactivity of trench warfare. To be shelled without being able to reply irked him; he looked forward, he said, to the chance of fighting in the open, and he would be glad to get his men away; the conditions under which they lived had told heavily on them. Before I returned to camp I saw a bombing party start out—looking like a party of strange mummers as they emerged, just after sunset, from behind a ruined wall. It was urgent some prisoners be taken, to identify German units opposite.

Before leaving our hosts, I offered a portrait drawing to whomever cared to sit. The proposal, I noticed, was met with an icy silence. I wondered why, and found that Kennington had drawn one of them, who, going up to the trenches shortly afterwards, was killed. But one day Colonel Holden said he would sit, he would like a drawing for his wife; and I drew his handsome head, with its thick curling hair. Poor Holden, he was killed some months afterwards in a cavalry charge in Palestine.

Kennington was as enthusiastic as I while drawing Indians, and I wrote to the War Office offering to devote myself for a time, together with Kennington, to making records of the Indian troops in France. The suggestion was not encouragingly received, though afterwards my friends at the India Office regretted that this was not done; such drawings would have been welcomed in India. I wrote too to Colonel Buchan, suggesting that some method might well be employed for the records we were to make. We had no instructions from H. Q., yet surely more might be done were each artist attached to a particular army. But people at home were too busy to take notice of so relatively unimportant a thing as the making of artists' records. John, who was with the Canadians, was as worried as I by the magnitude of the task.

A letter came from him:

Canadian War Records,
Canadian Corps H. Q.

My dear Will,

I very much hope you'll be able to look me up on your way to Arras. I am quite near Arras—at Antigny at the Château. You are quite right, scarcely anything can be done here in a short time. I have done actually very little yet. I am just beginning to form an idea of what my big canvas should contain. I hope you'll come out again. The British authorities seem strangely mean in their treatment of artists. I shall need to be about here for a year at least I feel and can only hope *I* shan't be interfered with before I have collected everything I want. Yes, the problem is immense and magnificent. One can only familiarise oneself as much as possible with all the multitudinous details and then set about arranging them in order. So much contraction is necessary.

Orpen is generally at Amiens. I have seen him several times. If you came my way as you suggest you could telephone to Capt. Robertson, Canadian War Records, to ascertain if I am at home as I am often out for entire days. Coming from the Somme where I imagine you to be you would anyway pass this way on your way to Arras. I don't know whether you hold a commission but presume you don't as Alice didn't mention it in her note when sending me your address.

Well, I hope to see you soon and perhaps hear from you before seeing you.

JOHN.

I met John more than once, looking superb in his uniform, the only bearded major, I think, in the army. He had refused to shave, much to the disgust, I gathered, of the authorities. I heard from Orpen, while I was visiting some of the famous Somme battlefields:

A. P. O. S/37.
23. 2. 18.

My dear Rothenstein,

I'm afraid I never answered your last letter, forgive me. I met a man yesterday who had seen you and he told me Kennington had been ill—I hope he's alright again=I am glad you had such a good time=you came to the right place =the Somme is 'it'. What a new world it all is=I am looking forward to going down to Italy soon=but I want to get back to London first in a week or so, just to look over what I have done quietly. I'm afraid most of it is tosh=it's hard to judge out here, things impress one that have no value as regards art, but they are very vital for the moment.

John is having a great time! No, his Headquarters were never Cassel—but they were mine—and he hunted me out there! John in the Army is a fearful and wonderful person. I believe his return to 'Corps' the other evening in a steel helmet will never be forgotten. He's going to stop for the duration. I was lent to the Canadians to do a 'sketch' of General Currie=this has turned into a group of twelve, and takes up half my time at present. I wish I could have met you when you were near P. I know every inch of the Somme off by heart and could have shown you places in one day that would have given you work for months.

I am very happy; but am slowly losing all the money
I ever made, so I expect a rough time after the war.

Yours ever,

ORPEN.

But I needed no guide; everywhere was the austere beauty of
desolation. Yes, I wanted to give up months to drawing these
places. The strange thing about the ruined villages and châteaux
was their look of immemorial age, as though, like the abbeys
of my boyhood, they had always been ruins. The worn,
attenuated rafters making pitiful shapes against the sky had
already acquired the silver-gray of age; the colours of wall-
papers had become delicate and flowerlike—'as though a
Queen long dead were young'. The bricks of houses and
barns and villas, so commonplace-looking as one saw them
outside the war zone, were now exquisitely coloured, and the
fragments of wall that rose above the rubbish were so
beautiful and shapely, that I wanted to draw them with the
care of a Van Eyck. Every hour spent in drawing was an
hour given to a sacred task. Had I asked myself, would I
rather there had been no war, and consequently no such
strange, livid beauty, I should have been at a loss how to
answer. Truth to tell, I never valued life more highly than
during the weeks spent in making these records. My
soldier friends could not understand what appeared to them
unnatural industry, and that I dreaded recall. Though I have
often wasted a day, it has rarely been without a morbid
twinge of conscience. Men say: you cannot always be working;
you must get knowledge of life. True, but the most industrious artist has still time enough to live actively; an artist
knows he must give his whole self to his art; this is his morality;
and though, in sinning against it, he may appear virtuous in
the world's eyes, he knows better. 'He was too lazy to write
a sonnet, so he made a revolution.' I have suffered more
when in the country keeping my word, carelessly given, to
go somewhere when the effect I have been waiting for
suddenly appears, or sitting on a committee, or speaking

333

instead of doing, or waiting for sitters who fail to appear, than from any vagaries of fortune. Happily a full day's work brings back self-respect. There were few days when I could not work in France; if it snowed or rained, I could find shelter somewhere. One of the things, indeed, from which my officer friends suffered was the boredom of life in the trenches, and of waiting in billets behind the lines. For war is by no means all fighting; there is much more of idleness.

Hearing from Maurice Arbuthnot that I was in the neighbourhood, Sir Hubert Gough kindly invited me out to his Headquarters. They were at Nesle, a busy little town, with its French inhabitants about the streets. That Nesle had escaped the fate of other places in the war zone was due, Gough explained, to a German general who disapproved of wholesale destruction. While lunching with Gough, I met many of his staff, among them General Uniacke, who was in charge of the artillery. In his room I saw plans wherein the machine-gun defences were shown—broad bands pencilled at all angles; to a civilian mind it appeared impossible that men could force their way through. I saw, too, some photographs taken from the air, one of which showed, when compared with others, that a bridge across a canal, on the German side, had recently been hidden by camouflage, a significant portent, it appeared. I recall, also, a long photograph, made from drawings pieced together, showing a considerable view of the German front. A Frenchman, Paul Maze, creeping, day after day, beyond our front lines, had made these notes for Gough, an act of rare courage and devotion. Had I been asked to perform a like service, I should certainly have funked it. But I was pleased when, after seeing some of my studies, Gough said he would like me to be attached to his Army.

During the early part of 1918 there was a general feeling that the rumoured German offensive would take place on the Fifth Army front. I became friendly with some gunners at Roisel and Hervilly, and early in March I painted some of their guns. The six-inch naval guns, with their snake-like

camouflage, were beautiful objects. I was shown various
guns skilfully hidden behind the front, none of which was
in action that their whereabouts might remain secret. But
other guns, further back, were now busy, trained on bridges,
hangars and roads on the German side. The shock one received when standing near a gun in action was like a sudden
blow on the chest. I used to carry my drawings with me;
while on a visit to a unit of the Third Army the Colonel sent
for me early one morning; was it not time, he asked, I took
my drawings to G. H. Q.? I took the hint, and motoring up
to Montreuil, handed my drawings over to Major Lee, and
asked him, in view of the hint I had received, if there were
any place on the Fifth Army front he might wish recorded.
I had been drawing guns, I told him, between Hervilly and
Hargicourt; and after I had drawn some guns discreetly hidden
in a sunken road, I was met with signs of embarrassment
by Captain Turnbull, the officer in charge; his orders
were, he explained, with many apologies, to place me under
arrest. He sent me down in my car, in charge of two armed
sergeants, to Brigade H. Q., where I was interviewed by an
indignant Brigade Major. He heard I had been drawing his
guns; he used strong language, and behaved, indeed, just
like a stage Major. I produced my White Paper, signed by the
Adjutant General, which allowed an official artist to go where
he wished. Next he could not decipher my name, and
asked me roughly what it was; more strong language
followed, and Lee was amused when I told how I pronounced
the first 'R' with a strong Teutonic accent, adding 'Now, I
suppose were my name Smith, you would have me shot'.
Lee hinted that important events were portending, and
gunners were naturally jumpy. I left him to return to the
front, and arrived late in the evening at Tincourt, where I
spent the night at a C.C.S. At dawn came the sound of a
terrific bombardment continuing without intermission.
Here at last was the preliminary to the expected offensive.

Major Lee had spoken of some tanks near Templeux
which I might like to draw. I started out in a dense

fog; the bombardment continued, growing ever louder. As we proceeded the road became encumbered with troops, some coming in our direction. My chauffeur looked anxious; he had had his share of fighting and never liked taking me near the front. Passing some Brigade H. Q., I stopped to make inquiries. Here some staff-officers flung at me the astonishing news that I should as likely as not find the tanks I asked about in German hands. I had better go back, they said. I told my chauffeur to go to Roisel, where I had lately been working. There I found the guns in action, and rumours of a German break through. There were doubts as to how long Roisel could be held. Wounded men were already being brought into the dressing station. To draw now seemed indecent, and I thought of returning to Tincourt, to offer my services in the C.C.S. there; but the hospital was to be abandoned, I heard, and I was advised to go to Marchèlepot where I had lately stayed with Howard Somervell. On the way thither I passed through Péronne, which was soon to be evacuated. Péronne was full of stores of all kinds which I believe fell into German hands. I went to the Officers' Club to get a bite, and found it empty save for a sergeant who was aimlessly, I thought, engaged in smashing the looking glasses, as though they could be of use to the Germans. Marchèlepot was well behind the front, yet even here numbers of wounded were being brought in and laid down on their stretchers. I offered to stay and help. My first task was to find out the names of the more desperately wounded men, so that their relatives could be written to, a ghastly business, for many were so fearfully mangled, it was often impossible to get at their identity discs.

As the day wore on more and more stretchers with their pitiable burdens were carried in. The beds in the wards were full, and stretchers were set down wherever there was space to receive them, while outside the wards they were laid in long close rows. One had to stride across dying men to get to the beds, whence came piteous appeals for water. But in the case of abdominal wounds, water must be refused;

and my heart was wrung to a pitch that, but for the
incessant call for activity, would have been insupportable.
I can still see the beautiful faces of the dead, calm, ethereal,
and strangely happy, whatever the previous agony endured.
The places of those who died were quickly taken by the
living, whose endurance was beyond praise. The zeal of the
nurses, and of the surgeons, was untiring. For three days
and three nights no one got more than an occasional snatch
of sleep. For three days and three nights I witnessed this
devotion; for Somervell had asked me to take charge of the
Officers' Ward. On the fourth morning, going outside for
a breath of air, I saw some staff officers sitting by the side of
the road studying maps. A few minutes later my chauffeur
came up, much perturbed: they wanted to requisition my car;
we must leave at once, before it was taken. Somervell had
heard that the Germans had crossed the Somme at St Christ;
a hospital train, the last likely to get through, had just come
in. I left the C.C.S. reluctantly, and to my chauffeur's relief
we were soon on the road towards Amiens, and were
scarcely out of Marchèlepot, when, at a cross road, I heard
my name shouted from a passing car; it was Captain Turnbull, who told me he had managed to get his guns away from
Hervilly. Passing through Villers Carbonnel some shells fell
not fifty yards away. At Amiens I could get into touch with
Neville Lytton, who was then head of the Press Bureau, and
would know what was happening.

When, in Amiens, I saw everything going on as usual, the
shops, and the women marketing, and the children playing
in the streets, as though nothing untoward was about, I
wondered if the horrors I had left behind me were real. I saw
the great pile of the Cathedral standing, beautiful and im-
passive, as it had stood for centuries; surely its existence
could not now be threatened? Amiens had long been, for the
officers, the great relief from the trenches. To come into the
town, to lunch or dine sumptuously, to spend lavishly,
to intrigue with the pretty waitresses, to disappear into
mysterious houses with less pretty 'waitresses', to enjoy the

questionable pleasures of a town which showed no marks of war was, for these nerve-racked youngsters, an escape from madness and filth to an ordered world. There were dangers at Amiens; but these seemed as nothing to those of the trenches; to motor from a landscape bare as that of the moon to the friendly cultivation of Picardy, to see trees and farms and the normal life of the fields again, was a solace to the spirit of these poor heroic lads. In Amiens, save for the sandbags round the base of the Cathedral, there was no sign of war; was this town, so full of cheerful life, to become a city of ruin, like so many others I had seen?

When I saw Lytton, and spoke of the rapid German advance, and how shells had fallen in Villers Carbonnel, he was frankly incredulous. So was a staff officer who came in. However, it was not my business to discuss military matters. On Lytton's advice I remained in Amiens to await events. I met General Uniacke in the town, from whom I heard news of the Fifth Army. Orpen's brother was staying at my hotel —so too was Kapp. I motored out and saw and heard much that was disturbing; going into Albert, some shells bursting near portended a renewed German attack, while during the night German aeroplanes visited Amiens, bombing at their own sweet will; there seemed to be no defence, and some thirty houses in the centre of the town were destroyed. It was a nerve-racking night, one of the worst I have ever experienced. In the morning I went to see the railway station which had been bombed, and there I met Somervell and my medical friends; they had abandoned the C.C.S. soon after I left.

Meanwhile John and Orpen and the other official artists had been recalled, my whereabouts being fortunately unknown to Major Lee, but it was not long before I received an emphatic order to report myself at G. H. Q. No artists were to remain any longer in France.

I left France with reluctance. At home I heard rumours about the Fifth Army which made me indignant; I saw Herbert Fisher and told him of my experiences, which in no way bore them out. He was going to breakfast with Lloyd George, and I begged him to deny these stories of rout and confusion which were abroad. I wrote to Sir Hubert Gough to tell him how proud I was to have been connected in some measure with his gallant army. Gough replied:

> *The Brae,*
> *Farnham.*
> *6th May.*

Dear Rothenstein,

Many thanks for your nice note. I have been ages acknowledging it, for which please forgive me, but I have been very busy since I came home.

Where are your pictures exhibited? I would like to go and see them. We had exciting times since I saw you. We had to withstand the most colossal storm that has ever been thrown at any army. More than double what any other army was called to face. For meeting and stemming this torrent with the most insufficient resources placed at my disposal, a miserable Government backed and supported by a grateful people, recalled me! I never heard such stories as were told against me and the 5th army in London when I got back!!

However I am quite happy and have plenty to do. I don't mean to soldier any more. If one cared what the politicians, their Press, and their friends say, life would not be worth living!

> Yours sincerely,
> HUBERT GOUGH.

I had seen enough of the war to understand why men on leave were reluctant to talk of their experiences. Of late many books have been written, telling of things which, during war time, could not well be spoken of.

One effect of the war was to make history more immediate and poignant. How lightly one was wont to read of past wars, and having Shakespeare's histories with me in France, I found that here they had a new meaning. Many hold that war, despite its horrors, gives to life an added value; that to the man in the trenches, the things that once seemed so commonplace now appear rainbow-hued. In this the artist and the soldier are at one; for emotions bring every man into touch with the substance of art. Every man has a moment of genius when in love, and the sight of the stars on a clear night and the presence of death have the same meaning for us all. To have walked on to the stage as a super has given me a proud sense of having stood near the true actors in a great drama.

CHAPTER XXXVIII

ANDRÉ GIDE AT FAR OAKRIDGE

Back at Oakridge, I busied myself with war-paintings, and in addition, with drawings of week-end visitors. Many came, Margaret Woods, the Binyons, the Fishers, the Batesons, the Walter Raleighs, the Johns, Galsworthy, Oliver Lodge, Henry Newbolt, Yeats and W. H. Davies. The poets in the country puzzled and amused me: I would take them to remote valleys, through flowering orchards and hanging beech woods, yet they never seemed to notice anything. Yeats would keep his eyes on the ground, and while Davies was with us, he would talk literary gossip, and ask my opinion of this or that poet, while cuckoos sang and rainbows arched the valley.

At this time I wanted to make drawings which should spring into being at one 'jet', a rhythm of lines made without taking eyes from sitter, or hand from pencil and paper. Why should not a portrait drawing be as lyrical as an imaginative one? Hence I placed my sitter opposite the light, thus avoiding shadows and disregarding local colour, on hair or skin. A few of these drawings have, I think, a lyrical quality; too many of them were failures. But mostly I painted, not landscape only, but interiors with my wife and children, and portraits of village neighbours. One old man, Eli Gardiner, noted hedger and thatcher, who looked like Tolstoy, had the wisdom of the unlettered. He knew his Bible, the Old Testament especially, and could interpret the sign of the skies—the sun, clouds, and the flight of birds—and he knew the secret life of field and hedgerow. Most of our neighbours were called Gardiner; the name was said to be of French

341

origin. A village nearby, France Lynch, had been the haven of Huguenot refugees. I also painted Mrs Seth Gardiner, a strikingly handsome old lady, who put me in mind of Mrs Leslie Stephen. She was the mother of several handsome sons, one of whom, Jim, had a shrunken leg. In spite of this, Jim, with the help of a crutch, could leap on and off a horse, could ride a bicycle, play cricket, and run as fast as others on their two legs. He was also the local carrier, kept sheep, poultry and a shop, baked bread and cakes and was a shrewd politician. I had many good friends among our Oakridge neighbours. I relished their rich Gloucestershire voices, their Shakespearean vocabulary. At Christmas 'socials' they would act plays—Heaven knows where they got them!—so trivial and character-less, that I bethought me of a play *The Village Wedding*, by Charles McEvoy, a brother of Ambrose McEvoy, which I had seen in London. I asked, and readily obtained, his assent to produce this play at Oakridge. The rehearsals were a difficulty; the players attended or stayed away at their pleasure. But on the night they surpassed themselves, and so pleased Lady Darwin, who came over from Brookthorpe with her husband, that she wrote a play especially for our villagers, which they acted so beautifully, its author was moved to tears. Each year we produced a new play. I was scene painter and producer; but before we left Gloucestershire a true stage-manager took my place. This was William Simmonds, who had lately come with his wife to live at Oakridge. I had heard vaguely of Simmonds as a painter, and as a carver of puppets. I was henceforward to become intimate with a beautiful character and an enchanting artist.

Now I put Gimson and my craftsmen friends above the average painter and sculptor, but I could never agree with Lethaby that any work well done is fine art. The creative artist feels the uniqueness of things, and of himself. The craftsman usually repeats his patterns, and thereby repeats himself. Simmonds however endowed every figure he carved with something of his own nature, yet each seemed possessed with an individual soul. It is this inner life, be it lyrical or dramatic, which outlasts that of its creator, and distinguishes a fine work of art from a merely skilful one. Whether this last resemble a Bouguereau or a Cézanne, a Canova or a Rodin, matters not; for if the quick soul be not within, it is but a doll to be thrown aside.

Few men—how words are abused by use!—have *taste*; can savour the flavour, the aroma, of man's precious vintages. Most are deceived by the label, the market price, or their habits have dulled their palates. Yet now and again a man's work is assessed at its true value; A. E. Housman's *Shropshire Lad* became, almost at once, an English classic. Similarly the purity of William Simmonds's puppets is recognised by all who see them, young and old.

Housman came sometimes to stay at Woodchester, when he would walk over to Oakridge; and I was more than once his guest at Cambridge. I said earlier that one might never foresee Housman's views, on men and their works, on politics and on life. He was the only conservative poet I knew, one who had no patience with idealism, vague or otherwise. I delighted in his grim, dry comments; and as I had no claim to precise knowledge or scholarship, he was an indulgent listener. His rooms, like his talk, his dress and his austere bachelor ways, rejected all ornament.

Max once wrote in a book Housman gave me:

T. H. and A. E. H.

How compare either of these grim two?
Each has an equal knack,
Hardy supplies the pill that's blue,
Housman the draught that's black.

But at the High Table, and in the Common-Room afterwards, there was nothing grim in Housman's taste. He was the best of hosts, and a sure judge of wine.

André Gide was in England during the war, and he told me, with amusement, that when, on landing, he informed the Intelligence-officers that he was going to Cambridge, he was asked, was he a pacifist? They connected Cambridge, maybe, with Lowes Dickinson and Bertrand Russell. He came to stay with us for a time, and brought with him a young nephew, whose English was better than his own. The boy made friends with my son John, while Gide and I discussed everything under the sun. Once again I delighted in the range and subtlety of a Frenchman's intelligence; and I regretted my long severance from France. No one understood art more profoundly than Gide, no one's view of life was more penetrating; and while he talked, I made a dozen drawings of him, some of which seemed to please him, for he pressed me to come to Paris, to make a set of French drawings; I must draw Proust, and other of his friends. A book of such drawings, perhaps with comments by Gosse, would, he assured me, be welcomed in France. He was puzzled by my paintings, which had, he said, the vitality of French paintings, but were not abstract enough. But his writing was not abstract, I reminded him; he was careful to be clear, very clear, even about things other writers would wish to veil.

Gide had a half satanic, half monk-like mien; he put one in mind of portraits of Baudelaire. Withal there was something exotic about him. He would appear in a red waistcoat, black velvet jacket and beige-coloured trousers and, in lieu of collar and tie, a loosely knotted scarf. I missed Gide when he left us. Such talk as his, so alert, so profound, gave me a nostalgia for Paris.

The heart of man had no secrets from Gide. There was little that he did not understand, or discuss. He suffered, as I did, from the banishment of truth, one of the distressing symptoms of war. The Germans were not all black, and the Allies all white, for Gide. We were in the war, which had been brought about by Germany's megalomaniac ambition, and we must carry it on until Germany had been brought to her knees; but all Germans were not brutes, nor baby killers—they were Europeans, like ourselves. And Gide disdained men in haste to disclaim any regard for German philosophy and literature who made him, he said, ashamed of being an 'intellectual'. It was for us to uphold the honour of truth, threatened and shamed as she was from all sides. And I told Gide how, when with the armies in France, I found a more gallant spirit towards our enemies and more respect for truth than I met with at home.

CHAPTER XXXIX

A SHEFFIELD PROFESSORSHIP

DURING the year 1917 Herbert Fisher, now Vice-Chancellor of Sheffield University, asked me to come to speak at the University Luncheon Club. I was at first reluctant to go so far; then I bethought me that I might find a new subject in the armament works, so I went, and spoke at the club, not without some effect; for I was invited to give six annual lectures at the University, and in case of acceptance, a chair of civic art would be established. I was pleased to get into touch with Yorkshire again, and the country round Sheffield was beautiful. My lectures were well attended, though after a while deemed dangerous for the students of the School of Art. I began two paintings in the steel works of a friend, Samuel Osborn, but the noise and heat defeated me, and they were left unfinished. However I painted two buffer-girls. These girls wear scarlet handkerchiefs round their heads, scarlet neckerchiefs about their throats, and sleeveless blouses, lest, during the buffing process, anything catch in the machine. Though exhibited in Sheffield, this painting was acquired for a South African gallery.

I renewed, too, an old acquaintance with Edward Carpenter, who lived at Millthorpe not many miles from Sheffield in a house he had helped to build, with his friend Edward Searnehough. Carpenter had an affectionate nature and a real love for mankind, but his vision was too vague, and he was over-attentive to faddists and theorists. He lacked the power of men like Ruskin and Morris; the most concrete thing he achieved was the sandal. Carpenter rarely came to

346

the University. The bachelor's degree, he complained, rather than the humanities, was, in too many cases, the Sheffield undergraduate's final aim.

The Fishers lived at Ecclesall in a Georgian mansion with an ample garden overlooking a noble stretch of country, where undergraduates and professors were always welcomed. The influence of a man of Fisher's character and vision was an important element of university life. Although one missed the communal life of Oxford and Cambridge, which allows students to sharpen their minds one against the other, yet the University brought men of inspiring character into the industrial centres. No men of the calibre of Herbert Fisher or Sir Henry Hadow, G. C. Moore-Smith and J. B. Leathes at Sheffield, of Sir Michael Sadler, Sir William Bragg and Lascelles Abercrombie at Leeds, of Walter Raleigh, Oliver Lodge, Oliver Elton, W. L. Bragg and Samuel Alexander at Liverpool and Manchester, have yet been brought into similar relations with provincial art students. Moreover, such men might have a fruitful influence on the quality of our major industries.

The task I set myself was to plead for some practical encouragement of local talent; Fisher was hopeful, for during the war trade was flourishing. Others too encouraged me. Gordon Bottomley, who, a Yorkshireman born, remained faithful to the North, wrote in one of his enchanting letters:

' How splendid, how just, that the most enlightened of our modern Universities—and a Yorkshire one, too,—should found a chair of civic art and install you as its first occupant, is one of those ideal things that one loves to hear of, and so seldom may. I should like to offer my congratulations to Sheffield. *E pur si muove*: the good news of all the arts is still to be brought in a great measure to our North Country to make the young people aware of how much more there is to be got out of life than they are getting now.... How I wish you had been there when I was a youngster.'

I pleaded in vain; and when, later, I resigned the chair, no one was chosen to follow me. The sole effect of my

Sheffield activities was to move Sir Michael Sadler to make a gesture—a well-meant gesture—of the success of which I was doubtful. I had been wiser to be frank at the start. Sadler's plan was for several young painters to make designs for panels in the Leeds Town Hall. If the civic authorities could be persuaded to accept them, and to find the necessary money, the designs would be carried out *in situ*; failing this, Sadler would pay £20 for each design, and, in addition, all material expenses. I knew the municipal mind too well to be hopeful; yet when I put Sadler's project before Wadsworth, Stanley Spencer, the two Nashes, H. S. Williamson and my brother Albert, they agreed to accept it. At Sadler's suggestion, Jacob Kramer, a Leeds man, joined the group. The designs were to be approved by me; to reject any of these was disagreeable, but one by Stanley Spencer was, though admirable in itself, ill-adapted to the others. I was compelled, therefore, to tell him so. I find Spencer writing to me in his sincere and downright way:

> '*Fernlea*'
> *Cookham*,
> *Berks*.
> *April 23rd*, 1920.

Dear Mr Rothenstein,

I received your letter. I hope you received my telegram saying I could not come to Leeds.

Do not distress yourself over this misunderstanding. I make mistakes especially ones like these every day of my life.

Of course I felt very vicious at the time and could have done you any amount of harm but this was the result of disappointment and that makes me vicious always. And as I can easily forgive mistakes of any kind you must as I know you will forgive me for wanting to do unkind things to you.

You see I caught the 8-50 and went to Leeds; got out went to Town Hall, saw 6 panels: 4 in large Hall or Theatre and 2 in Vestibule. After that I thought possibly I might find Prof. Sadler at home but he was away, so I feeling intensely lonely, caught the 3-8 train back to London.

I am staying at Seaford with the Carlines and I did not want to break such a delightful holiday with another visit to Leeds. Your brother thinks I have seen all that is necessary.

Yesterday we all went out on to the downs and did paintings. The 'artists' were: Mr Carline (the father of the flock), Hilda, Sydney and Richard Carline and Gilbert and Stanley Spencer. We did the paintings first and set them in a row in a dear old barn and admired them for all we were worth because you see there was no one else to do so.

Yours very sincerely,
STANLEY SPENCER.

The Nashes' designs also came in for some criticism, but finally all were completed. Sadler deemed them insufficiently harmonious, while I knew they would shock the municipal eye. Had the work been commissioned, these gifted young men could have carried it out; but without a definite promise, they could scarcely be expected to achieve completed and harmonious designs. I agreed with Sadler that it would be wise to let the matter gently drop, without reflecting on the capacity of the artists to carry the scheme through. But I had been weak in furthering a project I did not believe would reach fruition. I learnt my lesson, and later was more happily situated when associated with the execution of wall paintings at St Stephen's Hall, and at Morley College.

Yet I hoped that, after the war, paintings illustrating local aims and achievements might be carried out; to that end a group of young men was prepared to go anywhere in England, to co-operate wherever possible with local authorities, to work for little more than their keep. For now for the first time there was a subject matter common to artists and laymen, and everywhere a spirit of devotion which must not be wasted. To this end I wrote a pamphlet, *A Plea for a wider use of Artists and Craftsmen*, which Clutton-

Brock reviewed generously, and which brought encouraging letters from Gilbert Murray, Mackail, Cornford, Conrad, and Masefield.

Our faith was justified by the exhibition of paintings, organised by P. G. Konody for the Canadian War Records, where Augustus John showed a superb cartoon, Wyndham Lewis an austere and impressive Calvary, while Walter Bayes, Paul and John Nash, Roberts, Nevinson, Kennington, and Meninsky contributed works of remarkable quality. Each painter was at his best, as though a great subject brought to the surface his sincerest and most personal powers. Aesthetic interest was, for once, perfectly united to a full and dramatic content; could this movement be continued, no Continental art would surpass our own. To my mind the work produced by English painters during the war remains a significant contribution to the European art of our time.

'Men, feelings, must descend the hill.' The heightened emotion produced by the war slowly cooled; the tendency to separate form from content spread to England from France, and a great opportunity for making painting a vital part of social and religious life was missed. A chapel near Newbury, filled with paintings by Stanley Spencer, bids fair to be the greatest example of decorative painting done during this century.

CHAPTER XL

CONVERSATIONS WITH RALPH HODGSON

THE saying of Jesus about the young man with great riches has aesthetic as well as moral significance. There are so many theories and influences that must be shed if the inner spirit is to be freed, so many time-wasting entanglements which attend on worldly success. But there is another, an apocryphal saying of Jesus, recorded in one of the gnostic books: 'Young man, first learn to use the wealth which is not yours, then you may use that which is yours in very truth'; which has an equal import. While we are young, and on the road, we may learn the methods and devices of an art; later, if we have faith, a personal method will come of itself; spirit will become flesh. But concentration on each part, that a life may possess the whole, is too hard a task for most. An artist with great intelligence, but wanting in will, and with a small equipment, is often more interesting as a man than one with the talents and tenacity to enable him to fulfil the responsibilities an artist has towards art. An organist, to give his attention to a multiple keyboard, must pull out first one stop and then another that the right sounds shall result; the minor artist, unequal to the complexities of such an instrument, draws pathetic notes from a penny whistle; and is belike (I have known several such) a reckless and a passionate theorist.

Rimbaud, Verlaine, Gauguin and Van Gogh sounded a note in their lives, to which others have since attuned themselves; indeed, a violent anti-social attitude has again become a convention among advanced poets and painters. Not so Ralph Hodgson, whose poems I had long admired, to whom

351

Silvia Baker introduced me. She had given me a notion of a rather 'doggy' person. I was the more delighted when I met him. I found in Hodgson, devoted to dogs (of pure breed) as indeed he was, one of the most remarkable minds I had hitherto known. Here was a man; with a powerful head, held rather high, his face irregular and deeply lined, with wide, sensitive nostrils and an ample, rather loose mouth. (Walter Raleigh once declared a loose mouth to be a feature of an imaginative man.) And when he talked, he gave his whole mind, as it were, to creating wealth—wealth of observation, on man's past and present, on folk lore, history, psychology, art and literature; of this last he was an exacting critic. His contempt for the dishonesties and pretences of writers was withering; his passionate admiration for true poetry was expressed in terms so powerful and convincing, that one was fain to go, with a new zest and understanding, to Shelley, Blake and Coleridge.

Here, to my delight, was no doctrinaire critic, with theories to which writers must adjust themselves or be damned, but a man after my own heart, with no bias in favour of any form of art, who waited to be convinced by the ring of the voice to which he listened. For though we may have little or no knowledge of the subject treated by poet or painter, something within us responds instinctively to truth, and rejects untruth. For our natures swing between passivity and action. Our critical sense is passive; we violate it when we hasten to praise or blame before our active senses are liberated by natural attraction or repulsion. Hodgson's sensitive spirit would respond, like the needle of the compass to a magnetic field; a stream of ideas came rushing out, a spring fresh, clear and transparent, now descending in a cascade of foam, now passing through fields and villages and towns, reflecting sun and clouds, moon and stars, and the lovely and evil doings of men. I know only one other poet-talker who evokes so wide a view of life, James Stephens. This country of the mind is dear as one's birthplace; 'Where the brain lies let the heart lie also'—not good poetry, perhaps, but good sense. One can be amused by a partial point of view, can understand and defend it, but only full enlightenment can command the whole soul. The lack of such has sometimes stood in the way of full sympathy between myself and others, has, indeed, in some cases, created a sense of actual hostility.

CHAPTER XLI

ON THE RHINE

WHILE I was hoping to be sent back to France, to continue my records, the military age was raised, and I now came under the new law. I was to report myself at Gloucester, travelling thither in a railway-carriage full of sturdy farmers; at least so I deemed them to be. After stripping to be examined, to my surprise I found myself classed as a C.1. man. Only one other had been thus approved. Something wrong had been found with all the rest—varicose veins, weak hearts, and what not.

Of course everyone at Oakridge laughed at the idea of my joining up—one could not make the villagers believe that herein no difference was made between the classes. What others had stood I could stand. I thought of Manning, and of what he had been through, and how small would be my troubles compared with his. Came the day when I had to present myself at Gloucester, when I bade farewell to Oakridge, and walked down to Chalford Station. On the way I met a telegraph boy: I was to report in London immediately. There I was told to go to Cheshunt College, Cambridge, to lecture to Australian Education Officers. There I found Albert Mansbridge and Hartley Withers, both assisting Bishop Long, who now became my chief. I was a little disappointed, having resolved to face the hardships of a Tommy's life, but I found myself in agreeable society; the Australians were warm-hearted and enthusiastic students. I lectured on town-planning, on the museum of the future, the decoration of buildings, and I took the young Australians round the colleges.

Peace at last

It was now November, and I went to spend a few days with H. G. Wells and his wife at Little Easton Glebe, near Dunmow; Mrs Wells's resourcefulness, good taste, and knack of discovering bargains, had transformed the house, and she and H. G. together had turned barns and out-houses into spacious play-rooms. Catherine Wells, well informed, wise in her judgments, restful and gracious in her ways, was a perfect hostess. Wells's energy was undiminished, his zest for life insatiable. Among his other activities he had been writing leaflets which were dropped in Germany by the hundred thousand—our propaganda work, under Lord Northcliffe, was, he said, remarkably effective. The German armies were now in full retreat. Success was at long last attending the allied armies; each day news of the German collapse led us to expect a speedy end to the war. On the morning of the eleventh, Wells drove me to the station, he on his way to London, I bound for Cambridge. There I heard the long awaited news of the Armistice. At Cheshunt my Australian friends were preparing to parade the streets in triumph. Mansbridge and I were created *Diggers*—the greatest honour, I was given to understand, that an Englishman can receive,—and were carried shoulder high through the streets of Cambridge. Oh, the ecstatic relief and gratitude that the long-drawn menace and wastage were ended, and, among tens of thousands of parents that their sons would be given back to them, though one could not help thinking of those who, having survived hideous dangers, met their fate on the very threshold of peace. It seemed incredible that peace, so long, so eagerly awaited, had really come, and that Germany, deemed invincible, was beaten to her knees. For days a sense of thankfulness filled all hearts, to be too soon displaced by less cheerful feelings. Unpleasant experiences were in store for us; but for the moment we knew only that the slaughter was over, Belgium and Northern France liberated, and England safe.

I had been impatiently waiting for a sign from the Canadians; now I was told to proceed to Bonn, there to report to Captain Douglas, who was in charge of the Canadian War Artists.

At Bonn I was to make studies for a mural decoration, to be added to others previously commissioned by the Canadian Government. Afterwards I was to proceed to France and Belgium to draw and paint sites where Canadian units had been engaged. Passing through London to get my papers, at the Café Royal I chanced upon Munnings. Hearing I was bound for the Rhine, he told me of a Canadian friend, Brigadier-General Paterson, who was going to Germany by car and might well take me with him. He there and then proposed to write a chit to the General, and as he sat reflecting on what he should say, he looked up and asked if it would be correct to describe me as a good fellow? I assured him that it would, and as 'a good fellow' I was invited by the General to join him. We went through Mons and Louvain, and I was surprised to see how little damage had been done compared with the destruction at Bapaume and Péronne. The roads through Belgium were encumbered by derelict transport abandoned by the Germans during their retreat. How hurried this had been I now understood. At the frontier I left my kind host and took the train to Cologne. The carriage was full of young officers who carried revolvers in their belts; they warned me I too would need one. They were soon to think otherwise—the only men I saw wearing revolvers in Germany were Americans, at Coblenz. Arrived at Cologne, I walked into the Dom Hotel, then the H. Q. for British staff officers. The first man I saw there was Henry Nevinson, who invited me to the pressmen's table. Here I met a pleasant and hospitable company: E. H. Lacon Watson, Percival Phillips and Ward Price. Next morning I reported at Canadian H. Q. at Bonn.

Of my many strange experiences as an Official Artist, perhaps the strangest was to find myself, but a few months after the terrible March retreat, actually in Germany, among a subdued and apprehensive people. I discovered this on being given my billet, when at my ring an old gentleman descended, perturbed and apologetic, since he and his wife had not yet had time to turn out of their bedroom. He seemed surprised when I chose the second best room. I was to paint, for the Canadians, some aspect of the German occupation; it was not at first easy to find a subject in Bonn, where there were few signs of military operations. The guns were parked in the square, opposite the University. But while lunching with Major Molyneux, the eccentric British Town-Major, and his staff, I chaffed them for their lack of imagination. Surely one British gun at least, a modest symbol of final triumph, should be seen somewhere on the banks of the Rhine. For I bethought me that a gun so placed would make an appropriate subject for a painting. My suggestion found favour. A howitzer was taken down to the Rhine and placed on the parapet with its muzzle poking across the river, and a sergeant and a small contingent of men sent with a lorry to guard it. It was bitterly cold; snow fell, and I was sorry for the men told off to look after the gun. The wind was icy, there was no shelter, and again and again I thought I should have to give up my work; but with a pair of fur gloves hanging from my shoulders, into which I could put my numb fingers from time to time, I struggled on. Every officer in the Army of Occupation came along and photographed that gun. It amused me to think that, but for my wish to paint this symbol of the final triumph, no gun had been seen on the Rhine. One thing struck me as curious. Germans walking by often stopped to look at my painting and would say 'O, wie schön!' Now, I thought to myself, had the Germans won and placed a gun on the Thames-side in London, and a German painter been painting it, no Englishmen would have said, 'How beautiful'. No one thought of putting his foot through my canvas,[1] which now hangs in the Imperial War Museum at South Kensington.

I would often go by tram into Cologne. I gave up using my car, as my Canadian driver was so anxious to kill any

[1] From this canvas I painted the mural decoration, commissioned by the Canadian Government, now, I believe, at Ottawa.

German walking in the road; perhaps he had not had the chance to kill one during the war. I explored Cologne, visiting churches and galleries, where are many notable paintings and carvings, these last especially beautiful, of the Cologne School. In the streets I was struck by the happy marriage between old and new. The recent buildings, howbeit very modern in construction, take their place naturally beside the stately old halls and houses. Indeed I admired the adventure shown in German town-planning. Towards evening the Höhestrasse was crowded with townspeople, among whom British Officers and Tommies mingled. The shops where cutlery, cameras and field glasses were sold were full of English soldiers; the exchange was then about ninety marks to the pound and trade was brisk. Elsewhere the goods displayed were largely *ersatz*; boots and shoes and even clothes were made, in great part, from paper. The Germans impressed one as being anxious to make amends for the havoc of the war. The Versailles Treaty was not then concluded and there were as yet no signs of bitterness. There could be no grievance against our officers or men, for they behaved with admirable restraint; yet many privileges were taken for granted. I soon found myself adopting the position of one in uniform attached to an occupying army; if some advantageous view over square or river seemed likely to be found in a particular house, I would ring and ask to see it, and facilities for drawing, if required, were willingly given. When I was with Nevinson, he would ask, 'Which of us shall take the salutes?' and each time I replied, 'Oh, you take them to-day'. For Nevinson, a noted pacifist, who looked like a Confederate General, had missed no war during the last thirty years, and really loved military life. I was always somewhat embarrassed, on crossing the Rhine bridges, when the guards gave the full salute. And I was amused when Canadian soldiers came up and asked for directions, for now I wore a Maple-leaf in my cap, and a green armlet with *Canadian War Records* embroidered thereon. With Nevinson I saw how effective our blockade had been.

Some of the journalists described the wretched conditions of the people at Cologne and Bonn, but one day during dinner a telegram came which was passed round. It was from one of the great newspaper magnates, saying that no news testifying to the plight of the Germans, likely to arouse sympathy in England, must be telegraphed home.

I was glad to be billeted at Bonn instead of noisy Cologne. Bonn has a modest charm. Its quiet streets, the University square planted with limes, the clipped lime-avenues and the gardens of the merchants' handsome villas by the Rhine, displayed the ordered charm which, in Germany, seems universal. How simply the old Rhinelanders lived can be seen in the 'patrician's' house, in an annexe of which Beethoven was born. Such a small house, and the Beethoven rooms scarcely large enough to hold a bed, or a kitchen table! but Major Molyneux took me late one night, accompanied by two British military police-sergeants and a German detective, into the less reputable streets. They were searching for hidden weapons—to retain firearms was strictly forbidden. The German would knock at the door of a suspected house; a light appeared and the door was cautiously opened, which, once we were within, was locked on the inside by the police-sergeants, who then went upstairs with the detective; the lodgers were turned out of their beds and their rooms thoroughly searched. Other houses were then visited, but a single experience was enough for me; it was an intensely dramatic one—the dark house, the frightened men and women on the stairs, the hushed voices and the sordid secrets of a lodging-house laid bare. I asked the German detective how he selected the houses to be thus searched. His explanation was a curious one; evil livers, it appears, habitually urinate outside their doors. Whether this applies to German criminals only, or to others as well, I have never inquired.

My painting finished, I went back to France to paint and draw chiefly round Cambrai and Bourlon, where Canadians had been engaged. At Bourlon, where all was in ruins, I lived in a cellar with some officers of a Chinese Labour Corps. I painted the ruined church there, made drawings of the château and of other places nearby. The Chinese coolies were big, truculent men. The few families who were trickling back, to live in such cellars as they could find, were afraid of them, and the Comte and Comtesse of X. when they returned to their château at Bourlon, were indignant to find it in the occupation of Asiatics. Alas, there was no sense of property in the War Zone; men lived whereever they could find shelter from rain and protection from cold.

A few peasants were beginning to return; it was pathetic to see them gathering bricks, timber, corrugated iron, beams and the like to patch together some semblance of a home wherein to live; a piece of ground here and there would be cleared, and vegetables sown. But as yet the country was scarcely coming to life; it was still desolate, treeless, the villages obliterated or reduced to heaps of stone and brick, with everywhere dumps of unexploded shells and bombs, shattered tanks, broken rifles and the litter of war. Here and there a German prisoners' camp made a centre of life; I stayed in one of them, on the Cambrai-Bapaume road, for a time. The Germans were found to be handy men, resourceful and willing. They were well treated, and though naturally homesick, were by no means discontented. The Austrians, who were in a French camp, were sad-looking men, poorly clad and, I thought, underfed. It seemed wrong that these men should still be prisoners, so many weeks after the Armistice.

At Cambrai I found all the men and boys in the town wearing British uniforms, captured during the March retreat, and sold to them by the Germans. I heard many stories of the German occupation—of how during the great attack round Bourlon when the Canadian Cavalry rode into Cambrai, the Germans left, taking all their equipment. But afterwards, finding that the British had not occupied the town, they returned, to the despair of the population.

But I had not forgotten Ypres; the vow I registered in

1915 could at last be fulfilled. I made carefully measured studies of the Cloth Hall and Cathedral, of the ruins of the Church of St Martin, and among other places of a ruined house which I discovered afterwards to have been Talbot House, the Ypres home of Toc H—a drawing I gave later to the War Museum, as a tribute to the Padre, P. B. Clayton.

While drawing the pitiful ruins of the Cloth Hall and Cathedral I felt that their stones were sacred; to move a single one would be an act of vandalism. The ruins, and the ground on which they stood, might have been of one substance. Outside Ypres, ruined tanks lay like wounded animals, and about German pill-boxes and English dug-outs lay the rubbish of war, cases of shells and cartridges, broken rifles and helmets, and here and there human bones and ragged remnants of uniforms. At Paschendaele one still needed to keep to the duck-boards to avoid the mud and slime. That anything could again grow in this desolate region seemed impossible.

I remained in France and Belgium, where Kennington (who was also attached to the Canadian War Records, and had been making remarkable studies of Canadian soldiers) joined me, until the end of May 1919. Kennington became as excited as I over ruins and battlefields, and now turned his attention to these. We worked at Cambrai, Bourlon, Mœuvres, Havrincourt, Flesquières—everywhere the fantastic shapes and colours of ruined houses and shell-shocked trees provided a constant stimulus; we could scarcely bear to waste an hour of daylight. After six months we were recalled, to our minds all too soon. No work has ever satisfied me so completely as that which I undertook while acting as a British, and later, as a Canadian, Official Artist.

CHAPTER XLII

RETURN TO TOWN

I CAME back with several paintings and a portfolio full of drawings in gouache, a number of which were selected by Arnold Bennett for Canada, whither they were sent. As for the War Museum, I found Martin Conway[1] in despair; Lloyd George had stopped the grant, hitherto available. He wanted several of my gouache drawings and, above all, the painting of the British howitzer on the Rhine, for his museum, and he carried me off with this canvas, in a taxi, to see Sir Alfred Mond at the Office of Works. Mond had no funds, but Muirhead Bone came to his assistance, and purchased, out of his own pocket, a number of works, including my canvas, which he gave to the War Museum. Bone's generosity equalled his enthusiasm; he gave up precious time, inducing others to buy, and lecturing on the war-paintings. Arthur Clutton-Brock was especially warm in his estimate of my war drawings; he even wanted the Dean of Westminster to exhibit them as religious paintings, for such he deemed them to be. He thought very highly of Kennington's work and bought, as well as wrote about, his drawings, while Campbell Dodgson, with the help of the Contemporary Art Society, acquired drawings for the Print Room of the British Museum. Then we heard that Orpen had been commissioned to paint the Versailles Conference, while Sargent (somewhat against his will) was to portray the British and Colonial Generals. Meanwhile the War Museum brought together at Burlington

[1] Sir Martin, now Lord, Conway had been made Director of the Imperial War Museum.

House the paintings and drawings commissioned, presented
and acquired. Again I was impressed by their striking qualities;
and lately re-visiting the Museum I found no reason to change
my opinion of their importance in the history of modern
painting.

I now set to work to paint, as a mural decoration for
Canada, the gun on the Rhine guarded by a single modest
Tommy, a subject that seemed symbolic of our unboastful
share in the final downfall of the German military power.
Would that this spirit, which I believe was active in the
minds of the best Englishmen, had been dominant at Versailles. The 'hang the Kaiser' election was indicative of the
fevered, not of the normal, national temperature. I remember
writing to Fisher, congratulating him on being a member of
the Cabinet at a time when the future of Europe was to be
decided; here was England's chance to show severity un-
tainted by vindictiveness. Fisher agreed; he had put a
similar view before Bonar Law, who, while of the same
mind, pointed out that it was their duty as a Government to
carry out the policy of the majority in the country; surely it
is for statesmen to lead, I argued, not to follow, popular
opinion. Our high hopes were to be dismally disappointed.
Orpen, who saw and heard much at Versailles, described
Clemenceau as he sat, gloved, grim, determined, obstinate
and watchful, day after day.

What a rare chance was Orpen's, to have passing before
his easel all the historical figures of Europe. He was modest
about his position. 'I am sorry to say', he wrote, 'that I
have scarcely got on with my work here at all this time—I
mean the official work, but I have been painting some quite
interesting people. They have also induced me to write a
book about people and things I saw in Picardy and the
North, and the Peace Conference—as I have no idea of
writing—this is a wearing task—but it's great fun trying.'
Orpen's book when it appeared showed him to be a witty
and observant writer—I wondered that he found time in the
midst of his heavy task to produce so considerable a work;

363

but Orpen was indefatigable. The portraits he painted during these years of the war and afterwards during the Peace Conference are brilliantly vigorous and alive.

During 1919 the question of a return to London had to be faced. Our children missed the companionship of others of their own age, and they were pining for concerts and plays. Country life suited me and my work, and it was hard to give up our beautiful home and the fields and woodland we had grown to love. To keep both a town and a country house was out of the question, though to exchange these for a London lease (for houses were now only for sale, not to let) seemed a sorry bargain. We found a house with a studio on Campden Hill, a pleasant quarter of the town, with its quiet lanes and sequestered houses and gardens.

While house-hunting I came across Walter Greaves at William Nicholson's studio. In spite of the stir caused by his exhibition at the Goupil Gallery, I gathered from Nicholson that he was extremely poor, so some of us got together and decided to give the old man a dinner, and to present him with a cheque. Lord Henry Bentinck presided and Walter Sickert and others made speeches. When a cheque for £150 was handed to Greaves he was quite taken aback; he had never, he said, had so much money in all his life! He spoke simply and unaffectedly of his years as a painter; had Pennell been present even his hostility to Greaves would have been disarmed. Max, who was a great admirer of Greaves, wrote, before the dinner, from Rapallo:

My Dearest Will,

I wish I could be at the dinner to Greaves. It would be a real pleasure. Put my name down by all means, and let me contribute to the 'purse'. How much are people giving? Would £5 be a correct sort of sum? If so, put me down for that, and I will send you a cheque. I got from you, just as I was on the wing for Italy, *such* a delightful letter about my new book. I am immensely glad the stories seemed to you to come out well in their new form. I think I read them all to you and Alice at the farm. *Braxton* and *Savonarola* especially shall I always associate with Far Oakridge, their birthplace. Your laughter, while I used to read them bit by bit from day to day, was such an encouragement. Had you looked grave, neither of these stories would have come to completion. I hate to think of your leaving the farm—though I dare say you will both enjoy being in London. You aren't leaving it altogether, are you? only letting it? I should like to think that you keep a firm hold on all those immemorial title-deeds and things, and can settle down again on your land when your land calls to you. Meanwhile, in London, what a whirl of committees you will inevitably find yourself in. You must not overtire yourself. You must not join more than two new committees a week, nor resign from more than one. It is lovely to be back here with Florence, I had forgotten how perfect life here could be. I expect you will rather miss your trees and valleys—but I expect you will enjoy the opportunity of doing portraits. I liked Mrs Albert immensely, a sort of fairy, and it was a joy to see Albert home from the wars and evermore, a civilian. What a nightmare the years of the war seem, don't they?

Your loving friend,

MAX.

There was as yet no whirl of committees, but shortly after our return to London, Fisher sent for me—Lloyd George had lately made him Minister for Education—and asked me to undertake the direction of the Royal College of Art; its prestige as the chief Government school of art must be raised and a change of policy was desirable. Fisher and Sir Amherst Selby Bigge believed I could effect something towards this end. They suggested a term of five, I agreed to one of three, years. The appointment raised a storm in the National Society of Art Masters; both Fisher and I were abused, questions were asked in the House of Commons, a protest was made at the Board of Education. Certain qualifications were required to entitle a man to become head of an art school; the Board had selected a man with none to be Principal of the chief school in the country, and moreover, a painter, with little knowledge of the crafts. To appoint a man without previous administrative experience was, I admit, a risky experiment, and I could understand the art-masters' soreness. But I do not think the students were displeased.

At the College were four principal Schools—Design, Architecture, Sculpture and Painting—presided over by Robert Anning Bell, Beresford Pite, Francis Derwent Wood and Gerald Moira. Later the Board agreed to make the engraving school a full-time one, to Sir Frank Short's satisfaction, for he had devoted wellnigh thirty years to its efficiency. From my colleagues, when changes were proposed, I got loyal and ready help. Among the staff were R. Constable Alston, friend to all the students, E. W. Tristram, George Jack and Edward Johnston, the last three devoted to Lethaby, whom they had assisted during his Professorship at the College. Had Tristram been an authority on Italian, or Chinese, instead of on English painting, he would have had a European reputation. He has helped to preserve, and has copied, every fragment of mural painting throughout England; and his copies retain all the energy and delicacy of the originals. Edward Johnston has given an impetus to good handwriting, not in England alone, but in Central Europe, where in addition his influence on typography, in its change from gothic to roman form, has been incalculable. I found my new chiefs at the Board of Education, Sir Amherst Selby Bigge, E. K. Chambers, and my immediate chief, W. R. Davies, ready to take me by the hand and guide me in the administrative path. I had heard hard things said about the Board, but I have known few abler or more enlightened men than my colleagues there. But I had still some months before I must get into harness. As I had no longer landscape to inspire me I concentrated on portraits. One figure, of whom I had heard romantic stories, I now met.

366

This was Colonel Lawrence (he was always then spoken of as Colonel). Shy, fair haired and ruddy, with blue eyes and a tendency to look downwards, he would slip into a room, and disappear from it, unnoticed. I took to him, as most men do, at once. I had heard of him as a man of action, but was also struck by his intelligence, his incisive judgment of men and books and by his political vision. He had been painted and drawn by John; he seemed to like being painted and was willing to sit to me. I began a small full length of him in Arab dress, wearing his famous gold dagger, made—by a goldsmith in Mecca—from 150 Turkish sovereigns he had captured, the only gift he ever accepted from Feisul. Lawrence—'Please no longer a Colonel' [he wrote] 'they used to pay me £700 a year for the pleasure of calling me that name, when they stopped, I stopped too'—had a taste for uncompromising writers and painters, for his namesake D. H. Lawrence especially and for William Roberts. Lawrence met Hudson more than once at our house, for whom he felt something akin to hero-worship; and Hudson liked Lawrence. I also brought him and Fred Manning together. Now Lawrence was reticent about his Arab campaign. People tried all manner of ways to get him to talk of his adventures, but in vain; yet before Manning Lawrence was ready to open out, for once to spread his peacock's tail, and again and again he began, to be interrupted each time by Manning, who broke in, to my amusement, to talk of himself!

Lawrence wished me to draw Doughty, another of his heroes, whose *Arabia Deserta* I had come upon many years before at the Hampstead Library, as a frontispiece to a new edition; but it was Kennington who, falling in with Lawrence, went down to make the drawing, a powerful presentment of the old man, which so pleased Lawrence that he took Kennington out to the Hedjaz, where he made the remarkable series of pastel portraits, later reproduced in *The Seven Pillars of Wisdom*. I referred to Lawrence as shy and blue eyed, yet when he spoke of his disillusionment, or of some act of moral cowardice, his eyes and mouth would harden, when I caught a glimpse of another, a cruel Lawrence. Churchill now was courting him, wanting him at the Colonial Office as Arab adviser, but for a time Lawrence was coy. When at last he reluctantly consented he was never comfortable, and soon retired, for he set a high value on his independence. He was happier at Oxford, at All Souls, where I stayed as his guest. He was *persona grata* there, and the Fellowship allowed him to buy the books he valued, and drawings by Roberts, Kennington and Nash. Never was any one more recklessly generous in his patronage of artists. For himself he needed no more than would keep body and soul alive—I was sometimes doubtful of the body. He was now commissioning drawings for his *Seven Pillars*. 'My picture gallery grows slowly,' he wrote. 'Nicholson (W.) has done a General for me. Roberts (W.) is to do another. Kennington has drawn an Admiral. If I could find Wyndham Lewis (he is in Venice) I'd ask him to attempt Hogarth, and I want Lamb to agree to Dawnay's brother: and I've got two other people whom I want Spencer or someone to draw. Only I don't know the last: and I can't get to know them till my self-exile ends.' I was to draw Alan Dawnay. 'You are the only possible executioner for him of all the artists I know.'

After eight years largely devoted to landscape painting, I was grateful for the stream of sitters who consented to be drawn or painted.[1] For Winchester College I drew H. A. L. Fisher and Lord Grey, drawings of Dean Inge and E. M. Forster were acquired for King's College, Cambridge, while Siegfried Sassoon, Aldous Huxley, Arnold Bennett, Walter de la Mare, Ralph Hodgson, Sir Frank Dyson, Sir Oliver Lodge, Sir J. J. Thomson, Sir Ernest Rutherford and Sir William Bragg and numerous others allowed me the freedom of their features.

These last were physicists; and when later, during a visit to Berlin, I had the privilege of doing Einstein's portrait,

[1] I find, in the catalogue made by my son John, 167 portrait drawings noted between 1920–22.

he told me that he placed English physicists above all others. In his study there hung but one framed print, a portrait of Clerk Maxwell. During one of the sittings, a solemn stranger, looking, I thought, like an old tortoise, sat listening to Einstein, who, so far as I could understand, was putting forward tentative theories, his expressive face radiant, as he expounded his ideas. From time to time the stranger shook his heavy head, whereupon Einstein paused, reflected, and then started another train of thought. When I was leaving, the presence of a third party was explained. 'He is my mathematician', said Einstein, 'who examines problems which I put before him, and checks their validity. You see I am not myself a very good mathematician!'

We had pleasant neighbours on Campden Hill, the Thomas Arnolds, the Malcolm Macnaghtens, the Sidney Colvins, the G. P. Gooches, the George Booths, Kenneth Barnes, Violet Hunt and Wynnard Hooper. At the Gooches I met Ramsay MacDonald, Dr Sthamer the German Ambassador, and the first secretary, Herr Dufour-Feronce. There were then few houses where Germans were welcomed; their social relations were not yet comfortable, but Gooch, a true European, was friendly to all men of fine character; he was learned as he was kind—Fisher used to say if he wanted a clear light on any subject, he consulted Gooch. With MacDonald I felt an immediate sympathy. Our sons had been at Bedales School together, and this gave a common interest to the acquaintance. I had known of him heretofore as a humane statesman; I now found him, in addition, acutely responsive to beauty. His life had been too fully occupied with practical matters to permit of his reading or seeing pictures as much as he wished; but his real interest I felt to be in the intellectual life. I recollect his coming up to me, at the dinner given to D. S. MacColl, just after the fall of the first Labour Government, to say with feeling, 'my chief regret at leaving office is that I have done nothing for the arts'. I was amused when one day Lord Balfour came to my studio, and seeing a drawing of Ramsay MacDonald, remarked with a twinkle, 'a born parliamentarian'.

During 1920 a book of twenty-four of my recent drawings was published, followed by a second series two years later. Conrad, always an indulgent critic, in acknowledging a copy of the first series, showed himself still diffident, both about himself and his writings.

Dearest Will,

Thanks ever so much for the admirable book of portraits. Every one is a revelation—especially of course those of the people one knows, if ever so little. Of course I don't know many; but one has in all the sense of looking at the final expression in art and psychology.

Thank you dear people for being good to Jessie when she was in town. I couldn't face the racket (!) of it. Perfectly ridiculous—but I can't help it. I don't know what to say to people when I do meet them. I came for a day, arriving late and leaving early.

I have been writing a series of short prefaces for Heinemann's Ld.Ed. which will be published separately, also in a 250 copies edition. I will send you a copy—not that the things are of any interest, I have done nothing for more than a year and feel as if I couldn't do anything. I'll try however to keep in the collar. One must.

Always yours,

JOSEPH CONRAD.

Max, equally modest about himself, hearing that our youngest boy was to attend his old school, gave an amusing account of his own school-days.

'I am thrilled when you say that the last named is going to a school in Orme Square—Mr Wilkinson's. As if I didn't know that school! I went there, as a new boy, just 39 years ago! I was there from '81 to '85, and I am greatly glad that Billie is going to follow in those obliterated old footsteps of mine. I wonder if the school has quite all the charm it had in my time. There were only 15 or 20 boys in my time. 16 or 21, counting Mr Wilkinson, who was just one of us. I believe the school is larger and more elaborate now; but I feel that it must have kept very much of its quality. For Wilkinson himself (who is an old member of the Savile and with whom in later years I have very often lunched at the table near the window on Saturdays—his whole-holidays) remains as boyish as ever, making me feel always like a nonagenarian in his company. Do, when next you see him, give him my love. He is by far the best teacher I ever had; wonderfully understanding and "enthusing". He did— and I am sure still does—so sympathise with the mind of a small boy. It was he that first taught me Latin, and gave me a love of Latin, and thereby enabled me to write English *well*. Also he used to play "touch-last" with me at the end of afternoon school! Mrs Wilkinson, in those days, used to teach drawing to the boys. Hers were the only lessons I ever had. The free hand system—(two illustrations)—and so on. I am afraid I can't say that any success I may have had as a caricaturist is due to her teaching. You can see from the above how little I have profited. Look at the second of those jars. How weak—how poor! And what a trial I must have been to Mrs Wilkinson! But perhaps in those days my work showed more promise than it seems to show just now.

'Yours affectionately,

'MAX.'

CHAPTER XLIII

A VISIT TO DUBLIN

DURING the summer of 1921 I went with my son John to Dublin to stay with Lennox Robinson, in a dower house in Sir Horace Plunkett's garden. We reached Dublin at five in the morning, too early to disturb the household; so we wandered about the city, seeing the sights, under the guidance of a handsome policeman, of whom we had asked our way. Later in the day, at Sir Horace Plunkett's, when we remarked on the amiability of the Dublin police, laughter went round the table. It was explained to us that the Force was an anomaly, was boycotted: Dublin was policed by Sinn-Feiners—of course a police officer was delighted to be noticed. We had come at a stirring time; the first Dail was shortly to be held; so, too, was the horse-show, when feuds are for the moment put aside, and all parties meet in seeming amity. I went with Mrs J. R. Green, who greeted, and was greeted by, friends and foes alike. At Sir Horace Plunkett's, too, men of all parties came together; yet his house was soon to be burnt down by Irishmen. At a party at Miss Purser's I introduced a newly made friend, afterwards a Dail Minister, to Miss G. 'I can't shake hands with a murderer,' said Miss G., putting her hand behind her back; yet a few minutes later I found the two in amicable conversation. My son and I were invited to the opening of the Dail; then we discovered that no invitation had been sent to Plunkett. The error was hastily repaired, but too late. The streets were patrolled by rather sinister looking youths, their peaked caps low over their brows, who ordered people about with scant courtesy. I spent much time with Dermod O'Brien, James Stephens, Stephen Mackenna (the translator of Plotinus) and George Russell. Stephen Gwynn, anxious and perturbed, was in Dublin also, sad that the Conference, which so nearly succeeded, had failed; sad, too, that assassination had now become an accepted political weapon. His house, like Horace Plunkett's, was afterwards burned. Gwynn had the courage to be moderate when moderation was suspect, and while his wife was among the advanced Sinn-Feiners. So, too, was Mrs Green; and her secretary, a fair young girl, lovely as a Fra Angelico angel, was fiercely intransigent. I had lately seen something of war; now I breathed the strange air of revolution—strange, for there was so much friendliness everywhere. Only the youths in the street, with their jaunty caps and truculent manners, reminded me uncomfortably of sinister happenings. Dermod O'Brien and his wife took us over the Wicklow hills to Glendalough; we seemed to drive into the past when we left the high road, and crossed the wild, uninhabited hills, marked here and there with prehistoric stone walls. The little churches at Glendalough and the quiet lakes there, spoke only of peace. Yet nature's peace is an illusion. In an hour the quiet lake, like the heart of man, may change from peace to turmoil; and not rain and hail alone, but the blood of men, and of women and children, has splashed the stone walls of the tiny peaceful-looking churches. Nature and man are alike in this; they both forget quickly their own bloody history.

I was glad to have seen this bit of true Ireland and vowed I would some day return to see more. A country for a painter, I thought; A. E., who loved painting the Irish landscape, agreed. At Sir Horace Plunkett's was a room filled with A. E.'s canvases; they were all to perish with the house. But A. E. did not then appear perturbed, he was full of zest for life and of hope for the future. We talked of painting and painters, of books and their writers. He was always ready to talk at his office in Merrion Square or at his house. He

looked the primitive poet, with his shaggy head and beard,
his kind eyes and rough, sweaty skin; yes, I could see him
coming into a bare hall, prepared to tell long heroic stories
to rough chieftains sitting by the fire, drowsy or drunken
with mead. How attractive they were, these Irish poets, and
how hospitable. I parted from them feeling I was leaving true
friends behind. Yet hard words were still to be spoken not
only betwixt English and Irish, but between Irish and Irish.
There were mines under men's feet, ready to explode, and
murder and cruel deeds were again to be done before peace
was to come to Ireland.

From Dublin we returned to Oakridge, where we still
kept a cottage, and where I continued to paint farms and
barns. I wandered again through the quiet valleys in which
lovely villages were hidden, Througham, Daglingworth,
Miserden, and the three Duntsbournes—Duntsbourne
Abbots, Duntsbourne Rouse, and Duntsbourne Leer—the
first two with little Norman saddle-back churches, simple
and plain as barns, and further afield Elkstone and Syde,
with similar churches.

Gordon Bottomley wrote to me about my paintings. 'I
shall look out eagerly for your new paintings of husbandry.
You will get the rich profound feeling which is what
matters in the life of the fields; I often feel that the delight
which one gets from the pastorals of S. Palmer and E. Calvert
is equally inherent in the farmer's year now and is waiting to
be shewn; the completeness with which nature absorbs
machinery is strange. In half a century the whirr of the
mowing or reaping machine has become as purely a country
sound as the chirr of a grasshopper. I suppose that once on
a time the cart and the plough seemed as much machines as
the self-binder and the tractor do now; the only difference is
that the implement-makers have not yet learned to use iron
so completely according to its nature as in long generations
they have learned to use wood; but that too will come in
time. One of the supreme things of my life was the sight of
two black plough horses suddenly appearing on the horizon,

twenty yards distant, of a steep brown furrowed field—
apparently from an atmospheric gulf of tall mournful wood
beyond—as I mounted the low ridge from the other side.
Two horses half rearing in the air, and a man's head below
and behind, gave me all the sensations that the ancients
received from the thought of the waggon of Dis suddenly
emerging from the cloven ground.'

What he here writes of the whirr of the reaping machine
is truly and finely observed. Indeed during my later years I
have enjoyed discussing life and art with writers, musicians,
and with men of science, too, more, perhaps, than with
painters. With men following parallel pursuits one exchanges,
as it were, understanding. 'I have found the chief reward
of being an artist is the friendship of kindred spirits that it
brings', Robert Bridges wrote in one of his letters. It is with
older or much younger men than oneself that relations with
others are often most satisfying. Walter Greaves, for example,
enjoyed the praise he now got from his juniors; how pleased
he was when his 'Hammersmith Bridge' was hung in the
Tate Gallery:

> 38 *Lillie Road*,
> *West Brompton*,
> *March* 14*th*, 1922.

Dear Mr Rothenstein,

I dare say you have heard about my picture of Boat Race
Day being bought by the 'Chantrey Bequest'. I do feel really
honoured that one of my pictures should be bought for the
nation, and as you have always been so kindly disposed
towards me and my work, I reckon that you have been very
instrumental in bringing me forward before the public, and I
told Mr Marchant that I should like to write and thank you
very sincerely for all you have done for me. Thank you also
for your kind testimonial for the 'Charterhouse'. I do hope
they will accept me. Yours truly,

WALTER GREAVES.

There was no difficulty in Greaves entering the 'Charterhouse'. 'No expenses, a pound a week pocket money, and everyone kind!' It was luxury for Greaves. But when I went to visit him, his hair, which had been unnaturally black, through the offices of the Matron and a cake of soap, had turned white in a single afternoon.

Orpen was now working almost entirely in Paris, he wrote from time to time from the Hôtel Majestic:

'I'll be back before Christmas and we will fix up a night and have a talk. You write "I hope work goes well" but when I am not at portraits I am painting nudes at an American's called Russell Greely's—and my word—can a nude ever go well—it seems to me the last word in impossibility. I struggle and struggle and the things get worse and worse. I spent this afternoon in the Louvre looking at nudes and there are none in the least like a woman—Rembrandt's seated one is of course a marvel—but it's not like a woman—Manet's nude after all is a poor show—as a woman—and Courbet's one in the Louvre is a shocker—though I remember seeing photographs of some nude women of his a long time ago which looked wonderful. Forgive me writing all this stuff—I'll have a drink and forget it. Best of luck.

'WILLIAM ORPEN.'

I know that feeling well—that no painting, however masterly, ever renders what one feels when a beautiful model takes one noble pose after another. One may say, everything has been painted and nothing has been painted.

For this reason works of art assume different values at different times; we bring something to bear on them from within ourselves, as we feel faith and liking or distrust in our intercourse with men and women, which likewise affect their conduct. Indeed, every artist knows how when he has a Pre-Raphaelite visitor he becomes uncomfortably aware of loose ends all over his picture, while before a modernist small details and insignificant forms emerge.

CHAPTER XLIV

CAMPDEN HILL

DURING 1922 we moved to another house on Campden Hill; without a garden we could not endure life in London, and now we shared a large garden with the neighbouring houses. Our next-door neighbours, the Sidney Morses (who owned many treasures, among them some early drawings by Blake, and Whistler's famous Chinese Cabinet), loved the garden as we did. Walking there, London seemed far away, for adjoining was Mr Montagu Norman's garden and beyond, the park of Holland House. Pigeons nested and cooed upon our upper cornices, and at night we heard the owls hoot. In our new home a brother of Joachim had formerly lived, and here the great man stayed during his visits to London. Miss Weisse told me an amusing story of an evening party when Joachim had found the company of the wife of a certain famous painter unbearable. Seeing him with Donald Tovey, studying a Bradshaw, Miss Weisse inquired whither he was going? Joachim, still bent over the Bradshaw, replied, 'Ich muss blos von der Frau fort!' I never saw the great Joachim, but I numbered among my friends many musicians, from the young Herbert Howells to the veteran Sir Walter Parratt. I like to think they found me companionable for the reason that I could not hum a bar of music in tune, nor ever attended a concert, nor spoke of music. To the violin, the spinet and the virginals I can listen with pleasure, but the piano is, to my belief, an instrument of torture invented by the Devil. I recall an evening when Jelly

377

d'Aranyi, meeting Tagore in my studio, played to him, piece after piece, as she declared she had never played before. The expression of her face, the beautiful movements of her arms and hands as the sounds she drew from her violin travelled wailing about the walls and roof of the studio, I tried more than once to record. Only Watts could have done her justice.

I did not know Mr Montagu Norman, behind whose lovely garden the sun set so gloriously; but being one morning with Mr Baldwin when Mr Norman was expected, I was asked to stay a while longer that I might meet him. When he came in, before Mr Baldwin could pronounce my name, he strode up and accused me of taking in more milk than any of his neighbours: during his early morning walks he counted the number of cans and bottles outside our door!

What a solace the garden was to us all! To return tired from work and to lie on the lawn, and, besides the blackbird's song, to hear the gay shrill voices of the Booth children as they gambolled about their own grounds—yes, the beauty of the face of the world, the green leaves against the blue sky, the noble shapes of the drifting clouds, the shadows on the grass, gave a solid answer to the wherefore of life. And after sunset I would join Sidney Morse, or another neighbour, Lord Southborough, who knew so much of the world, and had so genial an understanding of men, in walks round the garden.

Decidedly the change from country to Town was not all loss. I found other neighbours on Campden Hill—the Edward Wadsworths, with two delightful children. Wadsworth had lately made a series of remarkable drawings of Staffordshire slag-heaps. Then I found that Wyndham Lewis was living close by. I had known Lewis as a handsome youth, adventurous, but uncertain of direction. I now discovered a formidable figure, armed and armoured, like a tank, ready to cross any country, however rough and hostile, to attack without formal declaration of war.

I had lately read *Tarr*, of which he wrote: 'I had always regarded life as practically never-ending, until the war came to remind me of the contrary. Before enlisting I wrote practically the whole of *Tarr*; if I were killed, I thought, at least I would have that to my credit in the way of writing. I also finished a lot of drawings, which I wish I could show you.' I thought *Tarr* one of the powerful books of our time; Lewis was responsive; the understanding of a work, he said, was a portion of its life—he recognised what this signifies. He had also lately written a pamphlet, *The Caliph's Design*, a brilliant challenge to the modern English architect. Lewis was a master of controversy; with no social or party ties, he was more independent even than Shaw. He was not out against the Philistine, but the literary and artistic gun-man, an enemy as well armed as himself. I admired his bold demeanour, and though I remembered the talent he showed when, as a youngster, he sent me his sonnets, I was astonished at his range as a writer. In his studio were many drawings, both in pencil and pen-and-ink, made with swift nervous lines and showing a vivid quality of design. Lewis be-lieved in exploring fully contemporary tendencies. I hold him to be the most forceful and intellectual of English ex-perimenters. I regret that cubism, in reality an austere and logical attitude to form, which Dürer, amongst others, had studied, should have become an end in itself, and finally, a mere mannerism, a matter of entertaining shapes and colours, of more concern to stage, fashion and advertisement de-signers than to painters.

Lewis never remained long in any place; he continued his old habits of secrecy. He did not pretend to be a lover of his kind. When I asked him to sit for a drawing he replied, 'I am sitting for myself at present—in fact its a permanent job, and I never sit for anybody else!'

Through my son John going up to Worcester College, I had an excuse for renewing old Oxford friendships, also of meeting post-war undergraduates, who were in no wise less attractive than those I knew in the 'nineties. My son shared rooms with William Gerhardi, a retiring and hard-working student who had served in Russia and spoke half a dozen languages, but gave little sign of the irony which in *Futility* was to astonish Wells and Bennett. But who can foretell what will emerge from the chrysalis-stage of youth? There was John Strachey, too, then editing, with Lord David Cecil and my son, *The Oxford Fortnightly Review*, the undergraduates' most conservative organ. His father St Loe was delighted to find his son following in his own footsteps—little did he think when he gave him an important position on the staff of *The Spectator*, along what dangerous paths he was to move ! When Lord Balfour, a year or two later, asked me to explain present-day aesthetics, which he found so puzzling, I said he must ask his nephew, Lord David Cecil, now in the advance guard writing for *The Nation*. Lord Balfour was astonished —and amused: 'David writing for *The Nation*! does his mother know?' Richard Hughes, Tom Darlow and Edward Sackville-West, three budding writers, were also of the company. Lord Balniel was the discerning critic of painting, while Malcolm MacDonald and Robert Boothby were the ardent politicians. How well-mannered all these young people were and how flatteringly polite to their elders. Much is said of the decline in manners; for my part, I find young people charming.

Though it were best to have, for the pursuit of an art, all one's time, I found much happiness in close association with young people at South Kensington. But there were things that troubled me. The College was meant to fit students for particular industries and to train future teachers, but there was not the equipment needed for serious vocational training, nor was this training, to my mind, essential. For our task was to provide truly educated men—it is for industry, which needs such, to draw upon these for its particular needs. If general problems of art-education did not come within my province, I could at least aspire to make of the Royal College, with the help of a carefully-chosen staff and the sympathy of Whitehall, as useful an institution as lay in my power. My chiefs at Whitehall agreed to the gradual introduction of part-time teaching throughout the Royal College, and to the provision of working studios for the staff; and with the coming of a new Registrar, Hubert Wellington, who took from my shoulders much of the administration, and through his insight and sympathy in his dealings with students and staff, brought an inspiring energy and intelligence to the service of the College, a new spirit pervaded the students.

Another new spirit was sometimes trying. There stood the model, one of a succession of marvellous figures, each a miracle of form and colour. But God's work was no miracle to some students, who looked rather at Cézanne's and Picasso's. Cézanne's French progeny might legitimately be called, after their father, *ces ânes*; but these later ones I named, *ces mulets*, for they, I knew, would have no progeny, and, my goodness, they were obstinate ! Yet from teaching, whether helpful or not to my students, I learnt many things. Moreover, to leave one's work to join in that of others is to live in an atmosphere of constant effort, and I gained much through the varied activities of studios and workshops.

But advanced or moderate, what muddlers students can be ! Such disorderly palettes and brushes, with which, one thinks, no one can possibly paint ! The painters could learn from the designers and craftsmen, who still respect their materials. There is, among young people, a strong disinclination to work methodically. Nevertheless, at the end of each session, I am delighted at the quantity of good work done, of invention and imagination shown. Women students have a rare faculty, in their compositions, of making their figures live naturally, as though these, like animals, were unaware of being observed. I have often wished that women artists would respect this natural gift more, and strive less for the qualities they deem it important to acquire. But the same may be said of all artists, men and women, young or mature; it is so easy to lose touch with one's true self, to pursue the interests of another, a self maybe as real, whose claims make themselves felt, since they are in need of excuse, more insistently.

A great museum near by, with a splendid art library, has been of incalculable service to the College, with the Keepers,

Palmer of the Library, Martin Hardie of the Print Room, Maclagan, Kennedy, Kendrick, Rackham, Strange, Watts and their assistants, ever ready to help the students.

These two years at South Kensington brought new duties, and my life was a full one. If to be used, sometimes to exhaustion, is happiness, then was I a happy man.

To an official, things happen that do not occur to a mere painter: for instance, an invitation to the annual dinner of the Royal Academy! I well remember the surprise of my friends when the rumour reached them that I was to be present at Burlington House among Statesmen, Admirals, Generals and Museum-Directors. I recollect T. E. Lawrence saying, during his short term at the Colonial Office, 'Who would have believed a couple of years ago, that you and I would both become officials!' As an artist-official I have been found useful to more than one Government Department; I reflect often on Burne-Jones's complaint: that people would ask him to do everything but paint! Perhaps the painter is somewhat contemptuous of the official, the latter a mere parvenu with even now but twelve years to his credit, while the painter claims, from the time of his entering the Slade School in 1888, wellnigh four times that number. Yet though partly enslaved, I have found myself free enough, and with time enough, to attempt some of the things I thought during my youthful, greedy selfhood—one of those former selves into which Max Beerbohm's eyes have peered to so much purpose—to achieve triumphantly —some day!

END OF VOLUME II

INDEX

Index

Index

Index

Index

Index

CAMBRIDGE: PRINTED BY
W. LEWIS, M.A.
AT THE UNIVERSITY PRESS